Relational Database Design

A practitioner's guide

Relational Database Design

A practitioner's guide

Charles J. Wertz

CRC PRESS

Boca Raton   Ann Arbor   London   Tokyo

This book was acquired, developed, and produced by Manning Publications Co.
Copyediting: Karen Verde
Layout and typesetting: Peter Schoenberg

Library of Congress Cataloging-in-Publication Data

Wertz, Charles J.
　　Relational database design : a practitioner's guide/Charles J.
　Wertz.
　　　　p.　cm.
　　Includes bibliographical references　(p.　) and index.
　　ISBN 0–8493–7450–2
　　1. Data base design.　2. Relational data bases.　I. Title.
　QA76.9.D26W47　1992.
　005.75'6—dc20
　　　　　　　　　　　　　　　　　　92–31696
　　　　　　　　　　　　　　　　　　CIP

CRC Press Inc.
2000 Corporate Boulevard, N. W.
Boca Raton, FL 33431

Manning Publications Co.
3 Lewis Street
Greenwich, CT 06830

10　9　8　7　6　5　4　3　2　1

Printed in the United States of America

Contents

Preface

Database design books seem to fall into two categories.

Some, while theoretically sound and complete, are very difficult to read. There are also some real issues that many theoreticians seem to ignore.

Others are easy to read and practical but incomplete and lacking in theory. I don't believe you can design databases or systems by following "insert tab 'A' into slot 'B' " style instructions. You really need to understand the reasoning behind the practice.

"Now the trouble with rules is that they may fit one set of conditions, but if conditions change, they don't fit anymore" (Frederick C. Crawford, President of TRW from 1933 to 1958 in the November–December 1991 issue of *Harvard Business Review*.)

Numerous books deal extensively with details of a specific product such as Database2, Oracle, Ingres, or dBase. I have not attempted to compete with them. By providing an understanding of basic concepts and principles, I prepare the reader to learn the details of any product.

SQL has become the next thing to a standard programming interface for relational systems. There are now a number of books which deal with the use of SQL. I explain and use a limited amount of SQL to illustrate concepts but this is not a book about the use of SQL.

Few books deal adequately with the relationship between database design and the overall systems design process. Books on systems development by authors such as Gane, De Marco, and Page-Jones do a better job here than any *database* book I know of. I show the relationship between database design and other systems development activities.

Few books deal well with practical details such as selection of keys, development of adequate definitions, index selection, and the like. I have included practical advice.

There are now several books dealing specifically with distributed systems. Most general books deal with this issue superficially. I have included usable information on distributed database design.

As a matter of fact, there just weren't many books about relational database design available when I started this project a few years ago. Even though several good books have come out since then, I still believe that I have not duplicated the work of anyone else and that I have included some important material that has been overlooked by many others. I've also tried to keep it simple and not take a lot for granted while providing something valuable for the experienced and knowledgeable.

Traditional systems and database design approaches call for total definition of everything first, before any programming, while many of the more contemporary approaches seem to call for the opposite—that is they advocate the use of *rapid development* tools to develop a system specification by prototyping. Some people interpret this to mean system development by trial and error. I believe that prototyping can be useful, but I also believe you need some solid definitions of data and processing requirements before you make too many difficult to revoke decisions. Thus, I suggest that it is still necessary to develop definitions and specifications as soon as possible. I suspect some people will feel that I lean too heavily towards the *define it all* school. I do believe that you must exercise judgement. But, I can't see how you will ever build the right system without really understanding the data and processing. Well, you decide what you think as you read the book.

The best way to learn this material is by looking at examples. So I've included a lot of examples, some brief, some extended, some serious, some whimsical.

I have tested a lot of this material on my students at Buffalo State College and in training sessions I've conducted at various corporate sites.

This is not a text for a general database course. Most texts cover a lot more material on hardware, DBMS architecture, and older data models. I have focused on the things a designer needs to know. This book could be used as the text for a database design course.

You may already have noted that many books on database systems seem to go in circles. Because the topics are so interrelated it is very difficult to come up with a best order for presentation. I've *tried* to follow an orderly progression. You should find it beneficial to go through the book from beginning to end as opposed to skipping around. I've tried to identify sections that you might skip if you are already familiar with a particular topic. You may do better to scan sections rather than skip. This field is characterized by a lot of inconsistency in the use of terminology. It will be a good idea to make sure you are aware of the way some terms are used here.

Let's quickly review the content of the book and then get on with it.

Chapter 1 is a review of basic systems and database concepts. It also discusses the need for and nature of design methodologies.

Chapter 2 is a discussion of the relational data model and relational database management. While the SQL language is introduced, this is not a book about SQL. Since SQL has become the closest thing we have to a standard database language it is the best vehicle for examples and illustrations.

Chapter 3 explains normalization. Normalization is really a very simple idea. Simple ideas are often the hardest to explain.

Chapter 4 is an introduction to entity relationship modelling. This is another simple idea that can be difficult to explain.

Chapter 5 deals with advanced topics in entity relationship modelling. You will find that the techniques explained here solve a lot of tricky design and modelling problems.

Chapter 6 discusses the nature of the information that should be collected during a design study. This is one of my *pet* chapters because I feel this is an important area that does not get anywhere near enough attention.

Chapters 7 and 8 deal with hardware and software and physical database design. Technology has been changing very rapidly and will probably continue to do so. Keep in mind that a book cannot by its nature be as current as a newspaper. While all of the basic ideas presented in these chapters should remain valid, technical details of specific products will continue to change. You will need to consult up to date documentation for the latest details on these topics. Chapter 7 is a review of physical design issues. Chapter 8 discusses distributed systems.

Chapter 9 presents the elements of a database design methodology. I've taken the approach that the world really doesn't need yet another complete design methodology. Instead I've tried to show how the material covered in the first eight chapters fits into any methodology.

Chapter 10 is an extended example.

I hope you find the book valuable. I'd really appreciate any comments, positive or negative.

Charles J. Wertz

Chapter 1

Concepts

1.1   CHAPTER SUMMARY

This chapter introduces some basic concepts about data, databases, and database management. If you are already familiar with these, you can probably read it very quickly, although it may not be a good idea to skip it altogether. Some authors use some of the terms differently than we do. Reading about database is extremely confusing because there is so little consistency in the use of terminology. (It isn't even clear whether database should be one or two words. We will stick with one word except for quotations from authors who have written data base as two words.) This chapter will provide the basis for what follows. It is important to make sure we are talking the same language.

1.2   WHAT IS A DATABASE?

We'll start by defining what it is that we want to design.

Definition   *A database is an organized collection of data. It contains the data necessary for some purpose (or collection of purposes). The data is arranged to facilitate some set of activities. The data is arranged so that it may be accessed and altered in an efficient manner.*[1]

This definition is a little different from the usual one. Most texts call for many more features.[2] But it has become common usage to apply the term database to almost any collection of data gathered for almost any purpose.

The use of the term does imply a conscious effort to organize the data for some purpose. *We can identify several desirable properties which will greatly improve the value and usability of any database.*

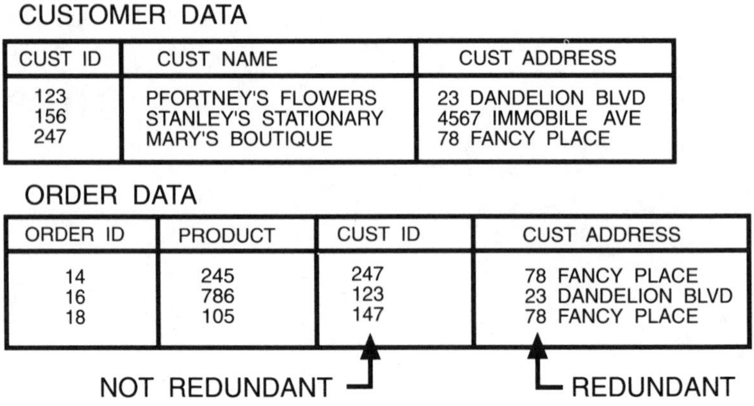

CUSTOMER DATA

CUST ID	CUST NAME	CUST ADDRESS
123 156 247	PFORTNEY'S FLOWERS STANLEY'S STATIONARY MARY'S BOUTIQUE	23 DANDELION BLVD 4567 IMMOBILE AVE 78 FANCY PLACE

ORDER DATA

ORDER ID	PRODUCT	CUST ID	CUST ADDRESS
14 16 18	245 786 105	247 123 147	78 FANCY PLACE 23 DANDELION BLVD 78 FANCY PLACE

NOT REDUNDANT ⅃   ⌐ REDUNDANT

Figure 1.1   Redundancy

It is beneficial to *eliminate, or at least minimize, redundancy.*

We want to eliminate duplicate representations of facts. Figure 1.1 illustrates what this means. If we store information about orders received from customers, and include the customer's address in every order record, there is redundancy. If, on the other hand, we store a customer identifier in each order record, and this is our device for recording the relationship between a particular customer and a particular order, this is not a case of redundancy. (You might also want to note that we must investigate before eliminating replications of customer address. It may be that some customers maintain establishments at more than one address and want different orders shipped to different addresses.)

Redundant representations of facts waste storage space. They require extra human effort for data entry and maintenance. They require additional computer resources for processing. Perhaps the most serious problem is that they lead to data *inconsistency.* Let's refer to the case of customer. If the address is repeated in every order record and a customer moves, we must take pains to assure that every record is changed. Our customers won't be impressed with our efficiency if we send some orders to the new address and some to the old.

It sometimes happens that separate computer systems with separate databases or data files are created for separate purposes. Thus a business may construct one database for customer orders and another for accounts receivable. If these are completely separate, there will be duplications of information about orders and information about customers. These redundant representations will require extra effort and resources for maintenance and will be susceptible to creeping inconsistency. *Integration* of the two systems with a shared database can eliminate these problems.

Why, you might ask, would anyone ever fail to share databases, especially in an obvious case like this? It may happen that the accounts receivable system was conceived and built before the order processing system and the data may be arranged in such a manner as to preclude sharing. It may be that the accounting department and sales department disagree in some fundamental manner about proper maintenance of customer data. Integrated systems and shared databases are desirable, but we can only achieve them by taking some extra time to research all the requirements and design a database which will satisfy all needs. And it often becomes necessary to deal with organizational conflicts and even change organizational structures and procedures in order to make integration work. It may or may not be possible to introduce the necessary changes.

It is highly desirable that it be *easy to change* the database when business conditions or requirements change. It is also desirable that changes or additions to the database have no impact on programs and systems which are not directly affected by the change. Thus, if order processing and accounts receivable share a database, changes in accounting procedures or data should not affect customer order processing. This property is often referred to as *data independence*. We often rely on database management software to provide for this. We discuss this again later on in this chapter.

Finally, it is desirable that a database be *logically organized* to simplify retrieval and maintenance by relationships. We'd like it to be easy to find all orders sent by a particular customer, all payments made by that customer, all orders for a particular product, all payments due on a particular date, and so on.

Thus, while our definition of a database is very broad and unrestrictive, we recognize that there are a number of desirable properties which a good database should possess.

In designing a database we strive for elimination of redundancy, consistency, ease of integration and sharing, ease of change, data independence, and logical organization in terms of processing required.

1.3   WHAT IS A DATABASE MANAGEMENT SYSTEM?

As is the case with the word database, there is more than one possible definition of database management system. We'll start with the broadest possible definition.

Definition   *A database management system (DBMS) is software that manages data.*

It is useful to view this from a historical perspective. In the past, programs included both business processing and data access processing. Programmers developed routines to instruct a tape drive to start up, transmit a unit of data, then stop and check itself for any errors. These input and output routines were intermingled with the instructions which accomplished the business processing. Figure 1.2 illustrates this.

This repetitive effort has been eliminated by the use of generalized input-output subroutines. The first versions of these were developed by individual programmers. Soon, hardware vendors began to provide input output control systems (IOCS). The vendors also began to provide control programs or operating systems. An operating system controls the operation of the computer system. IOCS routines were renamed access methods and became part of the operating system. Data access methods manage data manipulations while communications access meth-

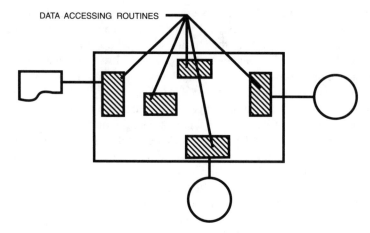

Figure 1.2 Data accessing routines in program

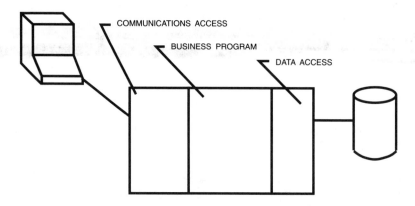

Figure 1.3 Data accessing separate

ods manage access from remote terminals or other computers. This is illustrated by Figure 1.3. Now the details of business processing are not intermingled with details of data transmission.

Access methods still do not eliminate data structuring functions from business-oriented programming. Modern computer languages such as COBOL and C free the programmer from involvement with the elaborate details of input and output operations, but do not eliminate the need for manipulating data relationships. Which order data goes with the specified customer data? Which course data goes with the specified student data?

Database management systems standardize the manipulation of structured data and eliminate tedious details of relationship processing. More details are moved from the program to the system software. This is illustrated by Figure 1.4.

It is useful for maintenance of data integrity, recovery from system failures, maintenance of audit trails, security checking, and the like to be provided by the database management system.

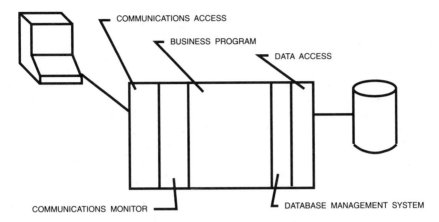

COMMUNICATIONS ACCESS

BUSINESS PROGRAM

DATA ACCESS

COMMUNICATIONS MONITOR

DATABASE MANAGEMENT SYSTEM

Figure 1.4   Database management separate

Selecting data to be reported, formatting reports and display screens, and summarizing data for reporting are additional functions provided by many database management systems. Some database management systems provide complete processing environments which neither need nor allow processing via traditional languages such as COBOL.

Figure 1.4 does look a bit more complex than Figure 1.2. But all these different types of processing must be accomplished. Isolation of specific functions into distinct software components actually results in simplification, ease of development, and ease of maintenance.

As this history has unfolded, various software vendors have taken various approaches. Thus, we can identify elements commonly found in database management systems. But we cannot state that all database management systems provide all of these elements. *Features commonly found in database management systems include data definition language, data dictionary, data manipulation language, query language, screen painter, report generator, integrity and recovery, data communications, distributed data management, and utility programs.*

A *data definition language* or DDL is the vehicle for defining the content and form of the database. Some systems provide complex definition languages which allow the designer to specify all details and select from many options. Some systems provide very simple languages and provide few choices. *The examples in this book utilize SQL, the Structured Query Language. SQL is used in a large number of database management systems. It is the closest thing there is to a standard database language.*[3] The selection of an appropriate product depends on the experience level of the system developer, the complexity of the requirements to be met, and the complexity of the computing environment.

This data definition is normally stored in a *data dictionary, data directory, or repository.* This is a special database which contains data about data, and is referred to as metadata. This is a large subject in itself. The interested reader is referred to the author's book about dictionaries [WERTZ89] for a much more detailed discussion. The systems which provide for a more complex data definition contain more elaborate dictionaries. Additionally, some dictionaries have been extended to contain much more than database descriptions.

A *data manipulation language* or DML is used to specify the retrieval and update operations to be performed by the database management system. Early data manipulation languages for mainframe computer database management systems were designed to be incorporated in computer programs written by professional programmers. These allow (and require) the programmer to express database search and processing strategies in great (and tedious) detail. Many of the newer database management systems and many of the systems designed for use on microcomputers are much simpler. These provide ease of use but sometimes are not as flexible or efficient. The choice should be based on the experience level of the system developer, the complexity of the requirements to be met, and the complexity of the computing environment. *One of the advantages of SQL is that it provides for both data definition and data manipulation in a fairly consistent manner.*[4]

Most microcomputer-based database management systems and most of the newer mainframe-based systems provide some means of specifying queries, screen designs, and report specifications without recourse to conventional programming. Some *query facilities* merely allow a user at a terminal to enter data manipulation language directly while some are designed to be very user friendly. The latter are often utilized by sophisticated end users. By end user, we mean some business person or, more generally, someone who is not a programmer by profession. The advent of easy to use database management systems has resulted in a blurring of the lines between professional programmers, end users who do some programming, and people who use computer systems developed by others. *Screen painting and report generating* facilities also vary in complexity and power. Screen painters make it possible to more or less draw the desired input or output arrangement on the screen of a video terminal. Report generators simplify the creation of printed reports. Many microcomputer-based systems incorporate special proprietary programming languages designed for ease of use. *While screen and report development tools do simplify programming, design is still necessary. The benefits of the tools will be achieved only with good database and system designs. A proliferation of rapidly developed but ill-conceived systems can do more harm than good.*[5]

Mainframe-based systems have traditionally provided for concurrent use of a database by several users. Airline reservation systems and bank teller systems are examples of systems which must provide for a high degree of concurrency. These must manage multiple updates of the same data. It is difficult for two different people to sit in the same seat on an airplane, for example. They must also provide for recovery of data lost via hardware and software failures. These *integrity and recovery facilities* have been common to mainframe systems for years. They were unnecessary in early microcomputer systems which were designed for single-user non-shared use. Contemporary microcomputer systems are multi-user systems and are also designed to be linked together in networks. These newer microcomputer database management systems provide features similar to those traditionally provided in mainframe systems.[6]

Shared systems such as those used on mainframes or in networks require *data security*. Thus, many database management systems provide a means for specifying who is authorized to access data. By now, you probably won't be surprised to learn that *SQL provides for data security definition along with data definition*. Sometimes it is a big problem to find out or decide who should, in fact, be authorized to access data. It may be that no one has ever thought about it. The issue may become part of a political struggle. We discuss this further in Chapter 6.

Some database management systems incorporate *data communications facilities*, some do not. Some systems provide for *distributed database management* and some do not. We discuss this in Chapter 8.

Many database management systems provide a variety of special *utility programs* for copying, rearranging, backing up, restoring, analyzing, and monitoring the database.

Thus, more elaborate definitions of database management are common. But it is then necessary to specify that not all features are found in all software products.[7]

In this book, we discuss general principles and concepts which will apply equally well to a variety of products. It will still be necessary for you to review vendor documentation for details of the specific database management system you intend to use. We do provide examples in SQL. Since this language is incorporated in many database management systems, the examples are portable. This book is a complement to your vendor's documentation, not a substitute for it.

1.4   WHAT ARE DATA MODELS?

It is difficult, if not impossible, for most of us to grasp all the details of a complex thing at once. A simplified representation can help us understand. Simplified representations are also useful to designers. Engineers, architects, and artisans frequently develop various kinds of models before constructing something complex. A set of drawings can be thought of as a form of model. Data models usually consist of diagrams combined with supporting explanations.[8] Chapters 2, 4, and 5 contain details of two particular model types, relational and entity relationship.

Definition   *A data model is a descriptive representation of a data structure. Data models are sometimes classified according to purpose. They are sometimes classified according to modeling style. A complete classification requires a specification of purpose and style.*

Models are used as an aid in database design and also as a reference to the content of existing databases. Different types or classifications of data models are often defined. Unfortunately, many of the terms are not used consistently by all authors.[9] We'll look at classifications according to *use or purpose* first.

A complete description of a database structure is often called a *physical data model*. This is a description of all the data as it is stored in machine readable form. The exact nature of this model will vary according to the nature of the database management system used and the type of computer hardware used. This physical model is sometimes referred to as an *internal model* since it is a representation of the data as it is seen inside the system. In case you don't think two names are enough, this model is sometimes referred to as the database *SCHEMA*.

A physical model can contain an overwhelming amount of detail. The complexity of the physical structure may obscure the information content of the database. It is often very useful to develop a model illustrating the types of data contained in the database or the concepts used in organizing the data. This is often called a *conceptual data model*, and is sometimes referred to as the *conceptual schema*. The conceptual model is intended for interpretation by humans and does not relate to a specific database management system or physical data representation.[10] The entity models we discuss in Chapters 4 and 5 are a form of conceptual model.

Conceptual model may sound imposing and complex. A model of some complex situation may be unavoidably detailed and complex. But the basic premise of conceptual modeling is really very simple. It is necessary to understand the data. A conceptual model is a representation of the concepts used to organize a particular collection of data.

Scope is an important issue in conceptual modeling. Many organizations have developed or are in the process of developing a conceptual model showing all data and data relationships used in all activities. Such a *global data model* can be useful in understanding the organization, planning systems, designing integrated databases, and so on. Developing such a model can be a demanding and time-consuming task. We are not opposed to this. It is a recommended activity. But it is not what this book is about.[11]

Some authors discuss a *logical data model*. The logical model is sometimes differentiated from the conceptual model by the scope or span. If the conceptual model deals with the entire organization, the logical model might deal with one sector or one computer system. Some authors add more detail to the logical model. In this approach, the logical model will often contain information about quantities of data items, volumes of transactions, and data accessing patterns. The important point is that a logical model, like a conceptual model, shows *what* is represented in the database while a physical model shows *how* it is represented.

We can note that different users of a database are interested in different subsets of the data. Different users may not only want to see different selections of data, they may also want to see it in different arrangements and different sequences. They may wish to retrieve data according to different relationships. The sales department cares about orders related to customers, the order processing department cares about orders related to products, while the accountant cares about receivables and payments related to customers. Models or representations of specific user requirements are variously referred to as *external models* (data seen from outside the system), *external schemas*, *subschemas* (portions of schemas), *user views*, and more simply *views*.

In the 1970s, the *ANSI/SPARC Study Group on Database Management Systems* developed and published the three schema architecture for database management systems. ANSI/SPARC stands for the Standards Planning and Requirements Committee of the X3 (data management) subgroup of the American National Standards Institute. The three schema architecture is discussed in most texts on database management, for example, [DATE86] and [MCFADDEN88]. Figure 1.5 is a diagram of this architecture as it is described above. The committee suggested that a database management system should provide for all three models and automatically translate or map from the conceptual model to the physical model and from the conceptual model to each view. Most contemporary systems provide for the internal model and a series of external models but do not directly support the conceptual model. However, this architecture is very useful in understanding database management and database design. Automatic mapping between external and internal representations provides the data independence we expect a database management system to afford.

A physical model is a representation of the database as it is stored in machine readable form. A conceptual model illustrates the data content of the database in a form suit-

VIEWS

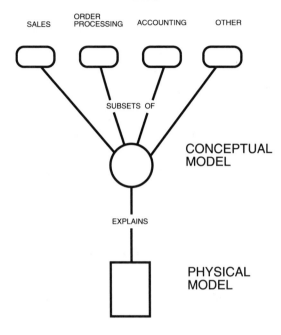

Figure 1.5   ANSI/SPARC architecture

able for interpretation by humans. A view is a representation of a subset of the data organized for a specific user or purpose. Now we'll look at classifications according to *modeling style*—the manner in which the model represents the data.

The *hierarchical model* organizes data like a traditional organization structure. The military, the Roman Catholic Church, many governments, and many businesses are organized in a hierarchical manner. Figure 1.6 illustrates a hierarchical structure. It is easier to draw than to describe in words. Database management systems which employ the hierarchical model require that data be processed in a specific order, top to bottom

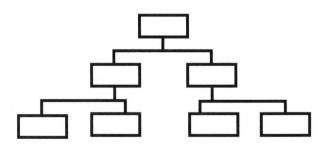

Figure 1.6   Hierarchical model

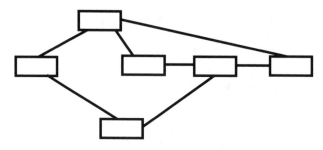

Figure 1.7 Network model

and left to right. This is because this model is derived from a particular method of storing data in the computer.

The *network model* organizes data in a somewhat freer manner. Data connections may be made in any direction and may be traversed in any direction. Again it is easier to draw a picture than it is to explain. See Figure 1.7. While the network model is not as rigid as the hierarchical model, the programmer or user must still be aware of many details of physical data storage. Once again this is because the model is derived form a particular method of storing data.

Most microcomputer-based database management systems and most of the newer database management systems do not employ the network or hierarchical models. These older models are of interest because many of the systems in use today were developed using older database management systems which embody them.

Hierarchical and network data models are based on physical storage formats. The user must be aware of the connections between collections of data.

The *relational model* views data in a tabular, row and column format. See Figure 1.8. E. F. Codd is normally credited with developing and introducing the relational model. [CODD70]

We discuss the relational model in much more detail in Chapter 2. Here are just a few significant points. The relational model differs from the network and hierarchical models in several important ways. It is not derived from any specific physical method for storing data. It severs the link between the specification of processing and how the data is stored. The design goal of the model is to facilitate use of data by humans, not to opti-

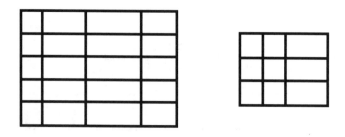

Figure 1.8 Relational model

mize machine utilization. The advent of faster, more powerful computers and storage devices has made this a worthwhile trade-off for most applications.

This model has a rigorous mathematical definition which provides a firm basis for consistent and logical data manipulation.

Most contemporary database management systems are based on the relational model.

It is possible to use the hierarchical, network, or relational model as the technique for constructing a conceptual model or a view or even a physical database. It may be convenient to use the same representation technique for all three purposes, but it is not essential to do so.

The final type of model is the *entity model*, which is usually employed for conceptual or logical modeling. The data is organized according to entities or things of interest, relationships between entities, and data items which describe entities and relationships. Although it is not essential that they do so, entity models usually assume a network form. A well-constructed entity model can be very useful in visualizing and defining data. We discuss this in some detail in Chapters 4 and 5. *Entity models organize data in terms of things of interest, relationships between things, and data about the things and relationships. They are very useful for visualizing and defining.*

1.5 WHAT ARE THE BASIC DATA BUILDING BLOCKS?

The basic data building blocks are individual atoms of data, such as customer names, order quantities, and shipping dates. While this seems obvious, simple, and easy to understand, it is actually very easy to misunderstand. Misunderstandings about basics can cause a lot of trouble. We develop some initial concepts here.

Programmers are accustomed to thinking of fields or variables. Those accustomed to COBOL or ASSEMBLY LANGUAGE normally talk about fields. Those accustomed to FORTRAN or PASCAL normally call the same things variables.[12] These are units of data which are not susceptible to further meaningful decomposition. (We can decompose character information into individual characters and numeric information into individual digits. This is useful for manipulation of data, but it is not meaningful in terms of what the data represents.) Each field or variable is given a name formed in accord with the rules of the language used and is then referred to by that name.

A programmer, using the PASCAL language, might write statements like these:

> READ(InputData, CustName, OldAmount, NewOrder);
>
> NewAmount := OldAmount + NewOrder;
>
> WRITE(Report, CustName, OldAmount, NewAmount);

This sequence will obtain values for the variables named CustName (a customer's name), OldAmount (a previous balance), and NewOrder (the value of a new order). It will then compute the value of the variable named NewAmount (a new balance) as the sum of OldAmount and

NewOrder and display the result. You probably realize that a program of any consequence is going to be a long series of such arcane appearing statements.

This simple example illustrates several points. These data elements are called variables because the data content of each variable will be constantly changing as we process a series of customer records.

Customer name might, for some other purpose, be decomposed into first name, middle initial, and last name, but it is not useful or necessary to do so here.

OldAmount and NewAmount both represent the amount the customer owes, but at two different points in time. We must establish two separate variables with distinct names because we need to deal with both simultaneously.

Haphazard naming schemes can lead to a lot of confusion if there are very many data items involved. We discuss this in Chapter 6.

Program and database design involves the identification and naming of all the different types of *data elements* used for the purpose or purposes at hand. It is necessary to understand the nature of each element, what it represents, and how it is to be used.

Some elements are atomic and cannot be decomposed, while others are groupings of atoms.[13]

It is not unusual to find two or more distinct elements which are instances of the same type of data item. This is sometimes a source of great confusion. We develop this idea further in later chapters.

Programmers and database designers must also be concerned about the nature or type of the data referenced by one of these names. We can add numbers but not names. We can put names in alphabetical order, but it this doesn't make sense for numbers. Amounts expressed in U.S. dollars normally have two decimal places. Processing rules and machine representations vary for different types of data.

Database and computer system design involves identifying and defining individual data elements, and then devising logical groupings for storing and processing them.

1.6   WHY HAVE A METHOD?

The process of designing and creating systems and databases is a unique activity. We are tempted to say "computer" systems and databases. But in most cases, we are called on to develop business systems which incorporate activities performed by both people and computers. The activity has some things in common with the design and construction of buildings and the design and manufacture of a product. We often use these as analogues. We have borrowed ideas and techniques from them. But computer systems are different from buildings and manufactured products. Probably the biggest difference is that a computer system embodies processes while buildings and manufactured things are artifacts. Yes, it is true that many manufactured devices perform processing, but systems tend to be closer to pure process.

Systems design is demanding and fascinating. We start with some need which an organization or individual has; at least we'd hope we do. A corporation might have a perceived need for improved customer order tracking. An instructor might need to keep track of student attendance and performance in order to assign grades at the end of the term. The goal of the systems activity is to design and implement a collection of computer programs, computerized data, and manual procedures which will accomplish the desired processes in an effective and correct manner. This can be very difficult because of the contrast between the ways of humans and the ways of computers. A computer program is an extremely detailed specification of the steps and decisions involved in some activity. A database design is a very detailed specification of the data to be stored and used. The smallest error or omission can cause all sorts of problems. Most of the time most of us just don't think with such precision. We are constantly interpreting and adjusting without even realizing that we are doing so.

Let's look at a simple example or two. Suppose you are asked to add a column of numbers. How much will you really stop to think about it?[14] You know that it is easier to add numbers if the decimal columns are aligned like this.

```
  12
   1.73
 101.6
2,305
```

But most people could add a mixed list like this with no trouble.

```
12
1.73
101.6
2,305
```

Given a longer list, you might copy it over and align the decimals without stopping to think at all. Notice by the way that you automatically incorporate some zeros and eliminate any commas and decimal points from the arithmetic. You really add these numbers.

```
0012 00
0001 73
0101 60
2305 00
```

If you want to write a computer program to add numbers, you must make sure that decimal places are aligned, decimal points and commas are omitted, and appropriate zeros are inserted.[15] You must make sure that all of the data is numeric. You must also be concerned with the specific technique to be used to detect the end of the list. While some programming systems take care of some of these details automatically, few will take care of all of them.

Let's look at a more data-oriented example. Many people have small books designed to contain names, addresses, and phone numbers. The pages of these books are usually marked out for individual entries, consisting of name, address, and phone number.

Have you ever noticed how useless these markings are? Most of us can't write small enough to fit even a short name in the space provided. There is rarely provision for a three or four line address. Suppose you want to keep track of your friend's home and office numbers. There is usually only enough room for one phone number, if there is that. Most of us make do by ignoring the little boxes on the page and using as much room as it takes for the data.

We can do this because we are able to tell a name from an address or a phone number just by looking at it. Sometimes we do have trouble with foreign names, addresses, and phone numbers because the people in other countries follow different conventions.

If this data is to be stored in a computer database, it is an entirely different story. Someone must decide how many characters to allow for a name, whether or not first names are to be segregated from last names and how, whether or not business names are to be treated differently from individual's names, how many addresses, how many lines of how many characters for each address, how many phone numbers, and on and on. Many companies are still working at converting computer databases from five-digit zip codes to nine-digit zip codes. Notice that, in this case, it is not only necessary to make room for the additional digits, it is also necessary to obtain and store the new data. Also notice that U.S. postal codes are entirely numeric, while many other countries use combinations of letters and numerics. Also notice that some readers in other countries may not have understood this issue until it became clear that zip code is another name for postal code. Some small countries may have no such thing. Possibly the European Economic Community will, in time, develop a universal code which will span national boundaries.

We could probably extend both examples. But for now, that should be enough to indicate the level of detail which must be examined. *Most of the time, most people do not think with the degree of precision which must be employed when designing computer systems. People are able to do a lot of things without really thinking about them at all. The jobs of the systems analyst and the database designer involve observing, studying things carefully, discovering things that are taken for granted, and developing precise, detailed specifications.*

Systems analysis and database design are often thought of as two separate activities, but it seems that they must be closely related and intertwined. The intended use will certainly affect how the data should be stored. The availability and nature of the data will certainly affect how things are done. It is often stated that data is more stable in form than is processing.

Today's traveller can obtain airline boarding passes from most travel agents along with the airplane tickets. Not too long ago, it was necessary to check in and obtain passes at the airport. In some situations today, this is still necessary. However, in either case the data is the same. A particular seat on a particular flight is not yet assigned to a passenger or it is assigned to a specific passenger. There does appear to be some truth to the claim that data design and process design can be to some extent separated.

At any rate, most newcomers to the information processing field are amazed to discover that detailed study of the simplest activities is difficult and time consuming, that it is often very hard to make the things that everybody knows explicit, and that the consequences of omitting the most minute detail can be far reaching and serious. As a matter of fact, old hands are continually amazed to rediscover this with each new project.

The obvious question is, "How is all this detail discovered and documented?" The obvious answer is, "Very carefully."

Many systems have been developed by a haphazard, trial and error sort of approach. Some have been successful. Some have been disasters. The consensus today is that an organized, orderly approach will greatly improve the chances for success. A well-organized approach does not guarantee success, but it seems to stand to reason that it will be beneficial. Numerous books, articles, training courses, and seminars have extolled the virtues and benefits of an appropriate methodology for system or database design. We are going to take most of the arguments for an orderly approach for granted and get on with our business. However, we do suggest some references which contain many good arguments for a sound methodology and also provide a sampling of worthwhile recommendations. [ATRE88] [DEMARCO79] [GANE79] [MILLS86] [PAGEJONES88] [PRESSMAN87] [SENN89]

1.7   SYSTEMS ANALYSIS METHODS

If this is all new to you, we recommend a standard textbook such as [SENN89]. We will merely provide an overview of an approach. There is a difference between a life cycle and a methodology. A *life cycle* defines the sequence of steps to be followed in developing a system. A *methodology* is a collection of techniques.

Now we'll introduce a generic life cycle. While various authors and various authorities differ on some of the details, most would accept the general concept of this sequence of steps.

First, we determine that there is a need to do something and why this is so. In other words, we *identify a problem and propose a solution*. In a large organization, a user[16] may write some sort of a formal request which is subsequently acted on by a systems analyst. In a small organization, things may be very informal. If you are experienced in the use of computers, you may identify a problem and develop a solution all by yourself. There are several things to observe here: We should probably have some good reason for doing anything; the true nature of a problem is not always readily apparent; and it is easy to confuse symptoms with causes. An excess of overdue accounts may be a problem with the accounts receivable system. It may also be the result of an inappropriate credit policy or a reflection of customer dissatisfaction with defective products.

This can be a tricky step because different people with different interests may have valid differences of opinion as to the true nature of the problem.

In some cases, a complete investigation might be very expensive and time consuming. The normal practice is to begin with a best approximation, document this, select an approach, and then gather additional information. At this point, it is also a good idea to attempt to determine if it is possible to solve the problem, what approaches might best lead to a solution, how long each approach is likely to take, and what each approach is likely to cost. These will be estimates, subject to refinement after more information becomes available. The amount of detail gathered at this point will depend on the nature of the problem and the policies of the organization. Too much study too soon will lead to *paralysis by analysis*. Too little thought can result in wasting a lot of time and money by working on the wrong solution to the wrong problem.

It is surprising that some organizations will embark on expensive system development projects with no agreement as to the benefits to be achieved, the means for achieving them, or the methods to be employed in conducting the work. It is not a surprise that
many of these fail. Sometimes the project fails because the developers and users do not
share the same concept of what is to be accomplished. Sometimes the developers do not
even agree among themselves.

It is as important to define what will not be accomplished as it is to define what will
be accomplished. This is often referred to as establishing the scope of the project.

The very important *second step* is to *draft a plan* for the next phases of the activity. If
you are embarking on a very simple project you will complete by yourself in a short
period of time, this plan might well be a few informal notes. If you are involved in a
major effort which may occupy scores of people for several years, the plan will be very
detailed. Be prepared for difference of opinion and organizational conflict if you are
involved in a major effort with a broad scope.

The *third step* is to *research all the details of the existing situation*. This might
involve determining how bills are processed. It might involve detailed analysis of the
activities of many people. It might involve the study of existing computer programs. A
large project may require extensive interviews and observations and produce volumes of
documentation.

Today, many organizations utilize one of the so-called structured methodologies for
this effort.[17] This results in a series of diagrams illustrating the various processes performed and the data passed from process to process. Considerable emphasis is placed on
documenting the processing steps, rules followed, and data used in appropriate detail.
We need to understand all the details in order to get it right.

The structured techniques place an emphasis on differentiating between the physical
system and the logical system. In this usage, *physical* refers to how things are done. In
Figure 1.9 we indicate that a form is filled out in triplicate. The white copy is sent to
manufacturing. The blue copy is sent to accounting. The salmon colored copy is retained
by the salesperson.

Logical refers to what is accomplished. Manufacturing and accounting are advised
that a particular customer has ordered a particular selection of products at a particular

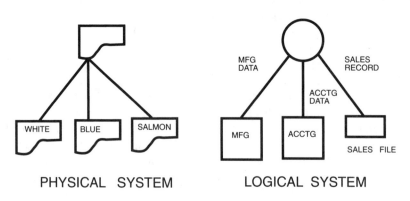

Figure 1.9 Physical versus logical

price to be delivered on a particular date. The salesperson retains a record of the order. The physical system might change without substantially altering the logical. We could, for example, substitute electronic mail messages for these colored forms.

It is very possible that a detailed study will result in a reevaluation and a redefinition of the problem. This does not mean that the initial definition was in error. It may have been fine based on the amount of knowledge which was available. The purpose of additional study was to gain further knowledge. Failure to use that knowledge in refining the definition of the problem and the plan for its solution would certainly be foolish. (But we all do have our foolish moments. And it isn't unusual for a project to continue on a wrong course because someone doesn't want to admit that the original concept was less than perfect.)

If a lot is at stake, it may be worthwhile to go through several iterations of study, redefinition, and refinement before proceeding. If this is the case, each iteration will add more detail.

The *fourth step* is to *develop the details of the proposed solution.* Depending on the situation, this may involve generating several proposed solutions, evaluating the costs and benefits of each, and selecting the best. Again, there may be several iterations, each adding more detail and refinement. Practitioners of the structured approach take great pains to distinguish between the logic of the proposed system and the physical means for carrying it out.

It is possible to repeat several cycles of step three followed by step four. That is, we might research some details, propose some solutions, evaluate, research more details, and repeat the cycle several times. Depending on the policies of the organization, the importance of the problem, the scale of the problem, and the disposition of the parties involved, this might be documented in a very formal detailed manner or in a very informal manner. The danger of the informal approach is that important details and issues will be overlooked. The danger of the very formal approach is that definition and redefinition will go on forever.

Many contemporary database management systems provide facilities for generating screens and reports very quickly. These can be used to develop a *prototype or working model of the proposed system* or a part of the proposed system. There are some cautions about this. This approach does not alleviate the need for discovering all details of what is to be accomplished, including procedural steps, rules, and data definitions. Prototyping does provide a way of working with users to discover the details through a s*how and tell* process. It is particularly useful for working out the details of the interaction between the user and the system.

The *fifth step* consists of *technical design and program creation.* This may be via traditional programming or the use of contemporary program generators. The obvious and important observation we make here is that the programs will only do the correct thing if we have determined what is, in fact, the correct thing and how to do it. And it is cost effective to determine this as early in the process as possible.

The *final steps* involve *testing, documenting, data conversion, training, and implementation.*

This has been a very brief summary of a difficult and time-consuming process.

1.8   NOW, WHAT ABOUT DATABASE DESIGN?

We just provide an overview here, as we did in the case of development methodology. We'll discuss database design by itself first, then show the relationship to system design. Again, various authorities espouse various methods which differ in detail but agree in overall concept. Much of the disagreement involves diagramming technique and terminology.

There are two possible approaches to database design. These are often referred to as *top down* and *bottom up*. *The bottom up approach consists of identifying and defining all atoms of data, utilizing user views as a means for organizing the elements, and synthesizing or integrating them into a database design.*

The top down approach consists of identifying the entities or things of interest, the relationships between the entities, and the data elements which describe each. This conceptual model then becomes the basis for the database design.

Both approaches have some advantages and failings. The bottom up approach should assure that nothing is missed but requires an immediate plunge into a welter of detail. A large business system may have hundreds or even thousands of separate data elements. The result may be a failure to organize the data in any reasonable manner.

The top down approach provides a clear organization of the data but can result in the omission of important details. It can also lead to a data organization which does not lend itself to the efficient processing of the data.

We recommend using a combination of the two approaches. Our *first step* is *the development of an entity model*. See Chapters 4 and 5. This model describes the things of interest, the relationships between things, and the data elements which describe them. It is necessary to develop complete, well thought out definitions for everything.

Our *second step* is to *identify the required user views along with all elements contained in each view*. If a user view contains an element which does not appear as an element in the entity model, we must define it, determine if it can be derived or computed from the elements contained in the entity model, and, if necessary, alter the entity model to incorporate the new element. It may or may not be necessary to add entities or relationships to accomplish this.

Steps one and two can proceed concurrently. They both can and should proceed concurrently with the first four steps of the systems development cycle. But it is necessary to avoid getting into too much detail too soon.

Step three is the *development of a normalized model*. Normalization is a technique for determining which elements should be grouped together. We explore this in detail in Chapter 3.

Step four consists of *augmenting the logical model with data volumes and data accessing patterns*. This becomes the basis for the final design. We discuss this in Chapter 7.

1.9   DO THE TWO CYCLES FIT TOGETHER?

We've discussed a *systems analysis life cycle* and a *database design cycle*. Many sources discuss one, the other, or both as if they are completely independent. Could they be independent of each other? It doesn't seem likely, does it? If we are developing a system which will utilize a particular database, there must be some connection between the two.

Here is a rough cut at putting the two together:

- Identify a problem and propose a solution.
- Draft a plan.
- Research the existing situation.
- Identify entities, relationships and data elements.
- Identify user views and elements contained in user views.
- Modify the entity model as required.
- Reevaluate and redefine if necessary.
- Develop the details of the proposed solution.
- Normalize the result.
- Determine data volumes and accessing patterns.
- Complete final database design.
- Complete technical design and programming.
- Conduct testing, documenting, data conversion, training, and implementing.

1.10   WHAT ABOUT INTEGRATED SYSTEMS?

We have ignored at least one thing. It is often suggested that the goal of database is to promote data sharing, eliminate all redundant data, and ultimately provide a single integrated database for an organization. The theory is that data modeling combined with the data independence provided by a database management system can make this happen. We do not say that this is not the case. We do, however, suggest that there are some difficulties.

It may be that this integrated database can only be implemented if a complete organizational data model is developed first. This is a very big undertaking for even a medium-sized organization.

There may be physical performance considerations which preclude the sharing of the same data by all processing. There may be organizational barriers which preclude sharing of data. This can be a very big problem. It is very difficult, if not impossible, to integrate data if an organization is not integrated.

We do recommend that an organization develop an entity model representing all data entities and relationships. We suggest that this cannot contain every detail because it will become unmanageable and will take too long to develop. We suggest that this be used as a basis for systems planning and be modified as new systems are developed. All of this, however, is beyond the scope of the present work. The principles and techniques contained in this book will be of use in this strategic data planning endeavor.

Endnotes

1. There is some question as to whether one should write "data is" or "data are." We are referring to the collection of data as a single structure and will usually say "data is" even though some language purists may object.

2. Here is an example: "A *data base is a shared collection of interrelated data designed to meet the varied information needs of an organization. A data base has two important properties: It is integrated and it is shared. By* integrated *we mean that previously distinct data files have been logically organized to eliminate (or reduce) redundancy and to facilitate data access. By* shared *we mean that all qualified users in the organization have access to the same data, for use in a variety of activities."* [MCFADDEN88] This might be called the purist (or data bigot) definition. We have no quarrel with the goals stated in this definition. We endorse them.

3. This is not a book about SQL. SQL is used in many of the examples because it is necessary to use some language and SQL seems to be a good choice at this time.

4. "Fairly consistent" is a relative term here. Many authorities have vigorously attacked SQL. This is discussed in more detail in Chapter 2.

5. This is a difficult statement to prove. We aren't going to try. It makes sense to the author. If it doesn't make sense to you, you may be reading the wrong book.

6. We discuss this further in Chapter 7.

7. It could be argued that products which do not provide all these capabilities should not be called database management systems. But there is no way to enforce this.

8. John Zachman has developed an extensive and useful correlation between architectural or engineering models and computer system models. [ZACHMAN87]

9. There was a big decision to make in writing the following material. Using only one name for each type of model would certainly have made it seem less confusing. But you won't be well prepared to read other sources unless you are aware of the different terms and how they are used. At the risk of making this a little harder to read, a variety of names have been listed for each kind of model.

10. This is one meaning of the term "conceptual model." As you will see, it has a slightly different meaning in the context of the ANSI/SPARC three schema architecture which is discussed later in this chapter.

11. If you are interested in this, you might refer to [GILLENSON84], [GOLDFINE82], or [MARTIN82].

12. At the risk of sounding patronizing, we'd best note that these are the names of various programming systems. These embody specific methods for describing data and processing in a manner which can subsequently be interpreted by a computer. Each has its own form and set of rules or syntax. Some concepts are basic to all programming. Some concepts are unique to specific "programming languages." The developers of different languages sometimes used different terminology in describing the same thing. Some individuals become dedicated and passionate aficionados of specific languages. And, of course, there are many more than the four we've mentioned here.

13. In Pascal, these groupings are referred to as records.

14. We'll ignore the fact that most of us are so used to calculators that we find it difficult to do arithmetic with pencil and paper. Your author is showing his age by demonstrating that he can remember the days before calculators.

15. Most calculators are programmed internally to do this.

16. Remember, when we say "user" we mean some business person who is probably not a systems analyst or programmer. This is a common expression in the data processing world.

17. The opening chapters of Meilor Page-Jones' book [PAGEJONES88] provide a summary of these techniques.

QUESTIONS AND EXERCISES

1. List and explain six desirable properties of a database.

2. List and explain ten common features of a database management system.

3. Explain the classification of data models according to purpose.

4. Explain the classification of data models according to modeling style.

5. How do logical and physical data models differ?

6. How does the relational model differ from the hierarchical and network models?

7. What is the value of a design method?

8. List and explain the elements of common systems design methodologies.

9. List and explain the elements of common database design methodologies.

10. Discuss the relationship between systems design and database design.

Chapter 2

Relational Database

2.1 CHAPTER SUMMARY

This chapter contains an explanation of the relational data model. We use the term *data model* in the sense of a particular way of looking at data. We discuss basic ideas, the theoretical foundation, and the standard manipulations of relational data. The definition of the relational model provides for representation and manipulation of data. This chapter also contains an overview of the SQL language. Most relational database management systems provide SQL capability. Most definitions for communication between disparate systems incorporate SQL. This is far from a complete exposition of SQL. It is included because the designer must possess some understanding of the possible data manipulations.

Please keep two important things in mind throughout this chapter. *First*, you will not learn all there is to know about SQL here. *Second*, it is possible that you already know SQL but have not yet become familiar with the theory of the relational model. In that case, resist the temptation to skip this chapter. Many texts on SQL do not deal adequately with relational theory, but an understanding of the theory is very important to a database designer.

2.2 WHY THE RELATIONAL MODEL?

The hierarchical and network data models require the user or programmer to be aware of the manner in which all data is stored. Discussions of database management systems based on the network model often mention *navigation through the database*. A good approach to programming in this environment is to picture oneself moving from record to record via predefined paths, like a rat in a maze. The result of a particular operation can vary depending on the position in the database from which the operation was requested.

We should be fair to the developers of earlier database management systems.

- Earlier computers provided limited memory and processing speed.
- The earlier disk storage devices were limited in capacity and speed.
- Earlier computer operating systems were not very sophisticated.
- Database management was a new concept.
- Initially, it seemed necessary in the development of computer software in general to emphasize efficiency over ease of use.

Developers of early data management and database management systems searched for effective and workable techniques for organizing data. The hierarchical and network models were then derived from the physical storage techniques.[1]

The relational data model was designed to enhance data independence and consistency by severing the connection to physical storage devices and by providing for rigorous definition of both data structure and data manipulation. In 1970, Codd [CODD70] wrote "[the relational model] provides a means of describing data with its natural structure only—that is, without superimposing any additional structure for machine representation purposes." Codd's seminal paper is, by the way, refreshingly clear and easy to read in comparison to many things which have been written about the relational model since 1970.

The results of this approach are improved data independence, more consistency in results, and greater ease of use in comparison to earlier approaches.

The relational model incorporates not only a definition of the view of data but also a definition of the manipulations which may be performed and the results to be expected.

Date [DATE86-3] writes "The relational model is *a way of looking at data*; it can be regarded as a prescription for how data might be represented and how that representation might be manipulated. More specifically, the model is concerned with three aspects of data: data *structure*, data *integrity*, and data *manipulation.*" Date has written extensively and authoritatively about the relational model.

Codd and others have taken pains to assure that the definition of the relational model is logically or mathematically consistent and rigorously defined. We specifically recommend [CODD70], [CODD90], [DATE86-1], and [DATE90] if you would like more detail than this book provides.

Relational theory draws heavily on mathematical set theory. Relations are akin to mathematical sets, and the operations which can be performed on relations are similar to the operations which can be performed on sets. This provides a useful way to understand the relational model. However, it should not be necessary for you to learn set theory in order to read this book.[2]

In our presentation we strive to keep the mathematics to an absolute minimum. But keep in mind that *this mathematical precision is the reason for the predictability and consistency of the manipulations defined as a part of the relational model.*

The benefits of the relational model do come at a price. It would not have been possible to implement a relational system on earlier computers. Today we can adopt the philosophy that the machine should do the necessary work to make things easy for humans. We discuss performance in more detail in Chapter 7. Relational systems can consume a lot of system resources because they make it possible to request manipulations which could not be readily specified using an older technology. Simple operations on a relational database do not have to be expensive. This does not, by the way, mean that complex operations must always be expensive.

2.3   THE RELATIONAL MODEL

The relational model views data in a tabular format. Here is an example.

PART_#	DESCRIPTION
27	UMBRELLA STAND
32	SPITTOON
48	BUGGY WHIP

A relation consists of a heading:

PART_#   DESCRIPTION,

and a series of rows and columns containing data:

27   UMBRELLA STAND

32   SPITTOON

48   BUGGY WHIP

The relational model is often described using special terminology. This is partly because some of the terms are borrowed from mathematical logic and partly to allow for precise definitions of everything. Many people do use simple terms like row and column, but if you want access to all of the literature, you do need to understand some special terms.

The columns are referred to as *attributes*. Attributes appear together in a relation because there is some relationship between them.

The notion of a relation in relational database theory is based on the mathematical concept of a relation. "A relation R on a set S is a set of ordered pairs of elements." [GELLERT75]

The rows are often referred to as *tuples*.[3] Often, each row contains a description of one occurrence of some thing (or entity) that exists in the world. It isn't absolutely necessary for this to be true, but it does often work out this way. In the present example, each row describes or stands for one kind of part. In a more realistic example, there would most likely be many more attributes. We might find something like this:

PART_#	DESCRIPTION	PRICE	WEIGHT	COLOR
27	UMBRELLA STAND	$20.00	5 #	SILVER
32	SPITTOON	$20.00	5 #	SILVER
48	BUGGY WHIP	$47.50	2 #	BLACK

We often desire to discuss the structure of a relation or table without reference to the specific data content. This is done by listing the attribute names, separated by commas, in parentheses, along with a relation or table name. Here are two examples.

PART_NAMES(PART_#, DESCRIPTION)

PARTS(PART_#, DESCRIPTION, PRICE, WEIGHT, COLOR)

The relational model provides for a special data value, *NULL*. It represents *no value*. This is different from zero or blank.

The complete definition of a relation calls for a number of important characteristics.

The ordering or sequence of the rows does not convey information. We frequently like to list data in some order, part number sequence, for example, to make it easier for humans to interpret the data. However, rearranging the rows does not really change the data content.

Traditional computer systems are sometimes designed to process sequential files. The programs and processing techniques often depend on a particular ordering of the data. If a data file is ordered by part number, the sequence... 27, 32, 48,... implies that there is no such thing as part 28 or 29 or 30 and so on. Should the sequence of the data be altered, a program which depends on it would fail to function correctly. The relational model avoids this pitfall by specifying that data sequencing is devoid of information content.

No two rows are identical duplicates. The premise is that there must be some way to tell them apart. Storage sequence can not be used to do this, because sequencing does not convey any information.[4]

Many relational database languages do, by the way, allow duplicate rows to be stored. Some consider this a serious flaw. Most of these provide a way to specify the elimination of duplicates. This is the case with SQL.

All attributes are atomic and can not be decomposed. The relational model does not provide for group attributes.[5]

If it is necessary to deal with a group, the individual components are stored as separate columns, then retrieved together. Many database management systems do provide special data types for dates. We discuss this in the section on SQL.

The ordering or sequencing of the columns does not convey information. Within a relation it is necessary to provide unique names for columns.

2.4 DOMAINS

The rule about column names brings us to a very interesting and important issue. We can, of course, have multiple occurrences of the same type of data element. We add some tables to our example to illustrate this.

PART	(PART_#,	DESCRIPTION)
	27	UMBRELLA STAND
	32	SPITTOON
	48	BUGGY WHIP

WHSE	(WHSE_#,	WHSE_CITY)
	A	BUFFALO
	B	HONG KONG
	C	NEW YORK

STOCK	(PART_#,	WHSE_#,	QTY_OH)
	27	A	10
	27	B	15
	27	C	7
	32	B	25
	48	A	8
	48	B	12

First we note that a part number is a part number and a warehouse number is a warehouse number, and therefore any reference to a part number or a warehouse number is a reference to a particular kind of data element. We also note that PART_# in the PART relation and PART_# in the STOCK relation are different columns in different tables and it may sometimes be necessary to differentiate one from the other.

This is one of the problems solved by introducing the notion of a *domain*.

Definition   *A domain is a set or pool of values of a given type.*[6]

We can, in this example, define a domain of part numbers. The specification of the domain can incorporate the characteristics of part numbers and the specification of what is and what is not a valid part number. The latter might be specified by enumerating all possible values or by stating some rule. In our example, part numbers might be defined as two digit numbers and the content of the PART table might specify the valid possibilities. We can deal with warehouse numbers in a similar manner.

Now, we can state that both the PART_# attribute of the PART relation and the PART_# attribute of the WHSE relation are drawn from the same domain. When two different relations are involved, it is common practice to form the attribute name by qualifying or prefixing the domain name with the relation name as in PART.PART_#, STOCK.PART_#, WHSE.WHSE_#, and STOCK.WHSE_#. The "." notation is normally used to indicate a qualified name. It is not a requirement that the domain name be incorporated in the attribute name. Completely different names may be assigned. If two columns in the same table are drawn from the same domain, unique names must be devised. It is convenient to incorporate the domain name whenever possible for clarity.[7]

This is a very simple concept which resolves a lot of problems about attributes, columns, and data elements. While it is simple, some people find it tricky. Perhaps you'd like to reread this section and think about it a little.[8]

2.5   KEYS

Each row or tuple in a table or relation must, by definition, be different from every other. If a row does actually describe or stand for some thing or entity in the world, we should be able to tell one row from another because we can tell one thing from another. Sometimes it does take all of the attributes to differentiate one item from another. But we can often select one or two attributes which can be used as a key or identifier.

In relational database theory and in database theory in general, the term *key* has a very precise definition. *The key for a relation is that attribute or combination of attributes which can be used to differentiate one tuple from another.* In the example given above, PART_# is the appropriate key for the relation PART_# and WHSE_# is the appropriate key for the relation WHSE, and the combination PART_# + WHSE_# is the appropriate key for the relation STOCK. *A key which is formed by combining two or more attributes is referred to as a concatenated key.*[9]

An appropriate key has two important properties.

- *It is not possible for two different tuples in the same relation to have identical keys.*[10]
- *A key does not have any unnecessary components. It is not possible to discard any attribute contained in a concatenated key.*

In some contexts, some books on programming for example, the term key is used to indicate those attributes used to identify data in a search. Thus, a program might search some parts data for all red parts and some would refer to color as the search key or key. In this book, we call this a *search argument* to distinguish it from a key. In our example, color could not be a key because there might be more than one red part.[11]

It occasionally happens that more than one set of attributes can be used as a key. *Any set of attributes which can be used as a key is called a candidate key.* We must then choose one of these as the primary key. In our example, if we can be sure that no two parts have identical descriptions, DESCRIPTION and PART_# are both candidate keys. Names do not make good keys because it is difficult to be sure that they are, in fact, unique.

If the key of one relation occurs as an attribute of another, it is referred to as a foreign key. In our sample relation STOCK, both PART_# and WHSE_# are foreign keys because each does appear as the key of another relation. Obviously the attribute which is a foreign key and the attribute which is a primary key must be drawn from the same domain. Notice that a foreign key is usually the vehicle for implementing a relationship between two relations.

Relationship and *relation* are different words. In discussions of database design they have completely different meanings. A relationship is an association or connection between two different things. A relation is a particular collection of data organized according to certain rules. In our example, PART_# appears in two different relations and so does WHSE_#. This is not a case of redundancy. These multiple occurrences are necessary to designate data relationships. In this case, we use them to indicate which parts are stored in which warehouses.

It is common practice to underline the key of each relation and designate a foreign key by dashed underline. The dashed underline is often omitted when the foreign key is contained within the primary key. We might write our sample like this.

PART (PART_#, DESCRIPTION)

WHSE (WHSE_#, WHSE_CITY)

STOCK (PART_#, WHSE_#, QTY_OH)

2.6   RELATIONAL DATA MANIPULATIONS

The relational model is complete in the sense that it incorporates not only a way of viewing and specifying data, but also a way of viewing and specifying data manipulations. In fact, the model possesses a property known to mathematicians as *closure*. This means that relational operations applied to relations produce relations for results.

Most people don't find this particularly exciting, but it is important to a mathematician or logician.

If we add or multiply two positive integer numbers, the result is a positive integer number. This is a closed system.

This property is valuable because it guarantees consistent results. It also means that *a series of relational operations can be performed one after the other with predictable results*. We take this for granted regarding a series of arithmetic operations.

Some of the more advanced texts discuss *relational algebra* and *relational calculus*. The differences between the two are not important to our presentation and use of relational concepts.[12]

Eight basic operators are defined. Some are of more practical interest than others.

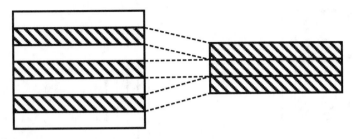

Figure 2.1   SELECT

SELECT is used to extract all tuples which meet some requirement. See Figure 2.1. In our part and warehouse example, we might care to determine which parts are stored in warehouse A. The result of this selection would be as follows.

RESULT 1

PART_#	WHSE_#	QTY_OH
27	A	10
48	A	8

PROJECT is used to extract desired columns from a relation.[13] See Figure 2.2. An obvious extension to the example at hand would be to omit the warehouse identifier from the preceding result. We certainly know which warehouse we asked for and don't need to see it in the result. And the property of closure guarantees that we can combine select and project in this manner. Here is our new result.

RESULT 2

PART_#	QTY_OH
27	10
48	8

A relation does not have duplicate rows. This means that the result of a project can not contain duplicate rows. If we project the single column WHSE_# from RESULT 1 above, the new table will contain a single row.

WHSE_#
A

UNION is used to combine two relations vertically. Union produces a result which contains any tuple contained in either table. Figure 2.3 illustrates this idea. The relations to be combined must have matching columns for this to be possible or even to make

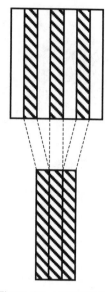

Figure 2.2 PROJECT

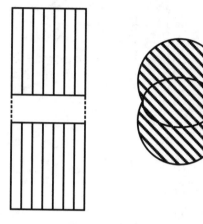

Figure 2.3 UNION

sense. Thus, we might select parts stored in warehouse A and parts stored in warehouse B and form the UNION of the two results,which would look like this.

RESULT 3

PART_#	WHSE_#	QTY_OH
27	A	10
48	A	8
27	B	15
32	B	25
48	B	12

Since relations do not contain duplicate rows, any duplication which results will be eliminated.

Suppose, in the current example, we would like to produce a listing of parts stored in warehouse A and warehouse B. Suppose further that we do not care which warehouse contains the part nor how many there are. Thus, we would create a projection of the preceding relation over PART_#. If duplicates were allowed to appear, our list would contain 27, 48, 27, 32, 48. We wouldn't be surprised to have someone tell us that this is a silly looking report. Elimination of duplicates produces this result.

RESULT 4

PART_#
27
32
48

An alternate sequence such as 48, 27, 32 would have the same information content.

Another approach would also be possible. We might select parts contained in warehouse A and parts contained in warehouse B. These would be the results.

WHSE_A	WHSE_B
27	27
48	32
	48

We could then form the union of these two intermediate results to obtain the same answer as RESULT 4. The union will contain any row which occurs in either table. But no row will be duplicated. Again, the property of closure makes it possible to combine operations in a variety of ways.

JOIN is used to combine two relations horizontally. A matching criterion establishes which tuples from the first relation are combined with which tuples from the second. This is shown in Figure 2.4. We might want to incorporate part descriptions in the preceding result. We could achieve this via a join with the PART table. Our matching condition is that the PART_# of the first match the PART_# of the second, producing this result.

RESULT 5

PART_#	DESCRIPTION
27	UMBRELLA STAND
32	SPITTOON
48	BUGGY WHIP

Strictly speaking, this join would contain two PART_# columns. This isn't very useful, so we omit one of the duplicate columns. The result with the duplicate columns would be called an *equijoin* because an equal condition was specified for the matching criterion. The form we've shown, with the duplication omitted, is referred to as a *natural join*. In most cases the natural equijoin is the desired result.

Now suppose we were to join RESULT 3 with PART, specifying that RESULT_3.PART_# = PART.PART_#. We'd achieve this result.

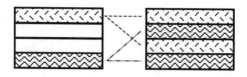

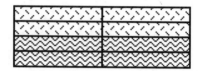

Figure 2.4 JOIN

RESULT 6

PART_#	WHSE_#	QTY_OH	DESCRIPTION
27	A	10	UMBRELLA STAND
48	A	8	BUGGY WHIP
27	B	15	UMBRELLA STAND
32	B	25	SPITTOON
48	B	12	BUGGY WHIP

Notice that our result is formed by making every possible match. Suppose we join RESULT 2 with PART in a similar manner. Here's what we'll get.

RESULT 7

PART_#	QTY_OH	DESCRIPTION
27	10	UMBRELLA STAND
48	8	BUGGY WHIP

Notice that since there was no tuple for part 32 in RESULT 2, the part 32 tuple from PART has been discarded. This is called an *inner join*, and is what is normally meant by the term JOIN.

There is also an *outer join*. The result of an outer join for the same example would be:

RESULT 8

PART_#	QTY_OH	DESCRIPTION
27	10	UMBRELLA STAND
48	8	BUGGY WHIP
32	–	SPITTOON

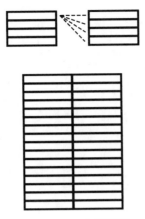

Figure 2.5 PRODUCT

Note that QTY_OH for part 32 is NULL. This does not necessarily mean zero. It means no value. Many relational database management systems do not provide for the outer join on the premise that it has no meaning.

PRODUCT is similar to JOIN. *PRODUCT produces a horizontal combination of two tables in which each tuple from the first is matched with each tuple from the second.* See Figure 2.5. The product of PART and WHSE is the following.

RESULT 9

PART_#	DESCRIPTION	WHSE_#	WHSE_CITY
27	UMBRELLA STAND	A	BUFFALO
27	UMBRELLA STAND	B	HONG KONG
27	UMBRELLA STAND	C	NEW YORK
32	SPITTOON	A	BUFFALO
32	SPITTOON	B	HONG KONG
32	SPITTOON	C	NEW YORK
48	BUGGY WHIP	A	BUFFALO
48	BUGGY WHIP	B	HONG KONG
48	BUGGY WHIP	C	NEW YORK

In practice, this is often the result of neglecting a required match condition from the specification of a join. It is sometimes referred to as a *cartesian product*. The product is useful in the theory, and it is also valuable to the designers of the database management system. In practice, it is usually an error one wants to avoid.

INTERSECT produces a result which contains any tuple contained in both intersected tables. Figure 2.6 illustrates this idea.

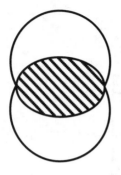

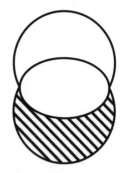

Figure 2.6 INTERSECTION

Figure 2.7 DIFFERENCE

Produce lists of parts contained in warehouse A and B, respectively.

RESULT 10

PART_#	DESCRIPTION
27	UMBRELLA STAND
48	BUGGY WHIP

RESULT 11

PART_#	DESCRIPTION
27	UMBRELLA STAND
32	SPITTOON
48	BUGGY WHIP

Here's the INTERSECTION.

RESULT 12

PART_#	DESCRIPTION
27	UMBRELLA STAND
48	BUGGY WHIP

DIFFERENCE produces a result which contains any tuple that occurs in the first but not the second. See Figure 2.7. Here's the DIFFERENCE between RESULT 11 and RESULT 10.

RESULT 13

PART_#	DESCRIPTION
32	SPITTOON

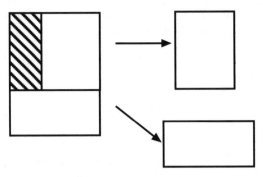

Figure 2.8 DIVIDE

DIVIDE "takes two relations... and builds a relation consisting of all values of one attribute [of the first] relation that match [all values] in the other." [DATE86-1] See Figure 2.8. This is analogous to long division, but it is a little hard to visualize.

PROJECT STOCK over PART_# and WHSE_#.

RESULT 14

PART_#	WHSE_#
27	A
27	B
27	C
32	B
48	A
48	B

PROJECT PART over PART_#.

RESULT 15

PART_#
27
32
48

To determine which warehouse, if any, contains all parts, DIVIDE RESULT 14 by RESULT 15. The result or quotient is as follows.

RESULT 16

WHSE_#
B

The remainder is a table containing part and warehouse combinations for all parts which DO NOT appear in all warehouses.

RESULT 17

PART_#	WHSE_#
27	A
27	C

You will find that all manipulations you care to perform on data can be readily expressed in terms of these operations. You will also find that, in practice, SELECT, PROJECT, and JOIN initially seem to be the most useful. As you become more experienced, you will begin to find many uses for the others also. *Thinking in sets of rows takes some getting used to. It is very helpful to draw a diagram of the table(s) to be operated on and the desired result.*

2.7   STRUCTURED QUERY LANGUAGE

SQL, the Structured Query Language, is a specific language for defining and manipulating relational databases. It combines elements of traditional data manipulation languages and data definition languages in a relatively consistent manner.[14, 15] In this section, we provide a general overview of the language and some illustrations of its use. You will find that SQL, like many *standard* computer languages, has both an invariant core and some details which vary from implementation to implementation. *It will be necessary for you to carefully review the documentation for the particular product you intend to use.*[16, 17]

A source of possible confusion is that *both the SQL language and most vendor documentation do not use many of the terms used by writers and relational theory.* In fact, some terms, such as SELECT, are used in a manner which is not consistent with the expositions of the theory. We will rarely encounter the terms tuple or attribute, or even relation. On the other hand, we can't completely understand what SQL is doing or how to use it without knowledge of the theory. So we have to make the best of this unfortunate situation.[18] *SQL and most implementations contain extensions which provide for data type definitions, presentation of results, special data transformations, and other practical details which are often omitted from theoretical expositions.*

Most of the more complete implementations provide two ways for accessing SQL. SQL statements can be entered directly from a terminal or keyboard. Or, they can be incorporated in programs written in conventional programming languages such as COBOL and C. The former is usually referred to as *interactive SQL*, the latter as *embedded SQL*.

2.8   SQL DATA DEFINITION

The primary unit of data organization in SQL is the table. A table is created via a CREATE TABLE statement. This statement gives the table a name which will be used to refer to it and lists the columns to be included in the table. Each column is given a name and data type, and, when appropriate, a size. It is also possible to specify that a column will not be allowed to contain NULL values.

It is necessary to specify a data type for each elementary item. Most computers make use of different internal formats for storing data of different types. Different operations are legitimate on different types of data. For example, it makes sense to add numbers but not character data. The nature of the specific types provided is one of the things that does vary from implementation to implementation. Availability of types and precision of numeric representations can be affected by hardware as well as by the whim of the implementor. The following is a list of types commonly provided.

CHARACTER or CHAR specifies character data. This would be used for names, descriptions, and other text. Notice that we can store digits in a character field. But if we do so, we can not do any arithmetic with them. We are normally required to specify a length for CHARACTER data. This must be the maximum length we want to provide for. If a particular data occurrence does not need all the room, some systems will add blank spaces at the right while others will truncate. The length is enclosed in parentheses.

NUMERIC (or sometimes NUMBER) specifies numeric data. This specifies that the data be stored in a form suitable for arithmetic. A length field may be required. It is generally possible (and necessary) to specify a number of decimal places as well as a length. Some systems provide a default length which will apply if none is specified. If no decimal places are specified, the default will be none; that is, the number will be an integer. NUMBER may be further subdivided into INTEGER and REAL or FLOAT. INTEGER numbers, by definition, have no decimal places. FLOAT calls for a special hardware format which provides for numbers which can be very large or very small.

Many implementations provide a special DATE type designed to contain month, day, and year in one element. This is usually accompanied by special functions for extracting month or day or year from the complete date and for performing DATE arithmetic.

Some implementations also provide a MONEY type. This is a number with two decimal places. Sometimes the size of a MONEY item is fixed, sometimes it can be specified.

Most implementations call for commas between columns. It is common to require a semicolon (;) as an end of statement marker. Parentheses must be in pairs. The entire list of columns is contained within parentheses.

Our sample tables might be defined like this.

```
CREATE TABLE PART
        (PART_#          CHAR(2),
         DESCRIPTION     CHAR(15));
CREATE TABLE WHSE
```

| (WHSE_# | CHAR(1), |
| WHSE_CITY | CHAR(10)); |

CREATE TABLE STOCK

(PART_#	CHAR(2),
WHSE_#	CHAR(1),
QTY_OH	NUMBER);

There are usually rules regarding the length and makeup of table and column names. Some systems allow as few as eight characters. Some allow thirty. Some allow more. Names are usually restricted to letters, numbers, and some, but not all, special characters. The underscore (_) is usually allowed as a separator for readability. Names such as CREATE and TABLE which have special meaning are usually restricted to SQL and not allowed as names. These may, however, be imbedded in a name like "EMPLOYEE_TABLE."

Current SQL does not provide for domains. It is necessary to repeat the characteristics of an attribute like PART_# every time it occurs in a table. The database designer is, however, well advised to keep a record of all columns drawn from common domains and take pains to assure that the type and size is always specified the same. If a data dictionary is used, it may be possible to record this information there.

Some implementations of SQL also use CREATE statements to define units of storage. These are variously referred to as CLUSTERs, PARTITIONs, or TABLESPACEs. The exact terminology and nature of these units varies from one hardware environment to another. Some systems require that these be specified. Some make it optional. We discuss this further in Chapter 7. It is usually also possible to CREATE INDEXes. Discussion of this is deferred to Chapter 7 as well.

A DROP statement is used to eliminate a TABLE or any other item which has been CREATEd.

2.9   SQL DATA MANIPULATION

In SQL, most data retrieval operations are specified via a SELECT statement. *The SQL SELECT is not quite the same as the select operator explained earlier in this chapter.* The SQL SELECT is used not only to call for a SELECT, but also to call for a PROJECT, a UNION, a JOIN, and all the rest! The usage might be defended this way. A query involves selecting a subset of the rows from some table. In some cases the subset consists of all the rows. This is mathematically proper. Thus, use of SELECT to designate any query is, after a fashion, correct. But it is, in this author's view, unfortunate and confusing terminology.

The basic form is like this.

SELECT	{specification of COLUMNs}
FROM	{specification of TABLEs}
WHERE	{criteria for retrieval}
	{presentation options};

Some of these items are optional. Some are not.

SELECT   {specification of COLUMNs}

It is necessary to specify the names of the columns to appear in the result. If all available columns are to be displayed, the asterisk (*) can be substituted for the list of column names. If more than one table is referenced and the same column name appears in more than one table, it is necessary to qualify the column name with the table name. Column names are separated by commas. There is no comma after the last column name.

FROM   {specification of TABLEs}

It is necessary to specify the table(s) from which the data is to be retrieved. Specification of more than one table results in either a join or a product. Multiple names are separated by commas. No comma follows the last name.

WHERE   {criteria for retrieval}
          {presentation options};

Criteria for retrieval specify the conditions for including rows in the result and the conditions for joining tables. The syntax doesn't require this, but it is often necessary in order to obtain the desired result. In other words, we can omit the criteria if we choose to retrieve all of the data.

Presentation options are used to specify characteristics of the output. These can be omitted if we desire standard or default output.

Let's look at examples of the various relational operations. Each of these is a complete query. These illustrations are indicative of results achieved via interactive SQL. Interactive SQL normally uses the column names as default headings. Most systems provide some form of scrolling to accommodate output which does not fit on the screen.

First we'll consider SELECTion.

SELECT *

FROM PART;

This statement will SELECT all columns of all rows from the PART table. The result will be like this.

PART_#	DESCRIPTION
27	UMBRELLA STAND
32	SPITTOON
48	BUGGY WHIP

A selection of parts stored in warehouse A as in RESULT 1 is achieved via the addition of a where clause.

SELECT *

FROM STOCK

WHERE WHSE_# = 'A';

will result in

PART_#	WHSE_#	QTY_OH
27	A	10
48	A	8

Comparisons involving character data are case sensitive. The result of a comparison with "a" would result in the retrieval of no data.

Character constants are enclosed in quotes (' '). Numeric constants are not.

Character data is compared according to a predefined (collating) sequence determined by the hardware.[19]

Comparison operators include

- equal   represented by   =
- not equal   represented by   <>   (or sometimes !=)
- greater than   represented by   >
- greater or equal   represented by   >=
- less than   represented by   <   and
- less or equal   represented by   <=

Additional possibilities include IN, which specifies that an item be tested for membership in a set of values, and LIKE, which provides a form of pattern matching.

A sequence of comparisons may be combined via AND and OR. We might write

    WHERE WHSE_# = 'A' OR WHSE_# = 'B'.

When AND and OR are combined in one WHERE clause, it is highly recommended that parentheses be used to clarify the meaning because

    WHERE (WHSE_# = 'A' OR WHSE_# = 'B')

    AND QTY_OH > 50

does not produce the same result as

    WHERE WHSE_# = 'A'

    OR (WHSE_# = 'B' AND QTY_OH > 50).

Let's discuss projection next.

The obvious way to achieve a project is to specify only the desired columns in the SQL SELECT statement. This, as it turns out, is not quite enough. *An SQL SELECT statement will return any duplicate rows unless we specify SELECT DISTINCT.* Now, for a language which we are actually going to use, this may be reasonable. If we have created a table with duplicate rows, we'd probably like to be able to view them. However, this deviation from the theory is considered by many to be a defect in SQL. At any rate, here are two queries with results to illustrate the point.

SELECT PART_# FROM STOCK;

PART_#

PART_#
27
27
27
32
48
48

SELECT DISTINCT PART_# FROM STOCK;

PART_#

PART_#
27
32
48

The keyword DISTINCT instructs SQL to perform a true project.

Most SQL systems allow us to specify UNION in a very straightforward manner.

SELECT PART_#, WHSE_#, QTY_OH

FROM STOCK

WHERE WHSE_# = 'A'

UNION

SELECT PART_#, WHSE_#, QTY_OH

FROM STOCK

WHERE WHSE_# = 'B';

PART_#	WHSE_#	QTY_OH
27	A	10
48	A	8
27	B	15
32	B	25
48	B	12

The SQL UNION operator does eliminate duplicates on most systems. You might also note that this UNION is functionally equivalent to the following.

SELECT DISTINCT PART_#, WHSE_#, QTY_OH

FROM STOCK

WHERE WHSE_# = 'A'

OR WHSE_# = 'B';

Now we'll review the JOIN. A JOIN is achieved by specifying two or more tables in the FROM clause and providing a match condition in the WHERE clause.

SELECT DISTINCT PART.PART_#, DESCRIPTION

FROM STOCK, PART

WHERE STOCK.PART_# = PART.PART_#

AND WHSE_# = 'A';

PART_#	DESCRIPTION
27	UMBRELLA STAND
32	SPITTOON
48	BUGGY WHIP

This is actually a combination of a JOIN and a PROJECT. Let's illustrate another point using the same data. Suppose we actually create a table named RESULT_2 containing the subset of the STOCK table relating to warehouse A.

SELECT * FROM RESULT_2;

PART_#	WHSE_#	QTY_OH
27	A	10
48	A	8

SELECT PART.PART_#, DESCRIPTION, QTY_OH

FROM RESULT_2, PART

WHERE RESULT_2.PART_# = PART.PART_#;

PART_#	DESCRIPTION	QTY_OH
27	UMBRELLA STAND	10
48	BUGGY WHIP	8

The above is the usual INNER JOIN. Only those rows which do have a match are shown. The following is an OUTER JOIN.[20] All rows are shown. Unmatched rows are extended with NULL values.

```
SELECT PART.PART_#, DESCRIPTION, QTY_OH
FROM RESULT_2, PART
WHERE RESULT_2.PART_#(+) = PART.PART_#;
```

PART_#	DESCRIPTION	QTY_OH
27	UMBRELLA STAND	10
32	SPITTOON	
48	BUGGY WHIP	8

The elimination of the matching condition from the JOIN results in a PRODUCT.

```
SELECT *
FROM PART, WHSE;
```

PART_#	DESCRIPTION	WHSE_#	WHSE_CITY
27	UMBRELLA STAND	A	BUFFALO
32	SPITTOON	A	BUFFALO
48	BUGGY WHIP	A	BUFFALO
27	UMBRELLA STAND	B	HONG KONG
32	SPITTOON	B	HONG KONG
48	BUGGY WHIP	B	HONG KONG
27	UMBRELLA STAND	C	NEW YORK
32	SPITTOON	C	NEW YORK
48	BUGGY WHIP	C	NEW YORK

We might really want to generate a list of all possibilities. But a result like this is usually obtained because of an error on our part. It is easy to make this sort of error when we are JOINing several tables. This error can use up a lot of machine time and generate a lot of output.

INTERSECT and DIFFERENCE might be specified like this.[21]

```
SELECT *
FROM RESULT_10
INTERSECT
SELECT *
FROM RESULT_11;
```

```
SELECT *

FROM RESULT_11

MINUS

SELECT *

FROM RESULT_10.
```

These might be simulated as follows.

```
SELECT *

FROM RESULT_10

WHERE PART_# IN

        (SELECT PART_#

        FROM RESULT_11);

SELECT *

FROM RESULT_11

WHERE PART_# NOT IN

        (SELECT PART_#

        FROM RESULT_10);
```

Several observations are in order here.

- First, these last two queries are not precisely the same as the INTERSECT and DIFFERENCE. We have checked to see if the part numbers match. We have not checked to see if the entire rows match,

- Second, we have introduced the IN operator. This tests whether or not the value is among those in a specified list.

- Finally, we've made use of subqueries. The result of the inner or nested subquery enters into the evaluation of the outer query. This is possible because the result of any relational operation is a table which can then be an operand for another relational operation. Sophisticated use of subqueries requires some thought and some practice. We aren't going into this at this point because our purpose is to show only enough about SQL to provide a basis for a discussion of relational database design.

We omit any discussion of DIVISION.

Suffice to say that any data manipulation can be clearly and unambiguously expressed, first, in terms of the relational operators, and second, in SQL.

2.10   ADDITIONAL DATA MANIPULATIONS

SQL also provides some useful features which do not directly derive from the theory.

If we are concerned about the sequence in which the data will be presented, we can specify something like this.

```
SELECT *
FROM STOCK
ORDER BY PART_#;
```

If we need totals of various parts, we can write this.

```
SELECT PART_#, SUM(QTY_OH)
FROM STOCK
GROUP BY PART_#;
```

This will be the result.

PART_#	SUM(QTY_OH)
27	32
32	25
48	20

GROUP BY asks the system to arrange the data in groups as specified and then operate on the groups. In this case, these would be the groups

PART_#	WHSE_#	QTY_OH
27	A	10
27	B	15
27	C	7
32	C	25
48	A	8
48	B	12

Each group has a unique part number, while each group does not have a unique warehouse number or quantity. Thus, we cannot specify warehouse number or quantity, as such, in the SELECT list. We can apply a group function to all members of the group and select the result. Most systems provide maximum and minimum functions as well as sum.

SQL implementations commonly provide additional functions for data manipulations including date arithmetic, extracting a portion of a character item, useful mathematical functions, and others.

It is also common to provide special commands for altering the appearance of the output. The usual features include report headings, page numbers, column headings, and insertion of commas, decimal points, and dollar signs. These extensions are beyond the content of the standard.[22]

2.11   UPDATE COMMANDS

To be useful, a database management system must provide for adding, deleting, and changing the data. In SQL, we accomplish this via statements like these.

> INSERT INTO STOCK
>
> VALUES
>
> ('59', 'C', 47);

Add a row to a table.

> INSERT INTO RESULT_2
>
> SELECT PART_#, QTY_OH
>
> FROM STOCK
>
> WHERE WHSE_# = 'A';

Add several rows to a table. Obtain the data via selection from another table.

> DELETE FROM STOCK
>
> WHERE PART_# = '59';

Delete a row from a table. Notice that if a table contains two identical rows, there is no simple way to delete one of them.

> UPDATE STOCK
>
> SET QTY_OH = QTY_OH * 2;

Multiply all quantities by 2.

> UPDATE STOCK
>
> SET QTY_OH = QTY_OH - 5
>
> WHERE PART_# = '27'
>
>   AND WHSE_# = 'B';

Subtract 5 from the quantity of part 27 held in warehouse B. Perhaps, in a book on design, we'd better note that this data manipulation alters an inventory record. It does not alter the actual quantity of goods in the warehouse. If we design a good system and the users are conscientious, the quantity shown in the database record will match the quantity in the warehouse. If this is not the case, we have a problem to solve.

2.12   EMBEDDED SQL

All of these examples have been presented as if we were entering them directly via interactive SQL. There could be a number of reasons why we would not want this.

- We really don't want to type these lengthy SQL statements over and over.
- We don't want to train users, warehouse clerks for example, in the use of SQL. We certainly wouldn't want it to be necessary for a bank customer to enter SQL statements at an automated teller machine.
- We may want to incorporate various tests for the validity of the input transaction and the data.
- The data manipulation or retrieval may be a small part of some elaborate process or calculation.
- We may want the manipulation to be a "batch process" which is run at some time when no user is present.

Thus, we need some means for incorporating SQL in a program written in some conventional programming language such as COBOL or C. This is what *embedded SQL* is all about. While we don't want to digress into programming here, we'd best note a few significant points.

- Most systems provide for the insertion of a standard SQL statement in a program. It is usually necessary to process the program through a special SQL pre-compiler.
- Programs must contain definitions of all data to be processed. This makes it necessary for the programmer to define variables to hold the results.
- Most programs are written to process one group of data (corresponding to a row of a table) at a time. Since SQL results are tables, it is usually necessary to define a data locator or CURSOR which is advanced through the result one row at a time.[23]
- It is necessary for the programmer to provide instructions which test a RETURN CODE to determine whether or not the requested operations were successful.

Figure 2.9 illustrates the basic concept of embedded SQL.

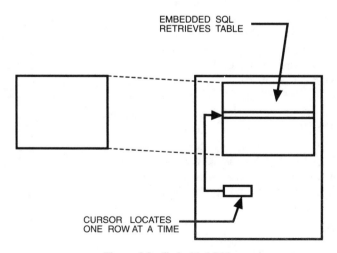

EMBEDDED SQL
RETRIEVES TABLE

CURSOR LOCATES
ONE ROW AT A TIME

Figure 2.9 Embedded SQL

2.13 VIEWS

User VIEWs, as described in Chapter 1, are provided for in SQL. VIEWs are created via a CREATE VIEW statement. Here is an example.

CREATE VIEW PARTS_ON_HAND (PART_#, LOCATION, QTY,
      DESCRIPTION)

AS

SELECT PART.PART_#, WHSE_#, QTY_OH, DESCRIPTION

FROM PART, STOCK

WHERE PART.PART_# = STOCK.PART_#;

CREATE VIEW, unlike CREATE TABLE, does not actually create a table. It creates a definition of a pseudo table (or virtual table). The TABLE or TABLES from which the VIEW is derived are commonly called the BASE TABLES. The user can access the VIEW as if it were a table. The statements which define the view are stored by the DBMS and are executed each time the view is called for. There is no savings in execution time. The benefits derive from the ability to define the VIEW once for many users and from the ability to use VIEWS as a way to control access to the data.

A VIEW can simplify programming by avoiding the necessity for repeatedly re-entering a lengthy SQL statement.

VIEWS are often used to provide data security. We discuss this in the next section.

A big advantage here is that the VIEW is defined once to the DBMS and may then be utilized by many users and by many programs. If it is necessary to alter the VIEW, it is only necessary to make one modification. It is not necessary to search out and instruct all the users or search out and modify all the programs.

It's worth noting that since embedded SQL, as discussed above, provides a way to incorporate specific SQL statements in specific programs, these might be thought of as a form of VIEW. The one big difference is that the definition and derivation is known to the program and is not known to the DBMS. If several programs require the same data view, each must specify the same derivation and each must be modified if the derivation is modified. Even though it may look like a VIEW to the end user, one of the significant benefits of the view mechanism is lost.

Updating data via SQL VIEWS is problematic. Since a VIEW is normally a subset of the data, adding new rows via a VIEW must result in NULL values for some of the columns. This may be all right if NULL values for those columns make sense. It is certainly not all right if NULL values are not allowed for some of the columns which are not in the VIEW. Any attempt to add rows by means of a view which does not contain the KEY or IDENTIFIER [24] for the BASE TABLE must be doomed to failure.

It is frequently difficult, if not impossible, to define precisely what it means to add or delete a row via a VIEW that incorporates a JOIN or a GROUP BY clause.

Let's refer to the VIEW that was defined just above.

CREATE VIEW PARTS_ON_HAND (PART_#, LOCATION, QTY,
      DESCRIPTION)

AS

SELECT PART.PART_#, WHSE_#, QTY_OH, DESCRIPTION

FROM PART, STOCK

WHERE PART.PART_# = STOCK.PART_#;

We previously populated PART and STOCK like this.

PART	(PART_#,	DESCRIPTION)
	27	UMBRELLA STAND
	32	SPITTOON
	48	BUGGY WHIP

STOCK	(PART_#,	WHSE_#,	QTY_OH)
	27	A	10
	27	B	15
	27	C	7
	32	B	25
	48	A	8
	48	B	12

Given this data, PARTS_ON_HAND would look like this.

PARTS_ON_HAND	(PART_#,	LOCATION,	QTY,	DESCRIPTION)
	27	A	10	UMBRELLA STAND
	27	B	15	UMBRELLA STAND
	27	C	7	UMBRELLA STAND
	32	B	25	SPITTOON
	48	A	8	BUGGY WHIP
	48	B	12	BUGGY WHIP

Suppose we delete a row from the view. Do we delete only the STOCK data or do we delete the PART data as well? In the case of the fourth row, we might delete both. In the case of any other row, we could only delete from STOCK. Similarly, what does it mean to add a row? It would depend on whether or not the part already existed in the PART table. On the other hand, we could reasonably alter QTY through the VIEW.

For this reason, most systems severely limit VIEW updating. It is common to restrict update to VIEWs that are derived from a single table and do not involve GROUP BY.

This does eliminate some updates that might be possible, but it is the approach taken by the designers of most DBMS's.

As a result, the database designer must really think to produce a design with VIEWS which can be used for updating.

2.14 DATA SECURITY

SQL and most implementations provide for security via the GRANT command. The first line of defense is that no one can do anything until privileges to do so have been granted either by the database administrator or the *owner* of the data. The owner of the data is usually taken to be the user identifier which was used to CREATE the table. This may not always be appropriate. *It can be very difficult to determine who, in fact, should be authorized to access data.* If you are working in a multi-user environment where there is a differentiation between programmers and users, you will find that you must devote a lot of attention to this. If the user is actually the person who defines the table and enters updates and queries, the assumption that he or she can control the use of the data is more valid. But there may be organizational policy problems even here. We discuss this further in Chapter 6. *This is a policy problem which can not be solved by technology alone.*

This owner can then GRANT privileges to others who may in turn be GRANTed the privilege of GRANTing (or delegating) to others.

By GRANTing access to VIEWs rather than entire tables we can restrict the amount of data which can be accessed by a user. We can restrict rows as well as columns in the following manner.

> CREATE VIEW WHSE_A
>
> AS SELECT PART_#, QTY_OH
>
> FROM STOCK
>
> WHERE WHSE_# = 'A'; [25]

The user who is authorized access via this VIEW will only be aware of parts stored in warehouse A. The GRANT command may authorize all privileges or only certain privileges such as SELECT, INSERT, or UPDATE.

2.15 OTHER SQL FACILITIES

Most contemporary database management systems provide additional facilities for report, screen, and program generation.

This is possible because the database management system must contain a description of all data in a CATALOG or DICTIONARY. A typical CATALOG will include, among other things, a table identifying table name, column name, data type, and position for each column in each table. Thus, we might find the following in a typical CATALOG.

TABLE	COLUMN	TYPE	POSITION
PART	PART_#	CHAR(2)	1
PART	DESCRIPTION	CHAR(15)	2
STOCK	PART_#	CHAR(2)	1
STOCK	WHSE_#	CHAR(1)	2
STOCK	QTY_OH	NUMBER	3
WHSE	WHSE_#	CHAR(1)	1
WHSE	WHSE_CITY	CHAR(10)	2

The system can then use this data about data in various ways. It is used in analyzing SQL statements. It can be used to generate an input or query screen automatically. Many systems allow the user (or programmer) to specify where on the screen each item should appear, add text (instructions) to the screen, and specify specific actions to be taken by the system given particular data values or conditions.

Thus, with a little practice, you can eliminate a lot of conventional programming and create a computer system much more quickly than was possible in the past. *This will be possible only if the database is well designed, is suitable for the application at hand, and does actually contain correct data.*

We must understand the data, the manipulations to be performed on the data, and the business purpose of the system in order to achieve this. In other words, we can achieve reductions in programming, but not in analysis.

Finally, it is possible that the processing may be too complex or the performance requirement too restrictive. Then we must revert to traditional programming.

2.16 CRITICISMS OF SQL

There have been numerous criticisms of SQL, [CODD88] and [DATE87] for example. Some criticisms revolve around failure to conform precisely to relational theory. We've already noted some issues such as duplicate rows, lack of support for domains, restrictions on view updating, and failure to provide for some operations in a direct manner.

Some criticisms revolve around facilities for maintaining data integrity. We return to this in Chapter 6. Some criticisms revolve around the lack of standard facilities for report and screen format specification. Some criticisms are of the performance of relational systems in general. This is worth further discussion.

SQL is nonprocedural. This means we specify a desired result but do not really tell the system how to achieve that result. With a network or hierarchical system, or in a traditional file processing environment, we must not only identify the desired result, we must also devise and specify a means for achieving it. It may be necessary to search all stock data, examining the part number for each item, in order to find out how many units of part 27 are available. It may be necessary to devise some sorting and matching strategy to produce the results which combine information taken from PART and STOCK. A critical aspect of traditional approaches involves the design and implementation of appropriate data structures and searching and matching strategies.

Most relational database management systems incorporate a component, often referred to as the *optimizer*, which examines the statement to be processed along with the data in the catalog and selects an appropriate search technique. This must be a relatively intelligent program. Selection of an inappropriate strategy can have a significant effect on the amount of processing and searching required. Early systems were quite primitive. Some contemporary systems have become very sophisticated.

There is another complication. SQL provides more than one way to achieve a desired result. Theory says the system should select the optimal strategy no matter how one writes the statement. In practice, this is not always the case. It is sometimes necessary to experiment with various approaches and select that which performs best. In addition, two different vendor's implementations may derive two different strategies for the same statement. The experience gained by trial and error may not be portable.

The power of SQL creates a curious sort of *performance* problem. It is possible, in a relatively few lines of SQL, to specify a search which would be very difficult to code via traditional means. There may be no alternative to an exhaustive and time-consuming search through all of the data. If all of the data means hundreds of customer records, this may be no problem. If it means millions, it can be a big problem. One does hear horror stories of elaborate queries which processed for days against large databases. If the information retrieved has real value, this is just the price which must be paid to get it. But it is necessary to use this tool intelligently and to evaluate and schedule some types of searches carefully. On the other hand, simple processes which retrieve and alter small amounts of data should perform adequately in a well-tuned environment. We return to this issue in Chapter 7.

SQL and relational systems are here, have been widely promoted, are beginning to be used extensively, and are here to stay. In some cases, they've been purchased for all the wrong reasons. In others they've been adopted for sound reasons. A relational system is, for many purposes, truly easier to use than a more traditional approach. It is necessary for today's practitioner (and today's user) to understand the nature of relational systems, SQL, and key principles of relational design.

2.17 IS IT REALLY RELATIONAL? DOES IT MATTER?

As we just noted, SQL and relational systems have become very popular. It has almost reached the point where no self-respecting DBMS vendor will attempt to market a system which is not relational.[26]

In 1985, Codd [CODD85] proposed a set of rules for determining whether or not a system is truly relational. As the developer of the relational model, he is probably more entitled than anyone else to do this.[27]

We'll briefly review the rules.

"Rule Zero: For any system that is advertised as, or claimed to be, a relational data base management system, that system must be able to manage data bases entirely through its relational capabilities."

The system must make it possible for the user to request any necessary retrieval or manipulation via the relational operations described above.

"Rule 1: All information in a relational data base is represented explicitly at the logical level and in exactly one way—by values in tables."

The user must be completely unaware of the manner in which the data is physically stored. Even the description of the database is stored and manipulated as relational tables. All requests are in terms of data values.

"Rule 2: Each and every datum (atomic value) in a relational data base is guaranteed to be logically accessible by resorting to a combination of table name, primary key value and column name."

Rule 2 seems necessary to provide the capability required by rule 1.

"Rule 3: Null values (distinct from the empty character string or a string of blank characters and distinct from zero or any other number) are supported in a fully relational DBMS for representing missing information and inapplicable information in a systematic way, independent of data type."

NULL means there is no value. That is different from blank or zero which are particular values an attribute may assume.

"Rule 4: The data base description is represented at the logical level in the same way as ordinary data, so that authorized users can apply the same relational language to its interrogation as they apply to the regular data."

The system catalog (or dictionary) is a relational database which may be manipulated just like any other relational database.

"Rule 5: A relational system may support several languages and various modes of terminal use (for example, the fill-in-the-blanks mode). However, there must be at least one language whose statements are expressible, per some well-defined syntax, as character strings and that is comprehensive in supporting all of the following items:

- Data definition.
- View definition.
- Data manipulation (interactive and by program).
- Integrity constraints.
- Authorization.
- Transaction boundaries (begin, commit and rollback)."

We will deal with all of these issues in subsequent chapters. This rule follows from Rule Zero.

"Rule 6: All views that are theoretically updatable are also updatable by the system."

As we've noted, this one is difficult.

"Rule 7: The capability of handling a base relation or a derived relation as a single operand applies not only to the retrieval of data but also to the insertion, update and deletion of data."

Some vendors grafted a relational-like query capability (and only a query capability) onto a pre-existing network or hierarchical system.

"Rule 8: Application programs and terminal activities remain logically unimpaired whenever any changes are made in either storage representations or access methods."

True data independence is to be achieved. "Logically unimpaired" means that the same statement will produce the same result. It is very definitely true that changes to the physical database will affect performance and response time.

"Rule 9: Application programs and terminal activities remain logically unimpaired when information-preserving changes of any kind that theoretically permit unimpairment are made to the base tables."

This goes with the ability to update views that are theoretically updatable. It should, for example, be possible to partition a table, define a view that joins the pieces together, and proceed as if nothing happened. This is another difficult one.

"Rule 10: Integrity constraints specific to a particular relational data base must be definable in the relational data sublanguage and storable in the catalog, not in the application programs."

This means that rules about the data should be part of the database definition and should be enforced by the DBMS. We discuss this in some detail in Chapter 6.

"Rule 11: A relational DBMS has distribution independence."

It should be possible to store different portions of the data at different locations. This should be hidden from the user. Relocation of the data should not require modification to programs or queries. We discuss this in Chapter 8.

"Rule 12: If a relational system has a low-level (single-record-at-a-time) language, that low level cannot be used to subvert or bypass the integrity rules and constraints expressed in the higher level relational language (multiple records-at-a-time)."

This was mainly a reference to the aforementioned pre-existing network or hierarchical systems with relational capabilities grafted on.

Since the publication of these rules, Codd and his associates have performed a number of *audits* to determine whether or not particular software products satisfy these requirements and deserve to be labeled relational. Since software products are subject to continuing revision and enhancement it does not seem appropriate to go into these ratings here. We can observe that as this is written (1992) there do not appear to be any systems which completely fill the bill. Many of the major mainframe-oriented systems come close. Many microcomputer-based systems do not come as close. Most SQL-based systems come reasonably close. Some vendors have argued that the ability to perform required functions, such as query and update, is more important than any set of rules. It does seem that any system which meets these requirements and provides adequate performance will be a useful one. We let it go at that for now.

In the next chapter we begin to address design principles by taking a look at the process of normalization. This is an important concept. You will have to read this chapter carefully in order to understand it. However, normalization is often made to seem much more complex than it really is.

Endnotes

1. The hierarchical model is based on the notion of storing data items one after another. We might store data about orders for a particular customer adjacent to the data about the customer. That would look something like this:

Customer1 | Order45 | Order27 | Order 92 | Customer3 | Order14 |
Customer7 | Order19 | Order32 |...

This could, in turn, be visualized like this:

Customer1
　　Order45
　　Order27
　　Order92
Customer3
　　Order14
Customer7
　　Order19
　　Order32

This can readily be viewed as a hierarchy. The network model originated with the concept of storing the storage location of one record as data in another. Thus, the customer record would contain a reference to the storage location of an order record for that customer and that order record would contain a reference to the storage location of another order for the same customer. This arrangement can readily be visualized as a network.

2. Learning set theory is, however, a very worthwhile undertaking. It provides a valuable way of looking at many database design and programming problems.

3. Most people pronounce tuple as "tuh-pul" with the accent on the first syllable.

4. To some, this is problematic. A common counter example is a cash register tape, which, it is said, can contain meaningful duplicate rows. But they really are not duplicates because we will mentally identify them as the first, second, third, and so on. We can convert the register tape to a relation in one of three ways. We can provide a unique item number to identify the first item on the tape, the second, the third, and so on. Or we can assign a tie breaker to identify the first of a given type of item, the second, and so on. Or we can add a quantity attribute and a total value attribute allowing one entry on the order of "six bars of soap at $0.50 each for a total of $3.00."

5. Codd [CODD90] explains. "In the relational model there is only one type of compound data: the relation... any additional types of compound data add complexity without adding power."

6. There are other meanings for the word domain. In discussions of communications networks, for example, a domain is a particular grouping of devices within a larger network.

7. We discuss names at some length in Chapter 7.

8. Codd has proposed relational operator and DBMS support for domains. At this time, a few products do make some limited provision for this. It is a useful and valuable feature.

9. The word concatenate is often used to describe the joining of two items. "ABCD" concatenated with "GOLDFISH" results in "ABCDGOLDFISH." We use the plus sign ("+") in this book because the process is a sort of addition. Some authors use a vertical bar ("|"). Use of the plus sign is common in structured analysis.

10. We have noted that many database management systems, including those based on SQL, relax this requirement. This is discussed further in the section on SQL.

11. Notice that we have to know enough about the data to know whether or not this is true. There could be situations where no two items have the same color. Then color could be a key. We've really made an assumption here.

12. We include this note for sake of completeness. Date [DATE86-1] states, "where the algebra provides a collection of explicit operations... that can be used to *build* some desired relation from the given relations in the database, the calculus merely provides a notation for formulating the *definition* of that desired relation in terms of those given relations."

13. This is usually pronounced "proh-ject" with a long "O."

14. As we note elsewhere, this means consistent compared to some of the other possibilities. Codd, Date, and others have been quite critical of SQL.

15. SQL, the Structured Query Language, has evolved from SEQUEL, the Structured English Query Language, which was defined by D. D. Chamberlain and others at the IBM San Jose laboratory in the early 1970s. This language was incorporated in System R, an experimental relational database management system constructed by IBM in the 1970s. It was subsequently incorporated in SQL/DS and Database2, IBM's mainframe based relational database management systems; OS/400, the operating system for IBM's mid-range AS/400 system; and OS/2 EE, IBM's extended operating system for the PS/2 personal computer line. All of these became available in the 1980's. (SQL/DS, Database2, OS/400, AS/400, OS/2 EE, and PS/2 are registered trademarks of International Business Machines Corporation.) SQL is also a feature of the ORACLE database management system which was released in the early 1970s. (ORACLE is a registered trade mark of Oracle Corporation.) Initially there was some competition among relational data manipulation languages. The INGRES system incorporated the QUEL language. (INGRES is a registered trademark of ASK.) INGRES and ORACLE are worth mention because they were the first widely known and generally available relational systems. dBase II, dBase III, dBase III plus, and dBase IV (these are all registered trademarks of Ashton-Tate Corporation) incorporate a proprietary definition and manipulation language. The dBase line may well be the best known relational database management system for microcomputers. (There are those who would not consider dBase to be a true relational DBMS because many relational operations cannot be expressed in a nonprocedural manner and because many of the rules are not enforced.) dBase IV does also provide SQL, as do the newer releases of INGRES, and as does almost every relational database management system available at this writing. While there has been some debate as to whether or not SQL is the best language, it has, since the announcement of the various IBM products, become THE standard. Standards documents have been issued by the American National Standards Institute and the International Standards Organization. [ANSI86] [ISO89]

16. For the neophyte, we can recommend Ageloff's primer [AGELOFF88] as an excellent book for getting started with SQL. In preparing these materials, we have also referred to [ANSI86], [DATE87], [IBM88-1], [ISO89], and [ORACLE87].

17. Many of the examples have been checked out using ORACLE SQL*PLUS on a VAX/VMS system. (SQL*PLUS is a registered trademark of Oracle Corporation. VAX and VMS are registered trademarks of Digital Equipment Corporation.) This particular combination was used because the author had convenient access to it while working on this book. The Oracle SQL does contain numerous extensions which are not available in some of the other implementations. You may find yourself unable to duplicate them exactly on whatever system you use.

18. And PLEASE don't blame the author of this book for the inconsistency. He is, quite frankly, at a loss to explain how it came to be.

19. Most computers in use today use one of two systems for encoding character data. The American Standard Code for Information Interchange is referred to as ASCII. This is common for micro- and minicomputers. The Extended Binary Coded Decimal Interchange Code is referred to as EBCDIC. This is common for mainframe computers. Each has its own sorting or collating sequence.

20. As noted above, the Oracle system provides extensions not available in many other products. The ability to directly specify an OUTER JOIN is one of them. Obtaining a similar result without the use of the special (+) operator requires a much more elaborate statement. Language extensions always pose an interesting problem. They can be very useful. They can also "lock in" a particular vendor's product.

21. Again, these are extensions which are available in Oracle and may not be available to you.

22. We have noted a remarkable degree of standardization in this, at least in systems we have personal experience with.

23. Programming embedded SQL with CURSORs can get tricky. Some aspects vary from implementation to implementation. You should study your vendor's documentation and make sure you understand this.

24. We discuss KEYS and IDENTIFIERS in some detail in a preceding section and also in Chapters 4 and 7.

25. If the VIEW columns are identically named with those from the base table, and there are no ambiguities, we need not specify them in the CREATE VIEW statement.

26. Take heart. The age of object-oriented systems has dawned. Many developers of new systems are labeling them object oriented instead of relational. A complete explanation of object orientation must be lengthy and detailed and is well beyond the scope of this book. Suffice to say that many systems marketed as object oriented only provide some parts of object orientation.

27. Unfortunately, there is no one who can authoritatively define a set of rules for the above mentioned object-oriented systems.

QUESTIONS AND EXERCISES

1. What are the advantages of the relational model?

2. Must relational systems be inefficient? Why? Why not?

3. Explain the terms relation, tuple, attribute, key, and foreign key.

4. Explain the distinguishing characteristics of the relational model.

5. What is a domain? Why are domains important?

6. What is the meaning and value of the property of closure?

7. Explain SELECT, PROJECT, PRODUCT, JOIN, UNION, INTERSECT, and DIFFERENCE. Provide an example of each.

8. What is the difference between the INNER and OUTER JOIN operations?

9. Do all authorities agree on the value of SQL? Explain your answer.

Use the following relations for the exercises which follow. Show the result of each relational operation.

ITEMS(	ITEM_#,	ITEM_DESCRIPTION,	PRICE)
	123	Pontoon Cover	$100.00
	124	Potato Peeler	$5.00
	125	Pimento Polisher	$55.00
	126	Pig Preener	$25.00
	127	Pain Preventer	$7.50
	128	Pretty Parrot	$87.50

ORDERS(	ORDER_#	ITEM_#,	QUANTITY)
	1234	123	1
	1235	126	12
	1236	128	7
	1237	124	65
	1238	123	2
	1239	128	3

10. SELECT all orders for item 126.

11. SELECT all orders for item 124.

12. JOIN the two relations on the basis of equal ITEM_#. Show INNER JOIN and OUTER JOIN.

13. PROJECT ITEM_# from the ORDERS table.

14. SELECT all items costing less than $10.00.
    SELECT all items costing more than $60.00.
    Form the UNION of the two results.

15. Find all items for which there are orders. Explain the relational operations you used.

16. Find all items for which there are no orders. Explain the relational operations you used.

17. Find all items which cost more than $50.00 and for which there are orders. Explain the relational operations you used.

Chapter 3

Normalization

3.1 CHAPTER SUMMARY

This chapter explains normalization theory and practice. Normalization is an important component of relational database design. It is also valuable in the design of conventional files, hierarchical databases, and network databases. It is even useful in the design of forms, reports, and screens.

It is possible to express the principles of normalization very concisely and many works do this. Unfortunately, *learning a definition and understanding how to apply it are two different things*. Therefore we provide a lot of examples and a lot of explanation. You will probably find it necessary to devote quite a bit of time and energy to the review of this material.[1]

3.2 WHAT IS NORMALIZATION?

Normalization is a procedure for deciding which attributes belong together in a relation (or, which fields belong together in a record). One of the basic concepts of relational database is that we group a collection of attributes together in a relation because there is a clear and logical relationship among them.[2]

The result of normalization is a *logical database design*, a fairly detailed design which captures the true nature of the data. Sometimes people with some computing experience are disturbed by normalized database designs that do not appear to provide for the greatest processing efficiencies. There are several issues to consider here.

- A normalized logical design organizes the data according to its meaning. It lies somewhere between the conceptual and physical designs.
- Contemporary computer systems are much more powerful than those which were available just a few years ago. It is sometimes reasonable to implement a design which gains ease of use at the cost of additional processing.
- The *logical* design may not be the final design. It represents the designer's best understanding of the nature and meaning of the data. If performance needs dictate, the final *physical* design may be different. We may discover that, in order to implement a physical design which will provide the performance we require or desire, we must, in a later step, *de-normalize* the relations we have developed.[3] This does not mean we have wasted the time and effort we spent normalizing. When you understand the rule you are breaking, you can take appropriate action to keep out of trouble. When you break the rules without understanding them, you are likely to have serious problems later. We discuss this in Chapter 7.
- A normalized design will be robust and will not be susceptible to a variety of anomalies[4] or problems. This is because normalization eliminates redundancy or duplication of facts.
- The process of normalization will force us to come to a complete understanding of each element of the data. This last benefit may actually be the most important.

We use the word normalization here in the sense in which it is often used by mathematicians. A *normal form*, the result of a normalization process, is a standard format used for consistency.

The rules of normalization are usually explained by describing a series of normal forms. We will discuss *First Normal Form, Second Normal Form, Third Normal Form, Boyce/Codd Normal Form, Fourth Normal Form, and Fifth Normal Form*. These are abbreviated as 1NF, 2NF, 3NF, BCNF, 4NF, and 5NF. Each of these involves a rule which addresses a particular type of problem. Each is a refinement of the preceding.[5] It is natural and customary to explain each normal form in turn by demonstrating the flaws in an unnormalized relation and illustrating that the normalized form avoids the flaws. This might lead you to conclude that it is necessary to begin with a poor design and remedy its flaws by applying the normalization rules in sequence. This procedure will certainly produce the desired result, but it is likely to require a lot of unnecessary effort. Familiarity with all of the normal forms will often make it possible for you to establish a sound design immediately.

The rules are based on common sense. It is very possible that you would intuitively follow them. The advantage of having them stated formally and explicitly is that you can consciously make sure you follow all of them.

Much of the work leading to the development of these rules has been performed by people with a mathematical background or inclination. There is a definite advantage to mathematical rigor. It assures a solid logical basis. To keep this book accessible to the widest audience, we make every possible effort to minimize the use of mathematical symbols and proofs. It is still unavoidable that you will have to read some sections very carefully and possibly read some material more than once. You will find it to be well worth the effort.

3.3   MATHEMATICAL FUNCTIONS

Normalization involves the use of *functional dependencies*. These are similar to mathematical functions.

Some readers can probably skip the following discussion of mathematical functions. You will have to decide if you are already knowledgeable enough to do this.

A function describes a relationship between two or more kinds of things. For example, if oranges cost twenty-five cents each, the cost of a bag of oranges will be the number of oranges multiplied by 0.25. We might then write

$\text{cost} = \text{quantity} \times 0.25$

The important point here is that *a unique cost will be determined for any given quantity of oranges*. In a more general form, the mathematician will write

$y = f(x)$

to indicate that there is some *rule or formula which associates a single value for y with any given value for x*.

A more abstract statement of the formula for the cost of the oranges is

$y = 0.25x$

In the case of this particular function, there is a unique y-value to go with each x-value and a unique x-value to go with each y-value.

Let's look now at a different formula:

$y = 0.25x^2$

For an x-value of +2, the y-value will be +2 times +2 times 0.25, or 1. For an x-value of –2, the y-value will be –2 times –2 times 0.25. This is also 1. Two different x-values produce the same y-value. This is still a valid function since it does provide a single y-value for any given x-value.

It is a requirement that for any given x-value there must be a single y-value. It is, however, possible for two different x-values to be related to the same y-value.

There are different possible ways to express a function. In the examples we have seen so far, the functions have been expressed as mathematical formulas. This is not the only possibility. A mathematician will be perfectly happy to apply the definition of a function to a table of values such as the following:

PRODUCT	UNIT COST
orange	$.25
banana	$.17
lemon	$.10
grapefruit	$.32
peach	$.25

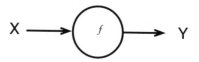

Figure 3.1   Function

By referring to this table, you can discover a single y-value or unit cost which is related to any valid x-value or product name. That is, given a product, we can identify a single unit cost. Bananas cost $.17 each. Notice that there are two different x-values with the same y-value assigned. Given a unit cost of $.25, we don't know if the product is an orange or a peach. Such a table might be developed by some calculation, by some arbitrary rule, or by observation. An example of the last might be the listing of today's closing prices for stocks listed on the New York Stock Exchange. The important thing is that we have a way to discover a single y-value that is associated with any given x-value.

We might think of a function as some sort of black box, which accepts an x-value as an input and produces a y-value as an output as indicated by Figure 3.1.

It is also possible for a function to involve more than one input or determining variable.[6] The cost of the oranges might be based on quantity and size. In a more abstract sense we might write

$$y = f(x, z)$$

to signify that for a particular x-value combined with a particular z-value we can determine a single y-value.

Understanding the mathematical notion of a function is fairly easy. So is utilizing a function which someone has provided. Determining that there is a function which relates two kinds of things and discovering the nature of that function can be much more difficult. This is the business of scientists and mathematicians. It frequently involves making observations about the world around us. It may involve trial and error.

For example, the student of elementary physics learns that if a constant acceleration (a) is applied to an object which is initially at rest, the distance traveled (x) at the end of a given time interval (t) can be determined by

$$x = \frac{1}{2}at^2$$

Once this is known, it is easy enough to find the x for a given a and t. But it wasn't easy for scientists like Newton to determine that this is, in fact, the correct formula.

We'll leave the rest of this to the mathematicians, scientists, and philosophers and return to relational database theory. Here we find we must deal with functional dependency.

3.4 FUNCTIONAL DEPENDENCIES

A *functional dependency* (often abbreviated as FD) is a relationship between two attributes, or data elements, or fields, and has characteristics similar to those of a function.

Definition   *We say that B is functionally dependent on A if, and only if, there must be a single B value associated with a given A value.*[7]

It is common practice to write this using the following notation.

A → B

This is used to indicate that *a single value for attribute B will be associated with any valid value for attribute A*. Several different values for A may or may not be associated with the same value for B.

We will discuss the hard part—how we might decide that this is the case—later. As you will see, finding a normalized form given the dependencies is actually quite easy. For now, we'll just work with this concept and assume that we have some way of deciding what is functionally dependent on what. Here are some reasonable sounding examples.

NAME_OF_STOCK → CLOSING_PRICE

NAME_OF_CITY → MAX_TEMPERATURE_PREDICTED

STUDENT_ID + COURSE_ID → GRADE_RECEIVED[8]

QUANTITY_OF_ORANGES + PRICE_OF_ORANGES → PRICE_PAID

Notice that it is perfectly legitimate to decide that one attribute is functionally dependent on a combination of other attributes as in the case of the last two examples.

We often see functional dependencies represented by bubble diagrams like Figure 3.2.[MCFADDEN85] An alternative representation is a diagram like Figure 3.3.[HAWRYSZKIEWICZ84] Both of these signify the following:

A → D
B → E
A + B → C

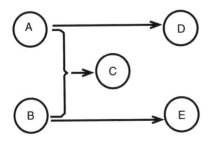

Figure 3.2   Bubble diagram

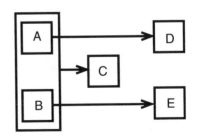

Figure 3.3   Functional dependencies

In words these would mean this. For each A value, we can determine a single D value. For each B value, we can determine a single E value. For each combination of a single A value with a single B value we can determine a single C value.

Diagrams like these are useful for explanations of normalization. They are also useful for simple problems with few data elements. They are not particularly useful for significant real problems with hundreds of data elements.

Some people use the term *determinant*. If D is functionally dependent on A, A is said to be the determinant of D. Some writers emphasize the concept of *full functional dependence*. C is said to be fully functionally dependent on A and B if and only if it does, in fact, take both an A value and a B value to determine a C value.

It is easy to be mistaken about dependencies on composites. This is particularly true when we are confronted with transitive or cascading dependencies. In mathematics, transitive properties are those which can be passed on from A to B to C. For example, if A, B, and C represent numbers and if A is less than B and B is less than C, then A must be less than C.

Suppose that the situation is really like this.

A → B

B → C

As Figure 3.4 indicates, A to B to C is transitive. A given A value determines a single B value which, in turn, determines a single C value.

We might notice that there appears to be a single C value associated with each A + B combination and mistakenly write

A + B → C

as we did in the preceding example. This is illustrated by Figure 3.5. We'd be making a mistake. Closer inspection would reveal that C is fully functionally dependent on B only, not on A and B.

We might also notice that there appears to be a single C value associated with each A value and write this:

A → C

B → C

A → B

This really doesn't seem to be completely wrong. But it will get us in trouble. Stating the dependency "A → C" not only doesn't add information, it may result in errors later on.

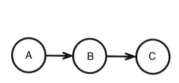

Figure 3.4   Transitive dependency

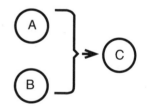

Figure 3.5   Error

Normalization   Chapter 3

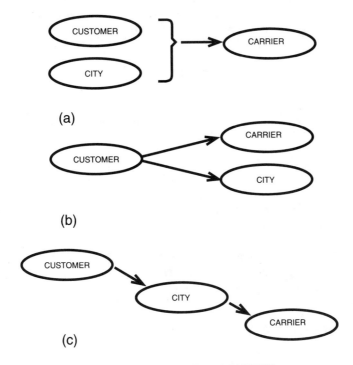

(a)

(b)

(c)

Figure 3.6   CUSTOMERs and CARRIERs

Here's an example. Suppose it is a company policy to use a particular shipping company to send material to a particular city. Thus, we might contact Fred's Friendly Trucking to send a shipment of oranges to Francine's Fruit Boutique in Fresno. As Figure 3.6 illustrates, there are several possibilities we might examine.

Possibility one:

CUSTOMER + CITY $\rightarrow$ CARRIER

Possibility two:

CUSTOMER $\rightarrow$ CITY
CUSTOMER $\rightarrow$ CARRIER

Possibility three:

CUSTOMER $\rightarrow$ CITY
CITY $\rightarrow$ CARRIER

Each of these possibilities would lead us to a different database design. How can we decide which is correct? We must carefully examine the particular situation. It is probably inherent in the nature of things that a given customer facility must be located in a particular city. However, *the choice of a shipping company is based on our business policy*. We will arbitrarily decide that, in this example which we have invented, possibility

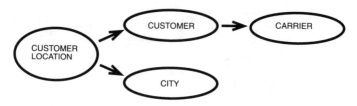

Figure 3.7   A more complex case

three correctly identifies the functional dependencies. Notice that while it is easy to settle an issue like this when we are inventing an example, it may be very difficult to sort out a real problem. *We've really said that it is our business policy to select the carrier based on the customer's city.* For some other business with a different business policy, the situation might well be different.

Suppose, for example, that we ship some product to a customer with locations in several cities and for accounting purposes we find it convenient to route all shipments to the same customer via the same trucking firm. Then, possibility two would be the correct representation. Actually, that is not quite true, is it? We must describe the situation like this (see Figure 3.7):

$$\text{CUSTOMER\_LOCATION} \rightarrow \text{CUSTOMER}$$
$$\text{CUSTOMER\_LOCATION} \rightarrow \text{CITY}$$
$$\text{CUSTOMER} \rightarrow \text{CARRIER}$$

Did you notice this? When you say that carrier is fully functionally dependent on customer, you are stating that you have concluded that it is the policy of our company to utilize the same carrier for all shipments to a particular customer no matter where the particular customer location happens to be. Also note that, in this example, customer is functionally dependent on location. This means that, given a specific location, customer identity is uniquely determined.

Now that we've got that all down we can proceed to a discussion of some normal forms. (Right now you need to be sure you understand what a functional dependency is. We say a lot more about discovering the appropriate dependencies in the next two chapters.)

3.5   FIRST NORMAL FORM

First Normal Form is easy. It is also a bit different in nature from all the other normal forms. It requires any relation we design to conform to the definition of a proper relation. One of the requirements of this definition is that for a given attribute and tuple (or for a given row and column) there can be but one value.

Suppose employees can be assigned to work on a series of projects. We might create a relation like this.

EMPLOYEE(<u>EMPLOYEE_ID</u>, EMPLOYEE_NAME, PROJECT_ID,
PROJECT_NAME, START_DATE, COMPLETION_DATE, PROJECT_ID,
PROJECT_NAME, START_DATE, COMPLETION_DATE,…etc.)

If the data is to be stored in a conventional file, we might actually get away with this. Many commonly used programming languages, COBOL for example, provide a way to manipulate data like this.[9]

But there are several problems with this arrangement. We can never be sure of a good number of project assignments to allow for. If we pick ten, some employee is sure to receive an eleventh assignment. We could play it really safe and allow for six thousand, but that would result in a tremendous waste of disk storage and memory.

While there are such things as variable length records and programming languages such as COBOL do provide for them, it is difficult to use them. Frequently, there are restrictions on their use. Consequently, most programmers prefer to avoid them.

The processing is also more complex. To find the particulars of a particular assignment, it is necessary to access the employee data and then scan it, examining one assignment at a time.

The relational model does not provide for these *repeating groups*. Most systems which are based on the relational model follow the rule. Occasionally, someone will subvert this rule by writing something like this.

EMPLOYEE(<u>EMPLOYEE_ID</u>, EMPLOYEE_NAME, PROJECT_ID_1,
PROJECT_NAME_1, START_DATE_1, COMPLETION_DATE_1,
PROJECT_ID_2, PROJECT_NAME_2, START_DATE_2,
COMPLETION_DATE_2,…etc.)

This will necessitate a data manipulation statement on this order.

SELECT PROJECT_START_DATE_1 FROM EMPLOYEE
 WHERE PROJECT_ID_1 = 'XYZ'
UNION
SELECT PROJECT_START_DATE_2 FROM EMPLOYEE
 WHERE PROJECT_ID_2 = 'XYZ'
etc.

If you've allowed for very many possibilities, you'll be saying "XYZ" and a lot of other things by the time you get done with this. (If there are only two or three possible repetitions, this may turn out to be a practical solution.)

In this example we might solve the problem like this.

EMPLOYEE(<u>EMPLOYEE_ID</u>, EMPLOYEE_NAME, <u>PROJECT_ID</u>,
PROJECT_NAME, START_DATE, COMPLETION_DATE)

This will result in an additional tuple (or row or record) for each employee assignment. Notice that the common attribute EMPLOYEE_ID will relate all assignments for a particular employee. *In a relational system, relationships are represented by common data values.*

This is now in First Normal Form.

Definition   *The rule for First Normal Form is eliminate repeating groups.*

3.6   SECOND NORMAL FORM

Second Normal Form involves the issue of whether or not we have a full functional dependency. Let's look at some sample data.

EMPLOYEE _ID	EMPLOYEE _NAME	PROJECT _ID	PROJECT _NAME	START _DATE	COMPLETION _DATE
123	Harry	XYZ	Space Shuttle	Jul 7, 1991	Aug 8, 1991
123	Harry	ZYX	Place Scuttle	Aug 9, 1991	Dec 24, 1991
231	Mary	XYZ	Space Shuttle	Jul 12, 1991	Dec 24, 1991
231	Mary	XYX	Face Shuttle	Dec 26, 1991	Mar 18, 1992
312	Larry	ZYX	Place Scuttle	July 27, 1991	Mar 3, 1992

Suppose that we have identified the following functional dependencies.

EMPLOYEE_ID   →   EMPLOYEE_NAME

PROJECT_ID   →   PROJECT_NAME

EMPLOYEE_ID + PROJECT_ID   →   START_DATE

EMPLOYEE_ID + PROJECT_ID   →   COMPLETION_DATE

Here's the relation we illustrated above.

EMPLOYEE(EMPLOYEE_ID, EMPLOYEE_NAME, PROJECT_ID,
PROJECT_NAME, START_DATE, COMPLETION_DATE)

Let's look the data over. We've stored the fact that employee 123 is Harry twice. We've also stored that fact that project XYZ is Space Shuttle twice. If we need to alter either kind of fact, we must be sure to locate and alter all occurrences. The data will be inconsistent if we do not. *This problem is often referred to as the update anomaly.*

When we enter data about a new employee, we must either assign a project or leave the project data NULL. When we enter data about a new project, we must either assign an employee or leave the employee data NULL. *This problem is often referred to as the insertion anomaly.*

Should we delete the data regarding the only employee assigned to a project, we will delete the project data as well. (In our example, deletion of all data about Mary will also delete data about project XYX.) Should we delete the data regarding the only project assigned to an employee, we will delete the employee data as well. (In our example, deletion of data about project ZYX will also delete data about Larry.) *This problem is often referred to as the deletion anomaly.*

How might we eliminate these problems? Let's begin by observing that no single attribute of this relation is an appropriate key. *It must be possible for a given key value to identify a single tuple.* Let's suppose that our knowledge of the situation leads us to the choice of EMPLOYEE_ID + PROJECT_ID as key for this relation. (This implies that an employee never has two or more assignments for the same project. If multiple assignments are possible, we'll have to include START_DATE in the key.)

We can also observe that the functional dependencies tell us that we are concerned here with three kinds of facts or relationships; employee names related to employee identifiers, project names related to project identifiers, and dates related to the assignment of particular employees to particular projects. We have combined several different kinds of facts or relationships in one table (or relation or record). The result is that the facts are stored redundantly. *The more formal way of stating this is that some of the attributes are functionally dependent on portions of the key of the relation.*

We can resolve these anomalies by following the rule for Second Normal Form.

Definition   *The rule for Second Normal Form is all nonkey attributes of a relation must be functionally dependent on the entire key.*

In our example, elimination of partial key dependencies results in the following.

EMPLOYEE(EMPLOYEE_ID, EMPLOYEE_NAME)

PROJECT(PROJECT_ID,PROJECT_NAME)

WORKS_ON(EMPLOYEE_ID, PROJECT_ID, START_DATE,
COMPLETION_DATE)

This decomposition could be produced by applying the project operation to the unnormalized relation. It results in three tables of data as follows.

EMPLOYEE_ID	EMPLOYEE_NAME
123	Harry
231	Mary
312	Larry

PROJECT_ID	PROJECT_NAME
XYZ	Space Shuttle
ZYX	Place Scuttle
XYX	Face Shuttle

EMPLOYEE_ID	PROJECT_ID	START_DATE	COMPLETION DATE
123	XYZ	Jul 7, 1991	Aug 8, 1991
123	ZYX	Aug 9, 1991	Dec 24, 1991
231	XYZ	Jul 12, 1991	Dec 24, 1991
231	XYX	Dec 26, 1991	Mar 18, 1992
312	ZYX	July 27, 1991	Mar 3, 1992

It might appear that a redundancy has been introduced. The opposite is true. Each instance of each kind of fact has been stored but once. The duplication of data values is the means for linking the relations. As a result, the anomalies we noted earlier have been eliminated.

Any time we need to view the data in the form of the original relation, we can recreate that view by means of join operations. Since the common attributes EMPLOYEE_ID and PROJECT_ID relate the three tables, we can write this:

> SELECT EMPLOYEE.EMPLOYEE_ID, EMPLOYEE_NAME,
> PROJECT.PROJECT_ID, PROJECT_NAME, START_DATE,
> COMPLETION_DATE
>
> FROM EMPLOYEE, PROJECT, WORKS_ON
>
> WHERE EMPLOYEE.EMPLOYEE_ID = WORKS_ON.EMPLOYEE_ID
> AND PROJECT.PROJECT_ID = WORKS_ON.PROJECT_ID;

3.7   THIRD NORMAL FORM

Third Normal Form involves transitive dependencies. Let's extend our example. Suppose that, for administrative purposes, each employee is assigned to a specific department and that each department has an identifier and a name.

Let's assume the following functional dependencies.

> EMPLOYEE_ID   →   EMPLOYEE_NAME
> EMPLOYEE_ID   →   DEPARTMENT_ID
> DEPARTMENT_ID   →   DEPARTMENT_NAME

Now suppose we design a relation like this one.

> ASSIGNED_TO(EMPLOYEE_ID, EMPLOYEE_NAME, DEPARTMENT_ID,
> DEPARTMENT_NAME)

This does not violate Second Normal Form. There are no partial key dependencies. (There can't be. A single attribute serves as key.) Let's suppose some data and see what happens.

EMPLOYEE_ID	EMPLOYEE_NAME	DEPARTMENT _ID	DEPARTMENT _NAME
123	Harry	ABC	Alpha Beta
231	Mary	ABC	Alpha Beta
312	Larry	BAC	Beta Alpha

Looks like we've duplicated the fact that department ABC is Alpha Beta, doesn't it? Suppose we need to alter a department name. We must be careful to alter it everywhere it appears. Suppose we assign an employee to a different department. We must alter the identifier and the name. *We still have update anomalies.*

Suppose we want to add a department before we assign any employees. We'll have tuple with NULL employee attributes. *We still have an insertion anomaly.*

Suppose we delete a department. The employees will be deleted along with it. *We still have a deletion anomaly.* The solution is to apply the rule for Third Normal Form.

Definition   *The rule for Third Normal Form is transitive dependencies are not allowed. Each nonkey attribute of a relation must be functionally dependent on the key and nothing else.*

The result will be two tables like this:

EMPLOYEE(EMPLOYEE_ID, EMPLOYEE_NAME, DEPARTMENT_ID)

DEPARTMENT(DEPARTMENT_ID, DEPARTMENT_NAME)

The data will look like this:

EMPLOYEE_ID	EMPLOYEE_NAME	DEPARTMENT_ID
123	Harry	ABC
231	Mary	ABC
312	Larry	BAC

DEPARTMENT_ID	DEPARTMENT_NAME
ABC	Alpha Beta
BAC	Beta Alpha

Once again we note that the original data can be recreated via a join if it is needed.

3.8   BOYCE/CODD NORMAL FORM

Boyce/Codd Normal Form (BCNF) resolves a special case which is not satisfactorily dealt with by the first three normal forms. The situation involves two composite and overlapping keys. This does not seem to occur frequently in practice.

BCNF also provides a single rule which incorporates both Second and Third Normal Forms. If this were theory, we might discard Second and Third Normal Forms in favor of Boyce/Codd Normal Form.[10] This has not been done so far.

Definition   *The rule for Boyce/Codd Normal Form is that every determinant must be a candidate key.*

Date states "A relation R is in Boyce/Codd Normal Form (BCNF) if and only if every determinant is a candidate key."[DATE86]

A *determinant* is an attribute or element upon which some other attribute is functionally dependent.

A → B

can be stated as "B is functionally dependent on A." It can also be stated as "A is a determinant of B."

A *candidate key* is an attribute or a collection of attributes which may be used for a key. It is possible for a relation to have more than one candidate key.

If the determinant is a single attribute and is the only candidate key, BCNF is merely a way of stating the rules for Second and Third Normal Forms in one sentence.

In our Second Normal Form example,

EMPLOYEE(EMPLOYEE_ID, EMPLOYEE_NAME, PROJECT_ID,
PROJECT_NAME, START_DATE, COMPLETION_DATE)

EMPLOYEE_ID + PROJECT_ID is a candidate key for the relation and also a determinant. The other two determinants, EMPLOYEE_ID and PROJECT_ID are not candidate keys.

The relation does not satisfy the rule for Boyce/Codd Normal Form. The resolution is the same as was given in the original example.

In the example given for Third Normal Form,

ASSIGNED_TO(EMPLOYEE_ID, EMPLOYEE_NAME, DEPARTMENT_ID,
DEPARTMENT_NAME)

EMPLOYEE_ID is a determinant for both EMPLOYEE_NAME and DEPARTMENT_ID and is a candidate key. DEPARTMENT_ID is a determinant for DEPARTMENT_NAME and is not a candidate key.

The rule for Boyce/Codd Normal Form is not satisfied.

In these two examples, each relation has but one candidate key. As a result, Boyce/Codd Normal Form does not add anything. You might find it easier to understand and apply than the combination of the other two forms. It allows us to simplify by substituting one rule for two. But the result will be the same no matter which form we use.

Now suppose the following.

PART_# → PART_DESCR
PART_DESCR → PART_#
WHSE_# → WHSE_DESCR
WHSE_DESCR → WHSE_#

PART_# + WHSE_# → QTY_OH

PART_DESCR + WHSE_DESCR → QTY_OH

PART_# + WHSE_DESCR → QTY_OH

WHSE_DESCR + PART_# → QTY_OH

PART_# is a determinant of PART_DESCR. PART_DESCR is also a determinant of PART_#. (There are no duplicate part descriptions.)

WHSE_# is a determinant of WHSE_CITY. WHSE_CITY is a determinant of WHSE_#. (There are no duplicate city names.)

PART_# + WHSE_#,   PART_DESCR + WHSE_DESCR, PART_# + WHSE_DESCR, and PART_DESCR + WHSE_# are all determinants of QTY_OH.

Suppose we form the relation

STOCK(PART_#, WHSE_#, PART_DESCR, QTY_OH)

There are now two candidate keys, PART_# + WHSE_# and PART_DESCR + WHSE_#. They overlap because they share the common attribute WHSE_#. Both are determinants of QTY_OH. However, part number is a PART_# of PART_DESCR and PART_DESCR is a determinant of PART_#, but neither is by itself a candidate key for the relation. This relation does not satisfy the rule for Boyce/Codd Normal Form. The anomalies we've noted earlier will occur.

Boyce/Codd Normal Form requires a separate relation

PART(PART_#, PART_DESCRIPTION)

3.9   MULTIVALUED FACTS

So far we have been able to resolve situations involving single-valued facts which can be expressed in terms of functional dependencies. We could say

EMPLOYEE_ID   →   DEPARTMENT_ID

because, in our example, there is but one department number for each employee identifier. Often, there can be many employees in the same department. We could write this in the following manner:

DEPARTMENT_ID   ↠   {EMPLOYEE_ID}

This notation, involving the double arrow and curly brackets, is intended to indicate that a department number determines a set or collection of employee identifiers.[11] We were able to ignore this *multivalued fact* because there is a corresponding functional dependency in the opposite direction.

Definition   *Multivalued fact means that a single A value determines a specific set of associated B values.*

Suppose we make this example a little more realistic by deciding that we desire to record an employee's entire work history. This means we need a record of every department where he or she has ever worked.

Now, we must write these multivalued facts.

$$\text{DEPARTMENT\_\#} \quad \twoheadrightarrow \quad \{\text{EMPLOYEE\_ID}\}$$
$$\text{EMPLOYEE\_ID} \quad \twoheadrightarrow \quad \{\text{DEPARTMENT\_ID}\}$$

Neither of these is a functional dependency. The rules we have learned so far do not help us.

Our recourse is to develop a new relation with the composite key of department number plus employee identifier.

WORKS(<u>EMPLOYEE_ID, DEPARTMENT_ID</u>)

This relation is all key. Neither attribute can, by itself, uniquely identify a tuple or row occurrence. But either attribute might be used as a search argument. We might select all tuples or rows involving a particular employee or a particular department. Key and search argument are not the same. This relation does not violate any of the rules we've discussed so far. There are no repeating groups, no partial key dependencies, no dependencies on attributes or elements other than the key. There will be no anomalies.

We would not include either employee name or department name in this relation because to do so would introduce partial key dependencies and would also violate the rule for Boyce/Codd Normal Form.

Let's make this a little more realistic by adding a start and end date to show the interval during which the employee worked in each department.

WORKS(<u>EMPLOYEE_ID, DEPARTMENT_ID</u>, START_DATE, END_DATE)

Neither of these dates is determined by employee identifier or department number alone, is it? We will write these.[12]

$$\text{EMPLOYEE\_ID} + \text{DEPARTMENT\_ID} \quad \rightarrow \quad \text{START\_DATE}$$
$$\text{EMPLOYEE\_ID} + \text{DEPARTMENT\_ID} \quad \rightarrow \quad \text{END\_DATE}$$

This relation also satisfies all of the normal form rules we have discussed so far. We are probably more comfortable because there are some functional dependencies involved.

Start date and end date would often be called *intersection data* or *junction data* because they are associated with an intersection or junction between the set or collection of employees and the set or collection of departments. The existence of intersection data which is functionally dependent on the composite or concatenated key seems to make it easier to decide what to do with this, doesn't it?

Now, the reason we can implement a relation or table like this without creating any anomalies is that there is only one set of multivalued facts involved. It's time for another definition.

Definition   *A multivalued dependency or MVD is said to exist when a relation or table contains more than one independent multivalued fact. (It is also said to exist if a relation contains both a functional dependency or FD and one or more independent multivalued facts. This is because a functional dependency is really a special case or subset of the class of multivalued facts.)*[13]

A multivalued dependency is usually expressed like this.

$$A \;\twoheadrightarrow\; B \mid C$$

The above means that B and C are both collections or sets associated with A and that there is no dependency or association between particular B values and C values.

This could be written like this.

$$A \;\twoheadrightarrow\; \{B\}$$
$$A \;\twoheadrightarrow\; \{C\}$$

This notation may be clearer but is not commonly used.

There must be at least three elements involved to form a multivalued dependency. Any of these could, by the way, be a composite.

3.10   FOURTH NORMAL FORM

Let's look at another example.[14] Suppose we want to record particular skills which our employee is certified to possess and also languages in which he or she is certified to be fluent. We might devise a relation like this one.

EMPLOYEE (EMPLOYEE_ID, EMPLOYEE_NAME, SKILL_CODE,
SKILL_DESCR, LANG_CODE, LANG_DESCR)

We could consider forming repeating groups for the languages and skills. This would result in a violation of the rule for First Normal Form. It would also be particularly nasty to deal with in practice because we would have two repeating item sets and there is no simple way to establish a maximum number of occurrences for either. We have not yet identified a key for this. Why don't you take a minute or two to think about it and then read on.

It would be reasonable to assume the following dependencies.

EMPLOYEE_ID $\rightarrow$ EMPLOYEE_NAME
SKILL_CODE $\rightarrow$ SKILL_DESCR
LANG_CODE $\rightarrow$ LANG_DESCR
EMPLOYEE_ID $\;\twoheadrightarrow\;$ SKILL_CODE | LANG_CODE

Using our alternative notation, we might restate the last dependency like this.

EMPLOYEE_ID $\;\twoheadrightarrow\;$ {SKILL_CODE}
EMPLOYEE_ID $\;\twoheadrightarrow\;$ {LANG_CODE}

Restating in words, we have this: Employee name is functionally dependent on employee identifier. Skill description is functionally dependent on skill code. Language description is functionally dependent on language code. An employee might possess multiple skills and also multiple languages. There is no particular connection between the skills an employee possesses and the languages he or she speaks and writes. (If there were a connection we would have a different problem. We'll discuss that problem next.) It is also the case that multiple employees might possess the same skills and multiple employees might possess the same languages.

At any rate, given these dependencies, the above relation does not meet the criteria for Second and Third Normal Forms or Boyce/Codd Normal Form. Do you see how to rectify that?

EMPLOYEE(EMPLOYEE_ID, EMPLOYEE_NAME)

SKILL (SKILL_CODE, SKILL_DESCR)

LANG (LANG_CODE, LANG_DESCR)

EMP_SKI (EMPLOYEE_ID, SKILL_CODE, LANG_CODE)

The first three look good. What about the fourth one? You have probably noticed that we still have not identified a key for it.

Let's invent some data.

EMPLOYEE_ID	SKILL_CODE	LANG_CODE
1	A	X5
1	B	X1
2	H	X2
2	A	X5
2	–	X6
3	A	X7
4	B	X5
4	C	–

The first thing we notice is that there is no one attribute or column which can be used to uniquely identify a tuple or row. It is also the case that there is no pair of attributes or columns which will serve the purpose. This relation is all key. The next thing we notice is that, if an employee does not have the same number of skills and languages, we must provide for missing or NULL values. NULL values within a key are not allowed. In addition, the method for inserting a new skill for an employee would be

IF THERE IS A TUPLE WITH A NULL SKILL VALUE FOR THE
EMPLOYEE,
  PLACE THE NEW SKILL IN THAT TUPLE,

OTHERWISE
  INSERT A NEW TUPLE CONTAINING EMPLOYEE IDENTIFIER, THE
  NEW SKILL, AND A NULL VALUE FOR LANGUAGE CODE.

The addition of a language for an employee or the deletion of a skill or language for an employee would pose similar problems. We might solve this difficulty with update, delete, and insert by adopting the strategy illustrated by the next example.

EMPLOYEE_ID	SKILL_CODE	LANG_CODE
1	A	–
1	–	X5
1	–	X1
1	B	–
2	H	–
2	–	X2
2	A	–
2	–	X5
2	–	X6
3	A	–
3	–	X7
4	B	–
4	–	X5
4	C	–

Somehow, this seems to be very wasteful, and we still don't have a proper key. A proper key will uniquely identify a single row and will never contain NULL values.

We might also consider storing all possible combinations. For employee 1, it would look like this.

EMPLOYEE_ID	SKILL_CODE	LANG_CODE
1	A	X5
1	A	X1
1	B	X5
1	B	X1

That doesn't seem right either. Think about the steps required to add either a skill code or a language code. The solution is to form two relations like this.

EMP_SKI (EMPLOYEE_ID, SKILL_CODE)

EMP_LAN(EMPLOYEE_ID, LANG_CODE)

This is what the rule for Fourth Normal Form tells us to do.

Definition *The rule for Fourth Normal Form requires us to eliminate anomalies by eliminating multivalued dependencies.*

We do this by making sure that no relation contains two or more independent multi-valued facts about something.[15]

Let's carry this example just a little further. We might like to record proficiency levels for each skill and language for each employee. We might periodically test each employee to determine if he or she had maintained or improved the proficiency level or perhaps even allowed it to deteriorate. Wouldn't we add this information in the following manner?

EMP_SKI (<u>EMPLOYEE_ID, SKILL_CODE</u>, SKILL_PROF, SKILL_DATE)

EMP_LAN(<u>EMPLOYEE_ID, LANG_CODE</u>, LANG_PROF, LANG_DATE)

Why? Because of this.

EMPLOYEE_ID + SKILL_CODE → SKILL_PROF

EMPLOYEE_ID + SKILL_CODE → SKILL_DATE

EMPLOYEE_ID + LANG_CODE → LANG_PROF

EMPLOYEE_ID + LANG_CODE → LANG_DATE

What has happened here? We have been able to detect some functional dependencies. The determinants are composite elements. In a case like this, we can often create a solid, normalized design without explicitly thinking about Fourth Normal Form. The rule does still apply, but we produced a correct result without actually making use of it.

3.11 FIFTH NORMAL FORM

So far, we have eliminated anomalies by increasing the number of relations. We have formed new relations more or less by applying the PROJECT operator to relations which contained redundant or potentially inconsistent information. Is it possible to carry this process too far? Let's look at another example.

Suppose that when we assign employees to work on particular projects we assign them specific tasks. Here's one way we might represent this.

EMPLOYEE_ID	PROJECT_ID	TASK_ID
123	XYZ	ABC
123	ZYX	CBA
321	XYZ	CBA
321	ZYX	ABC

There *appear* to be several multivalued dependencies here.

EMPLOYEE_ID $\twoheadrightarrow$ PROJECT_ID I TASK_ID

PROJECT_ID $\twoheadrightarrow$ EMPLOYEE_ID I TASK_ID

TASK_ID $\twoheadrightarrow$ PROJECT_ID I EMPLOYEE_ID

Suppose we determine that Fourth Normal Form applies and form two relations like this.

EMPLOYEE_ID	PROJECT_ID
123	XYZ
123	ZYX
321	XYZ
321	ZYX

PROJECT_ID	TASK_ID
XYZ	ABC
ZYX	CBA
XYZ	CBA
ZYX	ABC

Now let's join these two relations together on the common attribute, PROJECT_ID.

EMPLOYEE_ID	PROJECT_ID	TASK_ID
123	XYZ	ABC
123	XYZ	CBA
123	ZYX	CBA
123	ZYX	ABC
321	XYZ	ABC
321	XYZ	CBA
321	ZYX	CBA
321	ZYX	ABC

You'd better take a minute to check this out. We seem to have picked up some additional rows. How did that happen? This situation results in what is often called a *lossy* join. This is contrasted with a *lossless* join. The *lost* information in this case is that employee 123 did not perform task CBA on project XYZ. One obvious solution to this problem is "do not decompose the original relation." An alternative might be to decompose it into three new relations instead of two. Try it if you like. In this particular example it won't help.

The theory for *Fifth Normal Form* involves the detection and elimination of something called a join dependency. This artifact has been defined and methods for detecting one have been proposed. [AHO79] [FAGIN77] So far, however, it has not been possible to devise and present a clear and simple method which is of use to the average practitioner. Please be assured that the author does not intend to belittle or minimize the research that has been done or the work that has been published. This is just a problem that is very difficult to resolve.[16]

We propose a solution which appears workable. Determine the precise nature of the kinds of facts to be stored and develop relations which contain the complete facts.[17]

Definition   *The rule for Fifth Normal Form is do not create sets of relations which are susceptible to lossy joins. Be sure that the relations do represent the facts to be recorded.*

In our example, it is necessary to store the fact that a particular employee performs a particular task on a particular project. We need a relation containing all three attributes. This is really another form of the "connection trap" problem. We discuss this further in Chapter 5.

3.12   ONE, TWO, THREE, FOUR, FIVE NORMAL FORMS

The existence of numbered normal forms suggests that one might be required to begin with a poorly formed relation, cast it into one or more relations in First Normal Form, recast these into Second Normal Form, and so on. Many textbooks present running examples which do just this. This sort of procedure doesn't seem to be harmful. It may, in some cases, be necessary. However, it seems very likely that in other cases we might observe the dependencies, write down relations representing the dependencies, and use the rules to verify that the relations are normalized correctly.

Suppose that we have identified these dependencies.

$$DWARF\_ID \quad \rightarrow \quad DWARF\_NAME$$
$$DWARF\_ID \quad \rightarrow \quad CAVE\_ID \qquad (Where\ he\ lives)$$
$$CAVE\_ID \quad \rightarrow \quad NUMBER\_OF\_ROOMS$$
$$CAVE\_ID \quad \rightarrow \quad ASSESSED\_VALUE$$
$$DWARF\_ID \quad \twoheadrightarrow \quad SPELL\,|\,WEAPON$$
$$DWARF\_ID + SPELL \quad \rightarrow \quad POWER\_OF\_SPELL$$
$$DWARF\_ID + WEAPON \quad \rightarrow \quad PROFICIENCY$$

We might, after a little practice, examine these and write down a set of relations. Why don't you try it before you read on?

DWARF(DWARF_ID, DWARF_NAME, CAVE_ID)

CAVE(CAVE_ID, NUMBER_OF_ROOMS, ASSESSED_VALUE)

SPELLS(DWARF_ID, SPELL, POWER_OF_SPELL)

ARMS(DWARF_ID, WEAPON, PROFICIENCY)

Now let's check on ourselves.
- There are no repeating groups. First Normal Form is satisfied.
- There are no partial key dependencies. Second Normal Form is satisfied.

- There are no nonkey or transitive dependencies. Third Normal Form is satisfied.
- There are no multivalued dependencies. Fourth Normal Form is satisfied.
- Each relation represents one or more of the specific facts we want to store. We can not detect any possibility of a "lossy" join. We have done our best to satisfy the Fifth Normal Form.

3.13   IS THAT ALL THERE IS TO IT?

The first, very obvious, observation has already been made. Applying the rules for normalization to a given set of functional dependencies is a relatively easy procedure. *Unfortunately, discovering a correct set of functional dependencies is often quite difficult.*

To return to the comparison between functional dependencies and mathematical functions, we find ourselves in a position similar to that of a scientist who is trying to find a formula which will correctly express the rules implied by some observed phenomena. This is often a painstaking trial and error procedure. We can identify several approaches that scientists use.

- Utilize an exhaustive procedure of trial and error.
- Formulate a theoretical model, derive a formula from the theory, then test the formula against actuality.
- Make use of the solution to a similar problem.
- Have a flash of insight, then proceed as in the case of a theoretical model.
- Use some combination of these.

In a similar manner, we can identify some possible approaches to the discovery of appropriate functional dependencies.

- Document all the data elements. Examine every possible combination to see if there appears to be a functional dependency. (This is really impractical if there are a large number of data elements.)
- Document all known rules and constraints.[18] Some authorities use the term *business rules* to refer to statements on the order of "An employee works in a single department."
- Make use of known user views of the data to narrow the search for functional dependencies. By user views, we really mean the various reports, screens, and files. If we find a form containing vendor number plus a variety of information about a vendor, we might consider the possibility that there are functional dependencies between vendor identifier and the other data elements.[19] Admittedly, this is not a rigorous procedure. It is not possible to prove that it will lead to all functional dependencies. It is, however, a very useful labor saving device.[20]
- Formulate an Entity Relationship Model of the data. Derive functional dependencies from this model. Once again, this is not an exact procedure which guarantees a result. However, it is a very useful technique. This approach is the subject of the next chapter.

Normalization produces a nonredundant way of storing the data. As we've noted, the various forms of anomalies are eliminated. The normalization rules are really a formal statement of common sense. If the analysis has been done correctly, it should be possible to use the relational operators to recombine the data in any desired form. Unfortunately, in the real world of electromechanical data storage devices, this process of recombining may take too long. As a result, it is sometimes necessary to implement a database which is not in the ideal normalized form in order to achieve performance goals. This does not mean we wasted our time normalizing. The unnormalized form will be susceptible to the various anomalies. Only by being aware of this can we introduce appropriate programs and procedures to avoid these problems. And the normalization process forces us to discover the information we really need to know about the data. Thus, the accepted design procedure consists of normalization followed by analysis of physical design requirements.

Endnotes

1. To be perfectly honest about this, you are likely to find it a bit tedious to go through all of this. Unfortunately, there doesn't seem to be any easy way out. It will be worth the effort in the long run.

2. A normalized relation will behave much like a mathematical relation.

3. This should be done only if there are really good reasons.

4. Most discussions of relational database design and normalization use the word anomaly. It denotes something which is inconsistent or out of place, a deviation from the normal. You might mentally replace it with the word inconsistency. We choose to use the term because it is found in most of the references.

5. More than these 6 normal forms have been defined. This book will not be improved by including them.

6. In mathematics, these are referred to as independent variables or degrees of freedom.

7. Date [DATE86] states "…'R.X functionally determines R.Y')—if and only if each X-value in R has associated with it precisely one Y-value in R (at any one time)."

8. Using the plus sign (+) to indicate that two items are taken as one or concatenated is fairly common in works on systems analysis. It is less common in works on "database." We adopt it in this book because it is meaningful and useful. And, database design methodologies should be consistent with systems design methodologies.

9. This involves the use of arrays and subscripts. Many programmers consider these a big nuisance. If you are not a programmer, don't worry about it.

10. Frankly, the author was tempted to omit discussions of Second and Third Normal Forms and deal only with Boyce/Codd Normal Form. But this would seem like heresy to many people, and Second and Third Normal Forms are still better known. It's best to be familiar with all three forms.

11. This is not the conventional notation. It is, however, very clear and useful.

12. There may be a problem with what we've done here. Can you see what it is? We'll discuss it later on.

13. This terminology has always seemed particularly awkward to the author. It is retained in this book because it is widely used.

14. We are elaborating on one of Kent's examples. [KENT83]

15. We also make sure that no relation contains both a functional dependency and a multi-valued fact:
EMP_LAN (EMPLOYEE_ID, LANG_CODE, EMPLOYEE_NAME)
would violate the rule for Second Normal Form.

16. Date states "Hence the process of determining when a given relation is in 4NF but not 5NF…is still unclear." [DATE86]

17. We might state this as the simple rule for all of normalization. However, it really is not as easy to apply as the rules for the other normal forms. We only need to fall back on it when we come to this difficult situation.

18. We discuss constraints in some detail in Chapter 6.

19. If structured analysis is performed, one might think of data flows to and from external entities as user views. Data stores might also qualify.

20. There is another approach which consists of normalizing each user view separately, then combining them. This is sometimes referred to as *canonical synthesis*.

QUESTIONS AND EXERCISES

1. Why is normalization valuable? Give at least two reasons.

2. Explain normalization.

3. What is a functional dependency? What is a transitive dependency?

4. What is a multivalued fact? What is a multivalued dependency?

5. Which normal forms deal with functional dependencies? Which normal forms deal with multivalued dependencies?

6. Are functional and multivalued dependencies always easy to identify? Explain your answer.

7. Explain 1NF, 2NF, 3NF, BCNF, 4NF, and 5NF in simple English.

Base your answers to exercises 8 through 11 on these dependencies:

Bee_SS_# $\rightarrow$ Bee_Name		
Bee_SS_# $\rightarrow$ Hive_Identifier	(Bee Resides in Hive)
Bee_SS_# $\rightarrow$ Weight	
Bee_SS_# $\twoheadrightarrow$ {Flower_SS_#}	(For Flowers Pollinated)
Bee_SS_# $\twoheadrightarrow$ {Person_SS_#}	(For Persons Stung)
Hive_Identifier $\rightarrow$ Hive_Capacity	

Hive_Identifier $\rightarrow$ Hive_Phone_#

Hive_Identifier $\rightarrow\!\!\!\rightarrow$ {Bee_SS_#}   (Bees Reside in Hive)

Flower_SS_# $\rightarrow$ Kind_Of_Flower

Flower_SS_# $\rightarrow$ Color

Flower_SS_# $\rightarrow\!\!\!\rightarrow$ {Bee_SS_#}   (Flower Pollinated By Bees)

Person_SS_# $\rightarrow$ Person_Name

Person_SS_# $\rightarrow\!\!\!\rightarrow$ {Bee_SS_#}   (Person Stung By Bees)

Bee_SS_# + Person_SS_# $\rightarrow$ Number_of_Stings

Bee_SS_# $\rightarrow\!\!\!\rightarrow$ Flower_SS_# I Person_SS_#

8. Is the following relation normalized? If not, which normal form is violated? Provide and explain a correct normalization.
Bee(Bee_SS_#, Name, Hive_Identifier, Hive_Capacity)

9. Is the following relation normalized? If not, which normal form is violated? Provide and explain a correct normalization.
Stings(Bee_SS_#, Person_SS_#, Number_Of_Stings, Person_Name)

10. Is the following relation normalized? If not, which normal form is violated? Provide and explain a correct normalization.
At_Work(Bee_SS_#, Flower_SS_#, Person_SS_#)

11. Develop a complete set of normalized relations for the above. Explain in detail how it is that you are sure your relations are normalized.

12. Identify dependencies and develop a set of normalized relations for the following. Explain in detail how you know your normalization is correct.

Pigs are cared for by swineherds and live in pigpens. Each swineherd has a unique social security number (SH_SS) as well as a name (SH_NAME) and shirt size (SH_SIZE).

A swineherd may operate several pigpens. A given pigpen is operated by but one swineherd. Each pigpen is identified by a unique pigpen identifying number (PP_ID). Each pigpen also has a value in pig pence (PP_VAL) and a capacity (PP_CAP).

A given pig lives in one and only one pigpen. Each pig is assigned a pig number (PIG_NO) and has a weight (PIG_WT) and value (PIG_VAL).

13. Identify dependencies and develop a set of normalized relations for the following. Explain in detail how you know your normalization is correct.

Wizards are identified by social security numbers (WZ_SS). They have names (WZ_NAME) and daily rates which they charge for their wizardry (WZ_RATE).

Wizards belong to lodges. A wizard may belong to more than one lodge. And more than one wizard may belong to a lodge.

Each lodge is identified by a unique lodge name (LOG_NAM). Each lodge has a mailing address (LOG_ADD) and a telephone number (LOG_PHON).

The spells that the wizards can cast are described in the master spell catalog. Each spell has its own unique spell identifier (SP_ID), a descriptive name (SP_NAME), and a rating in terms of how astonishing it is (SP_AST).

Most wizards are capable of casting many different spells. It is possible for several wizards to cast the same spell. Each wizard has a spell competency rating (SP_CRAT) for each spell he or she is capable of casting.

14. Identify dependencies and develop a set of normalized relations for the following. Explain in detail how you know your normalization is correct.

Horses are cared for by trainers and live in horse barns.

Each trainer has a unique social security number (Train_SS) as well as a name (Train_NAME) and shoe size (Train_SIZE).

A given horse lives in one and only one horse barn. Each horse is assigned a horse number (Horse_NO) and has a weight (Horse_WT) and value (Horse_VAL).

A trainer may operate several horse barns. A given horse barn is operated by but one trainer. Each horse barn is identified by a unique horse barn identifying number (HB_ID). Each horse barn also has a value (HB_VAL) and a capacity (HB_CAP). A given trainer cares for all the horses kept in any barn he or she owns. Thus, you can tell who the trainer is if you know the barn. (You don't really need to store the horse to trainer relationship.)

15. Identify dependencies and develop a set of normalized relations for the following. Explain in detail how you know your normalization is correct.

Craftspeople are identified by social security numbers (CP_SS). They have names (CP_NAME) and daily rates which they charge for their work (CP_RATE).

Craftspeople belong to guilds. A given craftsperson may belong to more than one guild. And more than one craftsperson may belong to a particular guild. Each guild is identified by a unique guild name (GUI_NAM). Each guild has a mailing address (GUI_ADD) and a telephone number (GUI_PHON).

The crafts that the craftspeople can craft are described in the master craft catalog. Each craft has its own unique craft identifier (CRAFT_ID), a descriptive name (CRAFT_NAME), and a rating in terms of how crafty it is (CRAFT_CRAFT).

Most craftspeople are capable of crafting many different crafts. It is also possible for several craftsfolk to craft the same craft. Each craftsperson has a craft competency rating (CRAFT_COMP) for each craft he or she is capable of crafting.

SOLUTION TO PROBLEM 12

SH_SS → SH_NAME

SH_SS → SH_SIZE

SH_SS ↠ {PP_ID}   (It turns out you can ignore this)

PP_ID → PP_VAL

PP_ID → PP_CAP

PP_ID → SH_SS

PP_ID ↠ {PIG_NO}   (This can also be ignored)

PIG_NO → PP_ID

PIG_NO → PIG_WT

PIG_NO → PIG_VAL

SWINEHERD (SH_SS, SH_NAME, SH_SIZE)

PIGPEN (PP_ID, PP_VAL, PP_CAP, SH_SS)

PIG   (PIG_NO, PP_ID, PIG_WT, PIG_VAL)

SOLUTION TO PROBLEM 13

WZ_SS → WZ_NAME

WZ_SS → WZ_RATE

WZ_SS ↠ {LOG_NAM}

LOG_NAM ↠ {WZ_SS}

LOG_NAM → LOG_ADD

LOG_NAM → LOG_PHONE

SP_ID → SP_NAME

SP_ID → SP_AST

WZ_SS ↠ {SP_ID}

SP_ID ↠ {WZ_SS}

WZ_SS + SP_ID → SP_CRAT

WZ_SS ↠ LOG_NAM | SP_ID

WIZARD (WZ_SS, WZ_NAME, WZ_RATE)

LODGE (LOG_NAM, LOG_ADD, LOG_PHONE)

SPELL (SP_ID, SP_NAME, SP_AST)

WIZ_LOG (WZ_SS, LOG_NAME)

WIZ_SP (WZ_SS, SP_ID, SP_CRAT)

Chapter 4

Entity Relationship Models

4.1 CHAPTER SUMMARY

This chapter explains entity relationship modeling, provides some examples, and shows how this technique relates to normalization and database design.

You will see that there are frequently correspondences between components of a relational representation and an entity relationship representation of the same situation. It is often easy to translate one form into the other. This does not mean that entities are identical with relations. It means that we can note similarities between different representations of the same data.

4.2 WHAT IS AN ENTITY RELATIONSHIP MODEL?

The methods and techniques of analysis and design employ a variety of *models*. These are specific ways of organizing and understanding information. Entity relationship modeling is based on the notion that we think by identifying the things we observe as members of specific categories or entity sets.

An *entity relationship model* is a diagram, with supporting documentation, which illustrates the things or objects of interest and the relationships between or among them. The diagram provides a convenient visual overview. The documentation provides essential definition and explanation.

In Chapter 3 we discussed such things as Customers, Carriers, Cities, Parts, Warehouses, Employees, and Departments. These are all examples of *entities*: things that we are interested in and things about which we have data to store. *Relationships* are connections or associations that we are interested in. *Customer is located in city, carrier is used* for customer, *part is stocked in warehouse*, and *employee is assigned to department* are all examples of relationships. Relationship is a different word from relation and they do not mean the same thing.

4.3 WHY INTRODUCE THIS?

There are two good reasons for using this technique. *First*, it is not possible to design a system or database without some understanding of the real world objects involved. Thus, the designer of a system for accounts payable is aware of vendors, invoices, checks, and the like. The designer of an inventory database is aware of parts and warehouses.

Lacking a formal approach, the designer or analyst is likely to carry these concepts around in his or her mind. Given a simple project, a small development team, and few users, this approach can be successful. But we don't recommend it. As the complexity of the project grows, and the number of people involved grows correspondingly, it becomes necessary to document the ideas somehow. A standard form of documentation makes it possible for all involved to share a common understanding.

Entity relationship modeling also provides a method for arriving at an understanding in the first place. *Group modeling sessions are often marked by differences of opinion and heated debates. When this occurs it demonstrates a lack of a common understanding. The focus of the session should be to define and redefine until consensus is reached.* We provide some useful techniques for resolving problems in the next chapter.

Second, while normalization is a useful technique, it is difficult to apply because functional dependencies are not always easy to identify. Why, we ask, does one decide that color of part is functionally dependent on part number? Isn't it because we mentally attach both to the idea of a thing called part? Doesn't our sense of real world objects provide a focus which allows us to narrow the search for dependencies? Why not, then, recognize this and employ the technique formally?

These then are our main reasons for introducing this technique and employing it as a key element in our design methodology. *We use an entity relationship model to formalize, refine, and communicate our understanding of some situation or business. It's a diagram of a particular view of a slice of life. We use an entity relationship model as a convenient starting point for the process of normalization.*

4.4 DEFINITIONS

We'll try to keep this as simple as possible. Some partisans of entity relationship modeling endow this technique with near mystical qualities. Our approach is that the model should clearly show the things the database describes and should be as simple as possible. While formal definitions may seem to make this more complicated than it really is, we do need them.

An *entity* is essentially any thing. Customer, invoice, department, and the like are specific examples. An entity can be a person, place, thing, or abstract concept. In a college environment, student is an example of an observable, tangible entity. Course is more abstract. We know what it is, but it is difficult to point to one.

Sometimes, it is important to differentiate between the type of thing and a specific occurrence. Strictly speaking, entity refers to a specific person, place, thing, or concept. We use the term *entity set* to identify the type or class or category of thing. Often we are careless and use the word entity when we really mean entity set.

For our purpose, designing databases, it is important to select entity sets with unique identifiers. Eventually, we will want to extract specific information about specific entity occurrences from the database. We will need to be able to tell one from another. It is also because we will eventually want to make sure our design is normalized.

We will also want to restrict ourselves to things that are relevant to the activities which will be supported by the database. We will also restrict ourselves to entities about which we want to store information.

In Section 3.4 we discussed an example involving Customers, Carriers, and Cities. Customer, Carrier, and City are considered entity sets because they are classes of things of interest to us. We want to store information about them in some database. Occurrences of each can be uniquely identified. These happen to be samples of tangible entity types. It is possible to point to an example of each. Specific entity occurrences might by Francine's Fruit Boutique, Marvin's Marvelous Meats, Tailgate Trucking Company, and Punxatawny, Pennsylvania.

Definition *An entity is a person, place, or thing, concrete or abstract, which can be uniquely identified, which is relevant to the activity or business we are interested in, and about which we want to store information. An entity set is a type or class or category of entity.*

Definition *A relationship is a specific connection or linkage between two or more entities. Again, we differentiate between a specific occurrence and a type or category. The latter is properly referred to as a relationship set.* A relation in the relational model and a relationship in the entity relationship model are two different things.

In that same example from Section 3.4, Customer is located in City is an example of a relationship set, while Francine's Fruit Boutique is located in Fresno is an example of a specific relationship occurrence.

Sometimes, entity occurrences are important to us only because they are related to entities in which we have an interest. *A weak entity or dependent entity is one which is included only because of its relationship to some other. It cannot stand on its own.*

A classic example of a *weak* or *dependent* entity involves the family of an employee. We would most likely store information about these dependents in a Human Resources database only because of the relationship to the employee. We would normally access information about the weak entity via the primary entity. That is, we would search for the spouse or children of employee 123456789. We would not search for them by their own unique identifiers. When we delete the information about the employee from the database, we also delete the information about the dependents. Information about these is stored only because of our interest in the employee.

(Let's reword that. If what we have just said is true in a particular set of circumstances, then dependent is a weak entity. If the requirement is that it must be possible to access information about a child or spouse by a unique identifier for that child or spouse or if we retain information about the child or spouse after deleting the employee information, then this is not a weak entity. How can one decide? Examine the nature of the situation under investigation.)

Relationships involving weak entities are usually of a hierarchical nature. In the preceding example, employee can be considered the root or parent or owner node. All access to dependent is via the employee. Any identifier for dependent merely differentiates among dependents of a particular employee. The complete identifier consists of employee identifier plus dependent identifier. The opposite is not true. Hierarchical structures do not always involve weak entities.

Entities and relationships may have attributes. *Attributes are the specific data items which describe the entity or relationship.* The attributes of an entity or relationship will frequently become attributes of a relation or fields in a record. While attribute of a relation, attribute of an entity or relationship, and field in a record are similar in concept, they are not precisely the same thing.

We are concerned to identify the particular attribute or attributes which can uniquely identify a specific entity occurrence. This is referred to as a *key*. Here we use this term in the same sense as in the discussion of the relational model. We will often think of the keys of the associated entities as a combined or concatenated key for a relationship.

We also need to identify the *connectivity* or *cardinality* of each relationship. There may be a single carrier for a particular customer while the same carrier may relate to many customers. Thus we identify this as a one to many relationship. We commonly categorize relationships as one to one (1-1), one to many (1-M), many to one (M-1), or many to many (M-M). (Some people prefer to write M-N to show that there are not necessarily an equal number of occurrences of each of the related entities.

Suppose we are discussing the customer to carrier relationship.

One to one would mean that one customer is served by but one carrier and also that one carrier serves but one customer. (That would not be very realistic, would it?)

One to many would mean that one customer is served by many carriers. But each carrier would be restricted to serving only one customer. (Again, it's not very realistic.)

Many to one would mean that while a customer is served by only one carrier, a carrier may serve many customers. (This sounds better.)

Many to many would mean that a customer may be served by many carriers and a carrier may serve many customers. (This could be the most realistic.)

Connectivity refers to the possibility of a relationship set (1-1, 1-M, etc.). This information is necessary for normalization. *Cardinality* refers to the specific number of entities involved in a specific relationship occurrence. This information is necessary for physical design and tuning.

The number of links or the number of entity types participating in a relationship is referred to as the *degree* of the relationship.

In Section 3.11 we discussed an example involving the relationship employee performs task for project. This is an example of a ternary or three-way relationship, which is illustrated by Figure 4.8. We discuss it again below.

Most textbook examples deal with two-way or binary relationships. In fact, relationships of higher degree are commonly encountered. Four-way, five-way and higher degree relationships do exist. (There is a view that any relationship of any arbitrary degree can and should be reduced to a collection of binary or two-way relationships. See, for example, Section 3.4.12 in [FROST86]. This involves the introduction of artificial entities to represent the complex relationships. It does not seem useful for our purpose to deal with this here.)

4.5   TECHNIQUE

Many different diagramming styles have been proposed. It is quite possible that one is as good as another. If you concentrate on the concepts of entity modeling you should be able to see that different diagramming styles are just different ways of expressing the same ideas. Our technique is based on that originally published by Peter Chen. [CHEN77] It is widely used, is fairly simple, and is adequate to the job. We do take a look at some of the other styles later. The model consists of a diagram plus supporting documentation. *The supporting documentation is as important as the diagram.*

Entities are represented by rectangles. Each entity is assigned a descriptive name. Supporting documentation consists of a definition of the entity set, identification of the key, and a list of the attributes of the entity. (This is discussed in detail in Chapter 6.) Some people like to show the attributes on the diagram. See McFadden and Hoffer, for example. [MCFADDEN85] This can be useful for a simple model, but it becomes very unwieldy if the subject at hand involves a relatively large number of entity types and attributes.

Relationships are represented by diamonds. Lines connect the diamond to the related entities. Each line is labeled with a "1" or "M" to indicate whether one or many occurrences of the adjacent entity type may be related to one occurrence of the other entity type. Each relationship is given a simple name. Attributes of each relationship are documented. An arrowhead at the end of a line indicates a weak entity. Figures 4.1 and 4.2 illustrate the possibilities for the customers, cities, and carriers.

Figure 4.1a shows a relationship between customers and carriers. A specific carrier is associated with or related to each customer. Many customers may be related to the same carrier. The customer to carrier relationship is many to one.

The functional dependency would be

CUSTOMER   →   CARRIER

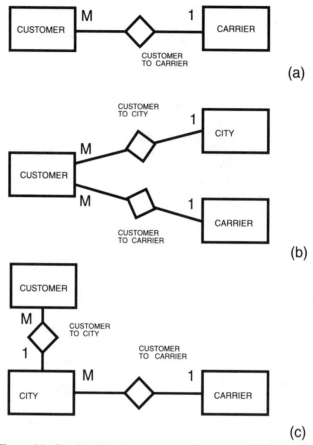

Figure 4.1 Possible CUSTOMER to CARRIER relationships

because, given the customer, we can determine the carrier, but given the carrier, we can not be sure of the customer. (Actually, the functional dependency would probably involve Customer Identifier and Carrier Identifier. Let's ignore that detail for now.)

Notice that we would not say

CUSTOMER + CITY → CARRIER

because City is not relevant to the determination of Carrier in this case.

Figure 4.1b indicates that we are also interested in cities and in customer to city relationships. The customer to city relationship is also many to one.

CUSTOMER → CITY

CUSTOMER → CARRIER

Figure 4.1c indicates that customers are not directly related to carriers. City to carrier is many to one. Customer to city is many to one.

CUSTOMER → CITY

CITY → CARRIER

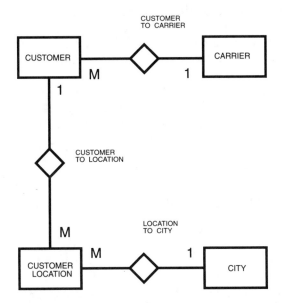

Figure 4.2 Another CUSTOMER to CARRIER relationship

Figure 4.2 indicates that we have an interest in specific customer locations. In this case, as in Figure 4.1a, specific customers are directly associated with specific carriers. More than one customer location may be associated with one customer. Each location is associated with a specific city.

CUSTOMER_LOCATION → CUSTOMER

CUSTOMER_LOCATION → CITY

CUSTOMER → CARRIER

These are not four different ways of drawing the same diagram. These are representations of four different business policies. Our intent in making such a diagram will always be to discover and document a view of the world which fits the circumstances and policies that exist at a given time and place.

It can be extremely difficult to arrive at a model which will satisfy everyone involved in a study.

Sometimes there are valid equivalent diagramming conventions. This should be the easiest type of problem to solve. It is merely necessary to select one of the possibilities. Unfortunately, it is often the case that one or more parties are extremely partisan to a specific diagramming style. Careful negotiation becomes essential in this situation.

Sometimes one or more parties will have different concepts of the same underlying situation. In this case, careful development of a precise definition for each entity and relationship, examination of the attributes for each, and careful examination of the relevant policies should resolve the difficulty. Open-mindedness and willingness to review and negotiate are essential to a solution. We repeat this for emphasis. *Precise definitions and a willingness to discuss and reevaluate are essential.*

Finally, it may be the case that different parties have different views which are valid and arise because each is concerned with a different aspect of the overall situation. In this case it is necessary to discover a broader underlying view which can satisfy all requirements. This is probably the most difficult problem. We discuss this in some detail in Chapter 5.

In the latter two situations, *drawing the diagram does not cause the difference of opinion, it brings it to light.* Any system or file or database which would be implemented without resolving the differences would not be satisfactory for all parties involved. *The model and the modeling process are a technique for communicating and refining concepts of reality and assuring that the database and system are appropriate to the need.*

4.6 WHY ENTITIES AND RELATIONSHIPS? HOW CAN WE TELL THEM APART?

Some modeling techniques do not involve a separate, explicit representation of relationships. Diagrams showing only entities are often referred to as Bachman Diagrams after Charles Bachman. [BACHMAN69]

Modeling techniques that do not differentiate between entities and relationships can lead to confusion and inappropriate assignment of attributes.

Consider the simple case illustrated in Figure 4.3. It involves the entity types man and woman and the relationship type marriage. It is our cultural norm that a person will be married to but one individual at a time even though over a lifetime one individual may be married several times. (Notice that this is not true for every culture.) It has also been our norm that a marriage involves individuals of opposite sex. Suppose we model only the two entities man and woman as shown in Figure 4.3a. Is DATE_OF_MARRIAGE an attribute of one party or of both parties? Since there is the potential for assigning multiple DATE_OF_MARRIAGE attribute occurrences to an individual, it is not convenient to think of it as an attribute of the man or of the woman. It would be arbitrary to assign it as an attribute of one or the other and redundant to assign it as an attribute of both. It is much more convenient and useful to think of it as an attribute of the marriage which relates two individuals as shown in Figure 4.3b.

The remaining question is whether or not marriage is really a different kind of object than man or woman. To a judge or a newspaper, a marriage itself might be a thing of interest—more so than the individuals involved. In this case, there might be a unique identifier for the marriage, possibly a docket number or announcement number. In such a situation, it might be appropriate to model marriage as an entity and either omit the man and woman or think of their identities as attributes of the marriage as shown in Figure 4.3d. If the database is about marriages and the man and woman are only of interest because of the marriage, they are represented by weak entities.

The choice illustrated by Figure 4.3a is suitable only if we are only concerned with the current marriage. The choice between the remaining three depends on which aspects we are most interested in. Another way to say this is that Figures 4.3b, 4.3c, and 4.3d represent three different viewpoints as to what is important. The choice illustrated by Figure 4.3c is the most comprehensive and flexible representation.

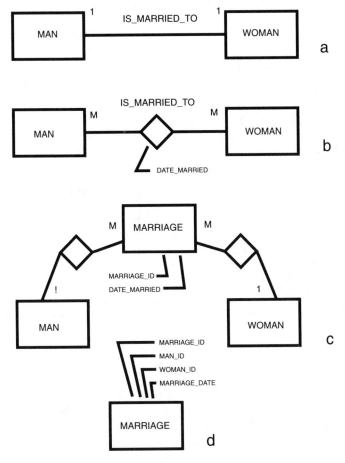

Figure 4.3 Different views of marriage

The first step in developing an entity relationship model is to identify the things that are to be represented in our database. The name of an entity set will almost always be a noun. Each will have an identifier plus other attributes. A specific value for the identifier must lead us to one and only one entity occurrence. Later on, after we have implemented the database, there will be times when someone will want to retrieve information about the entity using the identifier as a search argument.

Relationships are introduced to represent linkages or associations between entities. *It is possible to think of the entities without the relationship. It is very difficult to think of the relationship without the entities.* There will almost always be possible relationship names which are verbs. In the customer and city example we might have used IS_LOCATED_IN as the name for the customer to city relationship. It is unlikely that we would have any reason to establish a unique identifier for a thing called an IS_LOCATED_IN. Relationships normally are identified by the keys of the related entities. *If you just can't make up your mind, consider it an entity. It will fall out later on in the design process.*

4.7 ENTITIES VERSUS ATTRIBUTES

It is sometimes problematic whether something should be considered as an attribute of some entity or as an entity in its own right. This can be resolved by considering the purpose of the modeling activity. We think of something as an entity if it is something we will want to store data about.

Consider the color of a manufactured item such as a file cabinet or an automobile. Do the activities we have in mind require us to store data about the colors themselves? That is, is there an entity occurrence called "red" with its own attributes? If this is not the case, we think of color as an attribute of the product. If, however, we are concerned with specific formulas for manufacturing a product of a specific color or with attributes such as cost or reflectance which are associated with particular colors, then color will be an entity to which manufactured items are related.

If we just can't decide, we can arbitrarily call the thing in question an entity. It will fall out later on in the design process.

Would we ever have an entity with no explicit attributes? Yes, we might. The only attribute of interest might be that a particular occurrence does or does not exist. Later on, we might, for example, incorporate a record type or table consisting only of a color identifier and use this to validate the color associated with an input item.[1] The last comment might encourage the view that developing an entity relationship model constitutes designing a database. This is very definitely not the case. An entity relationship model is a form of conceptual model. It describes the kinds of information to be stored in the database. Our purpose is to refine, document, and communicate an understanding. If we desire to record that a particular color does or does not exist, color becomes, for us, an entity type. This is an important step in the design process. It will often—but not invariably—be the case that the database will eventually contain relations or records which represent or correspond to the entities and possibly to some of the relationships. Our current objective is to identify and define the things we have an interest in and the relationships between them. We will decide how to store the data later.

4.8 EXAMPLES

Let's review the remainder of the examples discussed in Chapter 3. Figure 4.4 represents the employee and project example used in Chapter 3 to illustrate Second Normal Form.

EMPLOYEE_ID → EMPLOYEE_NAME

PROJECT_ID → PROJECT_NAME

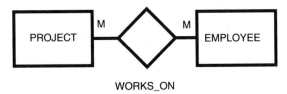

WORKS_ON

Figure 4.4   Many to many relationship

EMPLOYEE_ID + PROJECT_ID → START_DATE

EMPLOYEE_ID + PROJECT_ID → COMPLETION_DATE

EMPLOYEE(<u>EMPLOYEE_ID</u>, EMPLOYEE_NAME)

PROJECT(<u>PROJECT_ID</u>,PROJECT_NAME)

WORKS_ON(<u>EMPLOYEE_ID, PROJECT_ID</u>, START_DATE,

COMPLETION_DATE)

There should be little resistance to the notion that employee and project can be thought of as entity sets. Each is an object of interest. Each has a unique identifier. Each has descriptive attributes such as description.

Figure 4.4 represents the assignment of a particular employee to a particular project as a relationship between the employee and project. Start date and completion date become attributes of this relationship. The relationship is identified by the combination or concatenation of the relevant identifiers.

Notice that, in the relational implementation, each of the two entities and the relationship are represented by relations. Also notice that the attributes EMPLOYEE_ID and PROJECT_ID provide the linkage between the WORKS_ON relation and the EMPLOYEE and PROJECT relations. Individually, they are foreign keys. Together, they form the primary key of the WORKS_ON relation. We identified the functional dependencies based on this concept of the situation. If it seemed reasonable to you, it was because you shared the concept.

Could we think of WORKS_ON as an entity? We would do so only if there were a unique identifier, such as assignment number, associated with it. This would become the key for WORKS_ON. EMPLOYEE_ID and PROJECT_ID would still be foreign keys. The result would look like this.

EMPLOYEE(<u>EMPLOYEE_ID</u>, EMPLOYEE_NAME)

PROJECT(<u>PROJECT_ID</u>,PROJECT_NAME)

WORKS_ON(<u>ASSIGN_NO</u>, EMPLOYEE_ID, PROJECT_ID, START_DATE,

COMPLETION_DATE)

Should we explicitly include the foreign keys in a list of the attributes of the entities and relationships? In entity relationship modeling, this is really a matter of choice.[2] The foreign keys are implied by the diagram and can be omitted without loss of information.

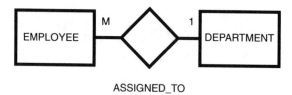

ASSIGNED_TO

Figure 4.5   Many to one relationship

Including them can be useful if it is likely that the lists will be viewed separately from the diagram. It is useful to include them if relations will be derived from the model. It is also useful to include them as a reminder that they will occupy space in the relations. We vote for including them.

Figure 4.5 illustrates the employee and department example that was used in Chapter 3 to illustrate Third Normal Form.

EMPLOYEE_ID → EMPLOYEE_NAME

EMPLOYEE_ID → DEPARTMENT_ID

DEPARTMENT_ID → DEPARTMENT_NAME

EMPLOYEE(EMPLOYEE_ID, EMPLOYEE_NAME, DEPARTMENT_ID)

DEPARTMENT(DEPARTMENT_ID, DEPARTMENT_NAME)

Employee and department are objects of interest and have unique identifiers. As in the preceding example, the relational implementation contains a relation which corresponds to each entity and the identifier of the entity is the key of the relation. In the relational implementation for this example, DEPARTMENT_ID becomes an attribute of EMPLOYEE because there is but one department for a given employee. We were able to identify this as a functional dependency. As such, it provides the link between EMPLOYEE and DEPARTMENT.

Notice that we have a many to one relationship between employee and department and that the relational implementation does not incorporate a relation which explicitly represents the relationship. *It is possible to represent a many to one relationship via a foreign key without introducing a relation to represent it.*

Notice the difference between the relationship for EMPLOYEE WORKS_ON PROJECT and EMPLOYEE ASSIGNED_TO DEPARTMENT. ASSIGNED_TO is many to one. It has no attributes. It is not necessary to provide a separate relation to represent it. It is not possible to maintain a history of employee to department assignments. (When we say it is a many to one relationship, we are really saying that there is only one department associated with an employee. If the model does not represent the situation the database will not work.) WORKS_ON is many to many. It has attributes. It is necessary to provide a separate relation to represent it. It is possible to maintain a history of all employee to project assignments.

Looking at this entity relationship model makes us aware of something that we've been overlooking so far. The functional dependencies which we identified in the preceding chapter were based on a hidden assumption. We assumed that an employee never has distinct assignments involving the same project. This is not realistic for most organizations. Thus the combination of EMPLOYEE_ID and PROJECT_ID is not enough to uniquely identify an occurrence of the relationship. It is necessary to introduce another element. START_DATE will be the most reasonable given the data we've identified so far.

In other words, we erred when we stated

EMPLOYEE_ID + PROJECT_ID $\rightarrow$ START_DATE

It is likely the case that

EMPLOYEE_ID + PROJECT_ID $\twoheadrightarrow$ {START_DATE}

We can resolve this by stating

EMPLOYEE_ID + PROJECT_ID + START_DATE $\rightarrow$ COMPLETION_DATE

and identifying the combination of the three elements as the key for WORKS_ON. In this case the relations look the same. But there is one significant difference. Identification of START_DATE as a part of the key tells us that we will not want to allow occurrences with null start dates. We also will not want to allow two different occurrences with identical EMPLOYEE_ID, PROJECT_ID, and START_DATE. (What would either of these really represent?)

Is COMPLETION_DATE also a possible component of a candidate key? One flaw is that it could have a null value for the current assignment. Including attributes which can be null in a key is not acceptable.

There are several things to note. The relational implementation of a many to one relationship can be accomplished by incorporating a foreign key in the relation which represents the entity on the many side.

The relational implementation of a many to many relationship usually requires the introduction of a relation which represents the relationship.

Foreign keys in the relation which represents the relationship identify the entity occurrences involved in the relationship occurrence. The concatenation of the foreign keys may form the key for the relation which represents the relationship, but this is not always the case.

It may be possible to develop a good design using only normalization or using only an entity relationship model or without using either. Using both, in combination, provides a good way of really examining the data and our concept of the data.

Figure 4.6 illustrates the example which was used in Chapter 3 to illustrate Fourth Normal Form.

EMPLOYEE_ID $\rightarrow$ EMPLOYEE_NAME

SKILL_CODE $\rightarrow$ SKILL_DESCR

LANG_CODE $\rightarrow$ LANG_DESCR

EMPLOYEE_ID $\twoheadrightarrow$ SKILL_CODE | LANG_CODE

EMPLOYEE_ID + SKILL_CODE $\rightarrow$ SKILL_PROF

EMPLOYEE_ID + SKILL_CODE $\rightarrow$ SKILL_DATE

EMPLOYEE_ID + LANG_CODE $\rightarrow$ LANG_PROF

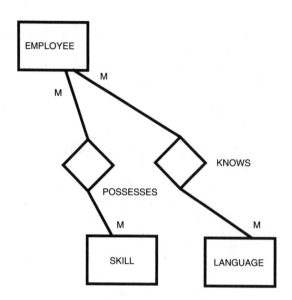

Figure 4.6   4NF example

EMPLOYEE_ID + LANG_CODE   →   LANG_DATE

EMPLOYEE (<u>EMPLOYEE_ID</u>, EMPLOYEE_NAME)

SKILL (<u>SKILL_CODE</u>, SKILL_DESCR)

LANG (<u>LANG_CODE</u>, LANG_DESCR)

EMP_SKI (<u>EMPLOYEE_ID</u>, SKILL_CODE, SKILL_PROF, SKILL_DATE)

EMP_LAN (<u>EMPLOYEE_ID, LANG_CODE</u>, LANG_PROF, LANG_DATE)

In this example, we have identified the employee, skill, and language as entities because each is a uniquely identifiable thing that we wish to record data about.

Employee to skill and employee to language relationships are many to many. As a result, our relational implementation requires the introduction of a relation to represent each relationship and the foreign keys appear in the relations which represent the relationships. Entity relationship modeling seems to make the analysis of this case a lot easier.

Let's review the example used in Chapter 3 to illustrate Fifth Normal Form.

EMPLOYEE_ID	PROJECT_ID	TASK_ID
123	XYZ	ABC
123	ZYX	CBA

Entity Relationship Models   Chapter 4

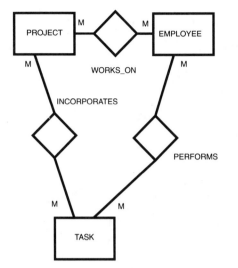

Figure 4.7 5NF example

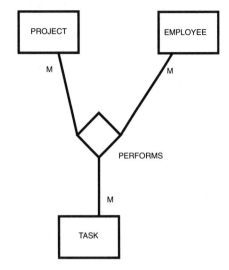

Figure 4.8 5NF: A better analysis

EMPLOYEE_ID	PROJECT_ID	TASK_ID (Continued...)
321	XYZ	CBA
321	ZYX	ABC

Figure 4.7 represents an incorrect concept of the situation which would lead us to a design resulting in *lossy* joins. The implications of this diagram are that there are no connections between the employee to project relationship, the project to task relationship, and the task to employee relationship.

Figure 4.8 represents a concept of the more likely situation. Here there is one three-way or ternary relationship. An example of an occurrence of this relationship is that employee 123 performs task ABC on project XYZ.

The appropriate relational implementation is to introduce a relation which represents the ternary relationship and contains foreign keys identifying each of the entities involved in the relationship. Here we have an example of a ternary relationship.

This type of misinterpretation is commonly referred to as the *connection trap*. Howe [HOWE83] provides a detailed discussion of this and other *traps*.

Figure 4.9 represents a comprehensive diagram of the entire example.

Figure 4.10 illustrates the entities and relationships which formed the basis for the dwarf, weapon, and spell example in Chapter 3.

DWARF (DWARF_ID, DWARF_NAME, CAVE_ID)

CAVE (CAVE_ID, NUMBER_OF_ROOMS, ASSESSED_VALUE)

SPELLS(DWARF_ID, SPELL, POWER_OF_SPELL)

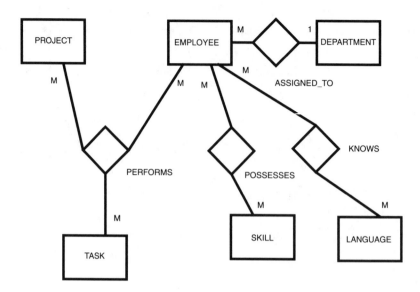

Figure 4.9 Combination of Figures 4.5, 4.6, and 4.7

ARMS (<u>DWARF_ID</u>, <u>WEAPON</u>, PROFICIENCY)

The entities are DWARF, CAVE, WEAPON, and SPELL.
DWARF LIVES_IN CAVE is a many to one relationship. In our relational implementation, this was handled by placing CAVE_ID in the DWARF relation as a foreign key.

DWARF USES WEAPON and DWARF CASTS SPELL are both many to many relationships. In our relational implementation, this was handled by creating a relation for each relationship.

Notice that, because we had no data to store about spells and weapons, we did not incorporate relations to represent these entities. In a more technically oriented and computerized society, we might find a need to assign weapon and spell identifiers and store characteristics of each. Then the dependencies and relations would look like this.

DWARF_ID → DWARF_NAME

DWARF_ID → CAVE_ID

CAVE_ID → NUMBER_OF_ROOMS

CAVE_ID → ASSESSED_VALUE

WEAPON_ID → NAME_OF_WEAPON

WEAPON_ID → WEIGHT_OF_WEAPON

SPELL_ID → NAME_OF_SPELL

SPELL_ID → LICENSING_REQ

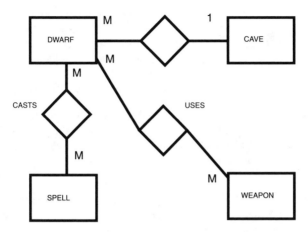

Figure 4.10   DWARF and WEAPON example

DWARF_ID $\twoheadrightarrow$ SPELL_ID I WEAPON_ID

DWARF_ID + SPELL_ID $\rightarrow$ POWER_OF_SPELL

DWARF_ID + WEAPON_ID $\rightarrow$ PROFICIENCY

DWARF (DWARF_ID, DWARF_NAME, CAVE_ID)

CAVE (CAVE_ID, NUMBER_OF_ROOMS, ASSESSED_VALUE)

WEAPON (WEAPON_ID, NAME_OF_WEAPON, WEIGHT_OF_WEAPON)

SPELL (SPELL_ID, NAME_OF_SPELL, LICENSING_REQ)

SPELLS (DWARF_ID, SPELL_ID, POWER_OF_SPELL)

ARMS (DWARF_ID, WEAPON_ID, PROFICIENCY)

4.9   LET'S REVIEW

We still have a few more refinements to add. We also need to formalize some rules and procedures. But let's stop and recap what we have gone over so far.

Entity relationship modeling is a technique for documenting our understanding of the things to be represented by data in a database. This is a useful documentation and system design technique in its own right.

An entity relationship model also provides a basis for further database design activities. It is particularly useful as a starting point for the identification of functional dependencies and normalization.

The entities are the things we are interested in. An entity should be something we may want to store data about. Individual entity occurrences should be uniquely identifiable by some key. We document the entity itself, the key, and the other attributes or descriptors.[3]

The relationships are the connections between the entities. Often, we are able to identify binary relationships (involving two entities). It is, however, possible for relationships to be ternary (three-way) or higher degree relationships. We identify the entities involved, the cardinality (or number of each entity type which may participate), and any attributes for each relationship.

Entity relationship modeling is not an exact science for several reasons.

- Our perceptions of entities and relationships are based on our perceptions of the world. Each of us has his or her own unique way of seeing things. What seems an entity to one seems a relationship to another. One way to resolve this is to say it is an entity if it has its own identifier or if it can be thought of independently. In case of doubt, model it as an entity.

- Sometimes the distinction between entity and attribute seems highly arbitrary. Usually it makes sense to model it as an entity only if there is information to be stored about it. In case of doubt, we model it as an entity.

- The purpose and scope of the activity will have a significant effect on the perception of what constitute entities, relationships, and attributes.

- *Real world* design activities differ from examples and cases in books in a significant manner. The designer of a real system starts with nothing but a blank piece of paper. It is necessary to arrive at an understanding of the situation by observing and questioning. Asking the right questions is very important and very difficult.

We must be flexible and willing to negotiate. When in doubt, we adopt the view which leaves the greatest flexibility. This usually means identifying an entity where we are tempted to identify a relationship or an attribute. We do this because we can always omit the entity later if it becomes evident that it is not needed.

Clear and complete written definitions for each entity, relationship, and attribute will clarify meaning and resolve many difficulties. We discuss this further in Chapter 6.

The next step in our design process will be to develop a set of normalized relations.

- We create a relation for each entity and for each many to many relationship.

- The entity identifier serves as the key for a relation derived from an entity. In the case of a weak entity, we add the identifier of the related entity on which the weak entity depends. Sometimes the identifiers of the related entities combine to form the key for a relation derived from a many to many relationship. Sometimes it is necessary to introduce additional attributes to form a proper key.

- One to many relationships are implemented via foreign keys. The identifier of the entity on the "one" side becomes an attribute of the relation which represents the entity on the "many" side.

- The remaining attributes are assigned to the relations which represent the appropriate entities and relationships.

- Now, it is necessary to examine the connection between each nonkey attribute of each relation and the key of the relation. Are there any nonkey attributes which are not fully functionally dependent on keys? Are there any hidden partial key dependencies, transitive dependencies, or multivalued dependencies? Is there any evidence of *lossy* join possibilities? If so, these are eliminated.

- Finally, any unnecessary relations are eliminated. These might involve only a key consisting of a single attribute. They might be imbedded within another.

4.10 ALTERNATIVE DIAGRAM STYLES

If there is anything that illustrates the fertility of the human brain, it's the number of variant entity relationship modeling techniques which have been developed. We'll take a little time to examine just a few.

Charles Bachman [BACHMAN69] is often credited as the original inventor of entity relationship modeling.[4] The original Bachman diagrams were very simple. Entities are shown as rectangles. Relationships are shown as lines connecting the entities. An arrow at the end of a line indicates the *many* side of a one to many relationship. There is also an extended form specific to the IDMS database management system which is used to show details of a physical database design.[5] When this technique is used, many to many relationships are often converted to entities. Figure 4.11a is an example. IBM [IBM90] [IBM91-1] has used a very similar approach in developing the data model for the MVS Repository.

Peter Chen's technique is one of the more popular approaches.[CHEN77] Figure 4.11b is an example. This style is used by a number of CASE tools. Minor variants include use of a single arrow to indicate the *one* side of a relationship and a double arrow to indicate the *many* side, use of a dot to indicate the *many* side of a relationship, and use of a double box to indicate a weak entity.

Ross [ROSS87] provides an elaborate set of extensions for diagramming integrity constraints, relationships that involve time, events which *trigger* or initiate other events, and subset superset relationships.

Finkelstein [FINKELSTEIN89] presents the *crow's foot* notation illustrated by Figure 4.11c. The *crow's foot* symbol is used to designate the *many* side of a relationship. He also uses a vertical bar to indicate a mandatory relationship and an open circle to indicate an optional relationship. *Mandatory* means that at least one relationship occurrence must be present for each entity occurrence. *Optional* means that an entity occurrence does not have to participate in a relationship. In the example, an order cannot exist unless it has a customer and at least one item. On the other hand, both customer and item may exist without order. Let's note once again that this is an invented example and that it is necessary to research the business rules for a given set of circumstances. It is fairly common to add a symbol for optional to the diagram; an open circle is often used. In this book, we've omitted this in order to keep the diagram simple. That is a matter of personal taste. In either event, we should be sure to describe the exact rules in the written documentation.

Bachman Systems (founded by Charles Bachman) is presently (1992) marketing a comprehensive CASE tool kit which incorporates a diagram similar to that illustrated by Figure 4.11d. The arrow indicates "many." Open and closed circles are used to indicate

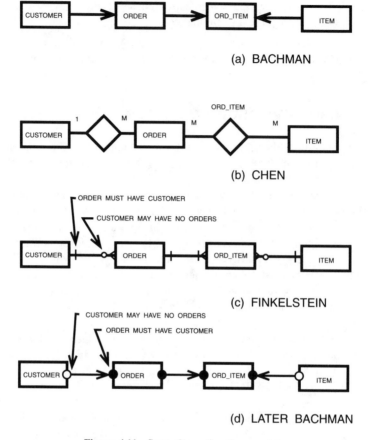

(a) BACHMAN

(b) CHEN

(c) FINKELSTEIN

(d) LATER BACHMAN

Figure 4.11   Some alternative diagram styles

optional and mandatory relationships. Note that the location for the open circle is different from in the preceding example.

We might carry this discussion much further. There is nothing sacred about rectangles. Some techniques use circles, or ellipses, or race track shaped symbols. The point is that most differences are cosmetic. The important issues revolve around recognition of the value of a model; identification of entities, relationships, and attributes; resolution of differences; and use of the model as a basis for subsequent activities.

Endnotes

1. The content of this relation would really constitute the definition of the domain of color identifiers.

2. Some people feel very strongly that a particular way of dealing with this is the only correct way. This sort of thing that can take up a lot of time and energy. Either approach is workable in practice. What is important is to understand the issue and how you have resolved it.

3. This is just used as an English language synonym. We are not introducing a new technical term here.

4. There is a story that his father was a football coach and the original technique was patterned after diagrams of football plays.

5. The original IDMS system was based on the network model. It is quite natural to use this type of diagram for documenting network database designs.

QUESTIONS AND EXERCISES

1. How does entity relationship modeling relate to normalization?

2. What is an entity? What is an entity set?

3. What is a relationship? What is a relationship set?

4. What are the connections, if any, between entities, relationships, and relations?

5. Both the relational model and the entity relationship model utilize attributes. Does attribute mean the same thing in each case? Explain.

6. Explain connectivity, degree, and cardinality.

7. Is written documentation an important part of an entity relationship model? Why or why not?

8. Does it matter what symbols are used in drawing the diagram? Why or why not?

9. How can one differentiate between entities, relationships, and attributes? Is it important to come up with the perfect answer on this? Why or why not?

10. How can you proceed from an entity relationship model to a set of relations?

11. Develop an entity relationship model for the *Bee Sting* example given in the exercises for the preceding chapter.

12. Develop an entity relationship model for the following. List the attributes for each entity and relationship.

    Show the attributes for each entity and relationship alongside the entity or relationship. Underline the KEY or IDENTIFIER for each.

Also provide a brief (one or two or three sentence) definition for each entity, relationship, and attribute.

This database will be used by the Central Pirate Registry located in the Lower Bermuda Triangle. (No doubt the database management system used will be unregistered pirated software!)

Pirates are identified by unique pirate Nicknames regulated by the Central Pirate Registry. Each pirate also has a given Christian Name, a Ferocity Rating, and a Date of First Piracy.

Pirate Ships are also identified by unique Pirate Ship Names. These are also regulated by the Central Pirate Registry. Important information about a Pirate Ship includes Number of Masts, Number of Cannon, and Date Commissioned.

Merchant Vessels are identified by unique Merchant Ship Names regulated by the Potential Victims Association in London, England. Important characteristics of Merchant Vessels include Weight and Number of Masts. The Pirate Registry only keeps track of Merchant Vessels that have actually been plundered or sunk.

A given Pirate is a Crew Member for a specific Pirate Ship at any given time. A Pirate may also be unemployed at some times. One and only one Pirate is Captain of one and only one Pirate Ship at any given time. (Assume that a history of past employment is not required.)

The Pirate Registry keeps track of each Incident of Plundering. The record identifies the Pirate Ship, the Merchant Vessel, the Date of the Plundering, whether or not the Merchant Vessel was sunk, and how many Innocent Seamen were forced to walk the plank. It is possible for the same Pirate Ship to Plunder the same Merchant Vessel more than once.

13. Identify Functional Dependencies and Multivalued Facts based on your model for exercise 12. Develop a normalized database design. Explain in detail how it is that you are sure your design is normalized.

14. Suppose the Central Pirate Registry does retain an Employment History for each Pirate showing beginning and ending dates for all assignments. Make the necessary changes to your entity relationship model and your normalized design.

15. Develop an entity relationship model for the following.

Show the attributes for each entity and relationship alongside the entity or relationship. Underline the KEY or IDENTIFIER for each.

Also provide a brief (one or two or three sentence) definition for each entity, relationship, and attribute.

Identify dependencies and develop a normalized set of relations.

Ron's repair performs warranty service on appliances which are sold with a lifetime warranty. The database will be used to keep track of Customers, Appliances, Technicians, and Specific Repairs.

It is necessary to keep track of all work performed on a particular appliance. The records must contain information about the Customer, the Appliance, the work done, and the Technician who performed the work. It is also necessary to know when the work was done and how many hours it took.

Customers are identified by Customer Numbers. It is necessary to keep a record of Customer name, address, and telephone and of all appliances owned by the Customer. An Appliance is registered as owned by the Customer when it is purchased. If necessary, new or revised Customer data is entered at the same time. Appliances are identified by serial numbers. Since it is conceivable two different types of appliance will have identical series of serial numbers, model number and manufacturer identifier are also recorded. Records of technicians include employee ID number and name.

When an appliance is brought for repair, a repair order is filled out. Each order has a unique identifying number. Date in and date out are recorded.

16. Develop an entity relationship model for the following.

Show the attributes for each entity and relationship alongside the entity or relationship. Underline the KEY or IDENTIFIER for each.

Also provide a brief (one or two or three sentence) definition for each entity, relationship, and attribute.

Identify dependencies and develop a normalized set of relations.

George and Marilyn's Creative Cleaning Service provides housekeeping and cleaning services. The database will be used to keep track of customers, employees, and specific cleaning jobs.

It is important to know which employee worked at a given customer's house on a given date in case there are problems or complaints.

It is necessary to keep track of each customer's name, address, and telephone number. A unique Customer identifier is assigned to each customer.

Specific dates for visits to the customers' houses are scheduled in advance. In addition to date and time, each visit is assigned a specific number of hours (to be worked).

If a visit is for any reason canceled, it is marked canceled but a record is retained. Once the visit is completed, the actual number of hours worked is recorded. There is also a notation as to whether or not and when the visit has been billed for and whether or not it is paid for. A specific employee will be assigned to go on a specific visit.

It is necessary to record each employee's name, address, and telephone number. Social Security number is used for employee identifier.

Chapter 5

Advanced Modeling Concepts

5.1   CHAPTER SUMMARY

This chapter continues the discussion of entity relationship modelling. Here, we deal with some trickier problems and introduce some advanced modeling concepts which help resolve them. Some of this material may appear a little *far out* to some readers. This is unfortunate, but it is really necessary to deal with some issues that seem philosophical, and you will have trouble if you don't appreciate them. We attempt to keep the presentation as simple and down to earth as possible. Be patient and it will make sense. The time you invest in digesting this will eventually prove to have been well spent. You may find it valuable to return to this chapter after you've had some practice.

The tools and techniques discussed in this chapter will help you work your way out of a variety of difficulties. It will be helpful if you understand the nature of each type of problem and if you appreciate that the data model (and the database) must organize the data in a way that is useful *for a particular purpose*. Concentrate on establishing and defining a set of entities and relationships that are useful here and now. That's what we really mean when we say that an entity is a person, place, or thing, concrete or abstract, which can be uniquely identified, which is relevant to the activity or business we are interested in, and about which we want to store information.

In this chapter we frequently switch back and forth between an entity relationship model and a set of relations. Entities and relations are not the same thing. But when each of these two different techniques is used to represent the same situation, there are similarities and it is possible to switch from one way of looking at it to another.

We also show sample SQL which might be used to implement some of the situations we discuss. Do not automatically assume that an SQL table is the same thing as a relation or an entity. Since it is another representation of the same data there will be similarity and it should be possible to make the transformation from one to the other.

5.2 DATA MODELING PROBLEMS AND SOLUTIONS

We've noted already that group data modeling sessions are often marked by controversy and debate. Let's examine some of the reasons for this. We begin with some discussion of how we think and what we are really doing when we design and build computer systems.[1]

The analyst or designer studies a situation (a business situation, a processing requirement, an organization—some *real world* phenomenon) in order to understand it well enough to design and implement systems which will facilitate or improve things. Our particular emphasis in this book is on designing data structures and databases which will be appropriate for whatever the need is. The database is in a way a model of the situation. The data attributes stored in the database represent the entities, relationships, and attributes of interest. If the branch manager of a bank finds it useful to record a customer's occupation and income, the database must provide attributes or *buckets* where this data can be stored.

A proper design requires at least two kinds of understanding. We must understand the data and its uses well enough to *provide for the storage of all necessary information*. This encompasses data values and data relationships.

We must understand the proposed uses and the processing environment well enough to *provide for efficient operation*. It may be extremely difficult to predict future processing and data requirements. So we need to store the data in such a manner that it can be used to meet unknown future requirements.

The development of an entity relationship model forces us to examine the important considerations about the situation. It provides a means for communicating and resolving conflicting views of the nature and uses of the data. The resulting model provides documentation of what has been determined and becomes an input to the next design step. This model is not, itself, the database design. It is a representation of information needed to complete the design.

To think about things, we assign them to named categories or classes. We have a notion or concept of the properties of a kind of object we call a chair. When an artifact in the world appears to possess the appropriate properties, we make the statement, "There is a chair." Notice that we have discussed more than one thing. There is the general idea of a chair and there is also a specific occurrence or instance of a particular chair which is one of the many chairs which may exist in the world. We are constantly identifying objects as instances of particular classes. Mostly, we do this without giving it a thought. This is not only the case for tangible objects like chairs, it is also true for less concrete things like customer orders, and even for very abstract ideas such as *freedom* and *good*. We use these named categories to think about things. And we also use them to communicate with each other. To the extent that we share the same notion of the thing or concept which is represented by a particular class name, we can communicate with each other. To the extent that we don't use the same system for classifying, we fail to communicate; sometimes we fail horribly.

Now, we can identify some problems.

It may or may not be possible to produce a single, perfect definition of what does and what does not fit into a particular category—chair, for example. We certainly encounter other artifacts that come close to being chairs but are not; stools, love seats, couches, for example. You might visualize a row of objects which begins with an obvious stool, ends with an obvious chair, but also contains a series of things, each slightly different from its neighbors, which gradually effect the transition from stool to chair. At some point, we must establish a boundary and state "Over here we have stools, over there we have chairs." If we encountered one of the borderline objects all by itself, we might have quite a debate about which would be the proper category. *It can be difficult to decide that something we encounter belongs in one category and not another.*

The label we use for the category is one thing. The observed object is another. One statement that Hayakawa [HAYAKAWA78] might be best known for is "The map is not the territory." We use the categories to organize our thinking about the world. We use the names of the categories to manipulate them and to communicate. Confusing the name with the thing or thinking that, having named it, we completely understand it can lead to a lot of problems.

We do not all attach exactly the same meanings to the same words. In the example above, one person may want to draw the boundary between stools and chairs in a different place than another. *It is very common for a particular usage to become normal in one place or one part of an organization and be unknown elsewhere.* Meanings of words also change over time. That's why the average person can't understand the writing of, say, Shakespeare without footnotes that explain the meanings and allusions of times past.

Some words, by common usage, have multiple meanings. And these meanings can vary greatly. Look on any page of any dictionary for examples. We can usually determine the appropriate selection from the context: the nature of the discussion, the other words, the way the term is used. You did not, it is hoped, confuse the *chair* one sits on with the *chair* who heads a committee or an academic department.

Some concepts, by common usage, have more than one name.

Concepts or categories are not mutually exclusive. There is a sort of hierarchy of classes. We can differentiate kitchen chairs from office chairs and living room chairs. We can also differentiate chairs from other items of furniture. A store might care to differentiate items of furniture from other types of merchandise. *Sometimes, the hierarchies of classes overlap.* We might care to classify furniture according to a hierarchy of types, as in a wooden chair is a kind of chair which is a kind of thing to sit on which is an item of furniture, and so on. We might classify it according to a hierarchy of uses, as in a kitchen chair is furniture for the home which is a category of furniture.[2]

The characteristics of an entity can vary over time. The status of your bank account, for example, may change significantly from day to day. It is necessary for the bank to differentiate your bank account as of February 1 from your bank account as of March 6 to the extent that these may, for some purposes, seem like two different things.

Different degrees of precision are appropriate for different purposes.

Simpler naming problems are resolved in terms of *synonyms*, *homonyms*, and *aliases*.

Two words are *synonyms* when they have the same or nearly the same meaning. We use the word in this sense here. In some database contexts, two separate representations of the same thing are referred to as synonyms. We do not use the word in this sense in this book. We normally resolve this latter issue via the notion of domains.

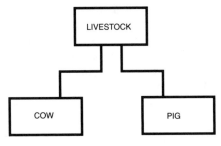

Figure 5.1 "Is a"

Two words are *homonyms* when they sound the same or are spelled the same but have different meanings. We use the word in this sense here.

An *alias* is an assumed or alternate name for something. Authors of treatises on database tend to use alias and synonym to mean the same thing.

Our recourse is to provide complete definitions of everything and to make appropriate cross references for synonyms and homonyms. We discuss this further in Chapter 6.

Issues regarding hierarchies of classes are often resolved by *generalization, aggregation, classification, and association.* All of these have to do with combining like things into broader types or decomposing the broad types into ones that are more specific. Robins, grosbeaks, and wrens are all birds and conversely the broad category birds may be decomposed into robins, grosbeaks, and wrens. *Generalization* refers to drawing broad conclusions from specific facts. *Aggregation* refers to grouping similar but different concepts together. *Classification* refers to categorizing based on some similarity. *Association* refers to forming a whole from two related things or ideas.[3]

Sometimes this problem is resolved by assigning *roles* to a base entity. Suppose the base entity is a person. We may desire, at various times and for various purposes, to view persons as employees, customers, prospects, and so on. A given entity occurrence may fit into several of these categories at a particular time. Employee, customer, and prospect are considered roles which person may assume.

For our purpose here, we can safely ignore many of the more subtle distinctions and combine all of these into something we might refer to as an *is a* or *is a kind of* linkage. The broader category is commonly referred to as a *supertype*. The more restricted categories are referred to as *subtypes*. We follow [HAWRYSZKIEWICZ84] in extending our entity diagram as shown in Figure 5.1. The connecting line differs from that used in the preceding chapter by the absence of the diamond symbol. When we connect two entities via a line (with no other symbol on the line) we are signifying an *is a* or *is a kind of* relationship between the entities. A connecting line broken by a diamond symbol (as in the last chapter) and supplemented with 1's and m's designates a relationship in which the items related are on an equal standing. We illustrate this with some examples shortly. (Other authors use a variety of symbols for this. Triangles seem to be becoming very popular.)

Temporal variations of entities are resolved identifying *versions*. A *version* is a particular form or variety of something. Software vendors normally assign version numbers to new (presumably) improved editions of their products, as in Version 1, Version 2, and so on. It is also fairly common to issue "Releases" of versions, such as Version 2, Release 3, which might be referred to as 2.3. Normally, a new version reflects major revisions, while a release reflects minor changes and corrections for problems. Manufacturers of a variety of products find it necessary to track versions in order to provide proper service and replacement parts. Few data modeling systems provide for temporal versions of entities and relationships.[4] In our examples, we deal with this by incorporating some date or version number in the key or by adding a separate "history" entity such as Customer History.

The data view which is suitable for one purpose or context may not be suitable for another. It is necessary to resolve these conflicts by finding a broader, more encompassing view from which we can derive those we need to support. This need is often brought to light by spirited debate between proponents of conflicting views. We must carefully examine all proposed views and all differences of opinion searching for the underlying reasons for them and appropriate resolutions. *It is less a question of who is right and who is wrong than of why it is useful to look at things a certain way.*

We'll attempt to keep our modeling technique as simple as possible and deal with more subtle problems and distinctions via careful definitions.

5.3   EXAMPLES

Let's work some example problems.

The purpose of a database is to track expenditures.[5] Figure 5.2 illustrates a possible entity diagram. Each *expenditure* is identified by an expenditure number and described by a date incurred, an amount, and a text description.

It is necessary to differentiate between capital expenditures, maintenance expenditures, and expenditures related to particular customer orders.

Each *capital expenditure* has an associated project identifier, depreciation schedule, amount depreciated to date, and date for complete depreciation.

Maintenance expenditures are associated with specific departments, and also classified according to a maintenance type category.

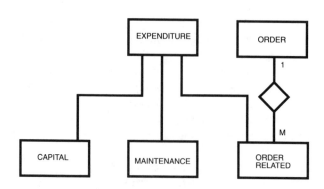

Figure 5.2   Expenditure types

Order-related expenditures are related to specific customer orders. This is a one to many relationship.

Thus, in one respect there is but one entity type, expenditure, and in another there are three, capital expenditures, maintenance expenditures, and order-related expenditures.

The following is a discussion of the way we might represent these entities and entity subtypes by relations. The entities are one thing and the relations are another. Since both are representations of the same business artifacts, it is not surprising that there are some similarities or that we can translate between the different representations.

Since there are some common attributes and some which are unique to a particular subtype, we might represent this situation via the following relations.

(Some SQL systems provide for the placement of comments between "/*" and "*/".)

EXPENDITURE   /* ONE OCCURRENCE FOR EACH EXP */

(EXP_#,   /* IDENTIFIES EXPENDITURE */

EXP_CLASS,   /* CAPITAL, MAINT, OR ORDER */

EXP_DATE,   /* DATE OF EXPENDITURE */

EXP_AMT,   /* AMOUNT */

EXP_DESCR)   /* DESCRIPTION */

This base relation contains data common to all expenditures. This table will contain a row for every expenditure.

CAPITAL_EXP   /* ONE FOR EACH CAPITAL EXP */

(EXP_#,   /* MATCHES AN EXPENDITURE OCCURRENCE */

DEP_SCHED,   /* DEPRECIATION SCHEDULE */

AMT_DEP,   /* AMOUNT DEPRECIATED */

COMP_DATE)   /* DATE DEPRECIATION COMPLETE */

This table will contain a row for each capital expenditure. The expenditure number will match one entry in the base table.

MAINT_EXP   /* ONE FOR EACH MAINT EXP */

(EXP_#,   /* MATCHES AN EXPENDITURE OCCURRENCE */

DEPT_ID,   /* ASSOCIATED DEPARTMENT */

EXP_TYPE)   /* TYPE CODE */

This table will contain one row for each maintenance expenditure. The expenditure number will match one entry in the base table. Department identifier might be a foreign key relating this expenditure to a particular department. We do not show department as an entity or relation in this example because we view it as outside the scope of this problem.

ORDER_EXP   /* ONE FOR EACH ORDER-RELATED EXP */

(EXP_#,   /* MATCHES AN EXPENDITURE OCCURRENCE */

ORDER_#)   /* IDENTIFIES THE ORDER */

This table will contain one row for each order-related expenditure. The expenditure number will match one entry in the base table. Order number is a foreign key relating each expenditure to a specific order. We include an order entity and an order relation to show how a one to many relationship is handled. We include order number in the expenditure table because a specific expenditure relates to a single order. An order on the other hand may relate to any number of expenditures.

ORDER_RECORD   /* ONE PER ORDER */

(ORDER_#,   /* IDENTIFIES THE ORDER *

ORDER_DATA)   /* REPRESENTS ATTRIBUTES OF ORDER */

This table will contain one row for each order. The order data attribute would most likely be replaced by a series of attributes relating to orders.

In this example we've made order an entity and department an attribute in an arbitrary manner. It's easy to do this when writing a book. In a real situation, we would ask these questions. Is there data which we must store about orders? Is there data which we must store about departments?

Now, we might list general info about all expenses with like this.

SELECT EXP_#, EXP_DATE, EXP_AMT, EXP_DESCR

FROM EXPENDITURE;

We might reference maintenance expenditures in this manner.

SELECT EXPENDITURE.EXP_#, EXP_DATE, EXP_AMT, DEPT_ID

FROM EXPENDITURE, MAINT_EXP

WHERE EXPENDITURE.EXP_# = MAINT_EXP.EXP_#;

We might list expenditures related to a particular order as follows.

SELECT EXPENDITURE.EXP_#, EXP_AMT, EXP_DESCR

FROM EXPENDITURE, ORDER_EXP

WHERE EXPENDITURE.EXP_# = ORDER_EXP.EXP_#

AND ORDER_# = '........';

Various combinations of selection, projection, union, and join can be used to retrieve any combination we need.

Let's look at another example. Figure 5.3 illustrates a simplified banking example.

- Mythical State Bank's *customers* are assigned unique customer identifiers. The bank stores name and address for each customer.

- In the case of a joint *account*, the bank treats each party to the account as a separate customer.

- A given customer may have several accounts. Thus, *customer to account* is a many to many relationship.

- Each account has an account identifying number. Date opened and branch responsible for the account are recorded for all accounts.

- For each *checking account*, the bank records a current balance, a fee schedule indicator, a count of checks processed, and a count of deposits processed.

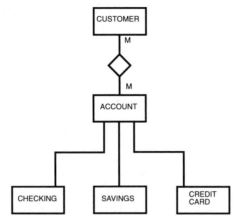

Figure 5.3   Mythical State Bank example

- For each *savings account* the bank records, a current balance, a daily average balance, and an interest formula identifier.
- For each *credit card account*, the bank records a current balance, a daily average balance, a credit limit, a count of charges process, and a number of cards issued.

  We might establish these relations.

CUSTOMER(<u>CUSTOMER_ID</u>, CUSTOMER_NAME,CUSTOMER_ADDRESS)

This table contains one row per customer occurrence.

CUSTOMER_ACCOUNT(<u>CUSTOMER_ID, ACCOUNT_#</u>)

This table contains one row for each customer and account combination. Customer to account is a many to many relationship. We create a separate table to represent the relationship. Customer identifier and account number are foreign keys. If there were data such as the nature of the customer's relationship to the account, we would store it here.

ACCOUNT(<u>ACCOUNT_#</u>, DATE_OPEN, BRANCH_RESP)

This table contains one row for each account. It contains data common to all accounts.[6]

CHECK_ACCOUNT(<u>ACCOUNT_#</u>, BALANCE, FEE_SCHED,
CHECK_COUNT, DEPOSIT_COUNT)

This table contains one row for each checking account. It contains data which relates only to checking accounts. The account number of each row will match a row in the base account table.

SAV_ACCOUNT(<u>ACCOUNT_#</u>, BALANCE, AVERAGE_BAL, INT_CODE)

This table contains one row for each savings account. It contains data which relates only to savings accounts. The account number of each row will match a row in the base account table.

CREDIT_CARD(ACCOUNT_#, BALANCE, AVERAGE_BAL,

CREDIT_LIMIT, CHARGE_COUNT, CARD_COUNT)

This table contains one row for each credit card account. It contains data which relates only to credit card accounts. The account number of each row will match a row in the base account table.

Let's do one more example. Henderson Hospital provides care for inpatients and outpatients.[7] Refer to Figure 5.4.

- All *patients* are assigned unique identifying numbers by the hospital. The same individual may be an *inpatient* on one occasion and an *outpatient* on another.

- Inpatients are *assigned beds*; outpatients are not. This is a one to one relationship.[8]

- Each inpatient is *admitted* to the hospital by a specific *physician*. This is many to many because the same patient may be admitted on different dates by the same physician or by different physicians. (We could treat admission as an entity identified by some unique admission number. Physician to admission would then be one to many, as would patient to admission. In practice we'd need to review this with the hospital administration. We'd ask if admissions are of interest in themselves, if unique identifiers are assigned, if there is data to store which is specific to admissions, and so on.)

- Patients *receive* a variety of *treatments* and services which may be *performed* by *physicians*, *nurses*, or *nonprofessional staff* members. Here, treatment means a specific service performed on a specific patient. Let's assume that the hospital assigns a unique billing identifier to each service. (This is also the sort of thing which must be researched carefully.) Patient to service is one to many. Staff member to service is

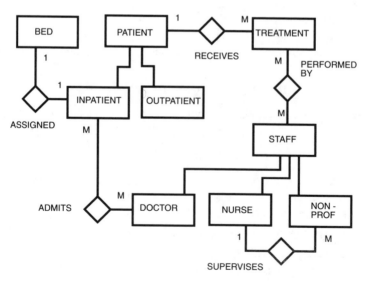

Figure 5.4 Henderson Hospital example

many to many. It may require several staff members to perform some services and over time each staff member surely provides many services.

- Staff members may be physicians, nurses, or nonprofessional staff. The information kept about each is different. Nurses *supervise* the activities of nonprofessionals. This is a one to many relationship.

We identify relations and keys here, but omit most other attributes in order to keep things as brief and simple as possible.

PATIENT(PATIENT_ID, NAME,…)

This table contains one row for each patient.

OUTPATIENT(PATIENT_ID,…)

This table contains one row for each outpatient. The patient identifier matches one found in the base table and may also match one found in the inpatient table.

INPATIENT(PATIENT_ID,…)

This table contains one row for each inpatient. The patient identifier matches one found in the base table and may also match one found in the outpatient table.

BED(BED_ID, PATIENT_ID,…)

This table contains one row for each bed. If the bed is occupied, the patient identifier is a foreign key identifying the related patient. Notice several things. Beds are permanent. Patients come and go. Patients may move from bed to bed. It does not make sense to combine the entities. Patient records may remain on file after the patients are discharged. Placing the patient identifier in the bed record seems to make more sense than the alternative.

STAFF(STAFF_ID,…)

This table contains one row for each staff member.

PHYSICIAN(STAFF_ID,…)

This table contains one row for each physician. The identifier matches one found in the base table.

NURSE(STAFF_ID,…)

This table contains one row for each nurse. The identifier matches one found in the base table.

NON_PROF(STAFF_ID, SUPV,…)

This table contains one row for each nonprofessional. The identifier matches one found in the base table. Supervisor identifier matches a staff identifier found in the nurse table. Since nurse to nonprofessional is one to many, we position the nurse identifier as a foreign key in the nonprofessional relation.

ADMISSION(PATIENT_ID, STAFF_ID, ADMIT_DATE,…)

This table represents the many to many relation, physician admits patient. Patient identifier is a foreign key identifying the associated inpatient. Staff identifier is a foreign key identifying the associated physician. Since the same physician may admit the same patient more than once, the key for admission must include some additional differentiating item, such as date.

TREATMENT(TREATMENT_ID, PATIENT_ID,...)

This table contains one row for each treatment, identified by the unique treatment identifier. The patient identifier appears as a foreign key in the treatment table because treatment to patient is one to many.

PROVIDES(STAFF_ID, TREATMENT_ID,...)

This table represents the many to many relationship staff member provides treatment.

5.4 LET'S REVIEW

Here is an expanded list of techniques for deriving relations from an entity model. (Some of the material in the preceding chapter is repeated in order to provide a single comprehensive list). [9, 10]

As a first approximation, *create one relation for each entity*. The entity identifier should be a candidate key for the relation.

Represent *one to one* relationships in one of these ways.

- If the existence of one implies the existence of the other and the two entities, once related, will remain related as long as either or both continue to exist, consider combining them into one relation. Most likely the identifiers of both will be candidate keys. See Figure 5.5. (The two solid lines designate the two candidate keys.)
- If it is possible for one entity type to exist without the other, or if the relationship between two particular entity occurrences is not permanent, represent each entity as a separate relation and insert the key of one as a foreign key in the other. If one of the two entities is optional in the relationship (or even more optional than the other), its identifier should be the foreign key inserted in the other relation. See Figure 5.6. (The

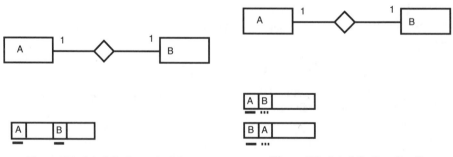

Figure 5.5   1-to-1 (both must exist)   Figure 5.6   1-to-1 (both optional)

two solid lines represent the two candidate keys. The dashed lines designate foreign keys.)

Represent *one to many* relationships by creating a relation for each entity, using the entity identifiers as candidate keys, and inserting the identifier of the entity which has one potential occurrence in the relationship as a foreign key in the relation representing the entity which can have multiple occurrences in the relationship. Thus, if one customer can send many orders while a given order can come from but one customer, customer number will appear as a foreign key in the orders relation. See Figure 5.7. (The two solid lines represent the two candidate keys. The dashed line designates the foreign key.)

Represent *many to many* relationships by creating a relation for each entity, using the entity identifiers as candidate keys, and also creating an additional relation to represent the relationship. The relation which represents the relationship will contain foreign keys designating each of the others. The key for this relation may be formed by concatenating the keys of the other two. It may be necessary to augment this with some other attribute, such as a date or sequence number. It often proves valuable to create a new attribute for use as the key. See Figure 5.8. (The two solid lines represent the two candidate keys. The dashed lines designate foreign keys.)

The key for a *weak entity* should usually be its own identifier concatenated with the identifier of the identity on which it depends. See Figure 5.9. (The two solid lines designate the two candidate keys.)

Given a *relationship with degree greater than two*, represent each entity as a relation with an appropriate key and represent the relationship as another relation. This should contain the identifiers of all related entities as foreign keys. This concatenation may be the key for the relation, or the key may be some other appropriate identifier. See Figure 5.10.

There is a choice of representations for the subset and superset situation. The determination depends on the degree to which the superset entity and each of the subset entities share attributes.

- *If all attributes are the same*, create one relation which has a "type of entity" attribute along with the others. See Figure 5.11a.

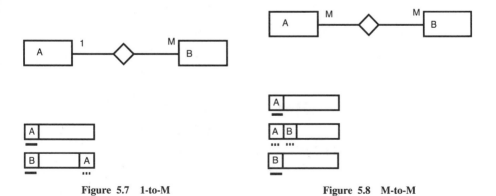

Figure 5.7   1-to-M   Figure 5.8   M-to-M

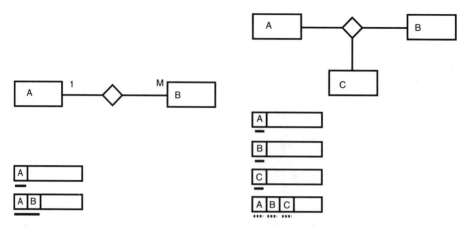

Figure 5.9 1-to-M with weak entity　　　　　**Figure 5.10 Ternary relationship**

- *If there are no attributes in common* (or even if there are relatively few), ignore the superset entity and create one relation for each of the subset entity types. See Figure 5.11b.
- *If there are shared and non shared attributes*, create a relation for the superset entity and for each subset entity. See Figure 5.11c. The combination of superset or shared data and subset or unique data can be retrieved via a join. All relations must have keys

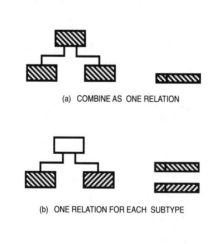

(a) COMBINE AS ONE RELATION

(b) ONE RELATION FOR EACH SUBTYPE

(c) RELATIONS FOR EACH

Figure 5.11 Subtypes and supertypes

drawn from the same domain or the key for the relation representing the subset entity must be the superset key plus some other attribute.

- *Versions* can be resolved by incorporating a version identifier in the key of the relation representing the entity, a date for example.

You will often find the relations derived in this manner to be fully normalized. It will sometimes be necessary to perform additional normalization steps.

5.5 RELATING TWO ENTITIES OF THE SAME TYPE—BILL OF MATERIALS

This is called the *bill of material* or *BOMP* problem because it often occurs in manufacturing and engineering databases. (BOMP is the acronym for Bill of Material Processor.)

A manufactured product is assembled from components. Some of these components may be subassemblies which are assembled from other components which may also be subassemblies. Eventually, there must be items with no components such as individual items or raw materials. (Strictly speaking, these might also be assemblies which are purchased and just require no further breakdown.) Figure 5.12a illustrates the general idea.

Thus a personal computer consists of a system unit, a display unit, and a keyboard. Each of these consists of a number of components. The system unit consists of a case, a mother board, disk drives, expansion cards, and so on. And these, in turn, have their components. And it is very possible that the same component (e.g., a particular connector) may be a component of more than one subassembly. A listing of all parts required for the manufacture of a particular item is frequently referred to as a *parts explosion* or *Bill of Materials*. A listing of all uses of a particular item is referred to as a *parts implosion* or *where used* list.

A similar situation arises in an academic environment where a particular course of study may have prerequisites which, in turn, have other courses as prerequisites. It can be seen in organizational structures (Mary supervises Fred who supervises Rex who supervises...). The general case is sometimes referred to as a *recursive* relationship.

An entity diagram might look like either of those shown in Figure 5.12b and 5.12c— a many to many relationship *turning back on* the entity part. This is a many to many since a given assembly may have many components and a given component may be a part of many assemblies. Some prefer something like Figure 5.12c which shows assembly and component as "roles" which may be assumed by part. Again, it is a many to many.

Since the data stored for assembly does not differ from the data stored for component, we need but one table for part in either case. As is usually the case, we also need a separate table for the many to many relationship.

PART(PART_#, PART_NAME,...)

This table contains one row for each part. Part number is the key. The remaining attributes are things like part name, quantity on hand, cost, and the like.

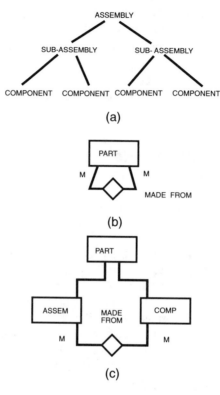

(a)

(b)

(c)

Figure 5.12 **Bill of material structure**

COMPONENT(<u>ASSEMBLY_#, COMPONENT_#</u>, QTY)

This table represents the many to many relationship. There is a row for every case of an assembly having a component. Assembly number and component number are both foreign keys, each matching the part number for one row in the part table.

Maintaining this structure and processing retrievals against it are both somewhat tricky.

SELECT COMPONENT_#, QTY

FROM COMPONENT

WHERE COMPONENT_# =...;

will retrieve all of the next level components of an item. The process must be repeated for each level.[11] Programming with cursors requires opening multiple cursors at the same time or making multiple selections for each level. The statement illustrated might return six items (B, C, D, E, F, and G) as components of item A. We must then repeat six times to find the components for each of these. We must then repeat more times to find the components of the components. There is an additional problem we must guard against—examine the data which follows.

Advanced Modeling Concepts   Chapter 5

ASSEMBLY_#	COMPONENT_#	QTY
123	456	1
123	567	2
123	678	5
456	777	3
456	778	2
567	887	1
567	888	3
678	222	1
678	223	2
678	224	4
222	123	5

123 is shown containing 678 which is shown containing 222 which is shown containing 123 which is shown containing 678 which… Clearly, there is something wrong here. Someone has entered some incorrect data. The difficulty is that, should this happen, our retrieval will be in an endless loop. The program which inserts this data must check the *where used* regression to make sure data like this is rejected.[12] Some designers find it worthwhile to incorporate level numbers in the part and/or assembly tables in order to track how deeply an item is nested.

5.6 GLOBAL MODELS, INTEGRATION, DISPARATE VIEWS

We've mentioned the possibility of a global data model that describes all data used by an organization. We noted that integration and elimination of redundancy are desirable. We've observed that different users have different views of data and that sometimes these differing views make it difficult to reach agreement on a data model. We now discuss the possibility for developing one underlying model which will support a variety of views.[13]

Our approach to resolving disparities between data models is to *treat the entities and relationships as if they were relations* derived via the methods discussed earlier in this chapter *and see if we can convert one to the other via relational algebra.*

Once again, keep in mind that the entity model and the set of relations are two different ways of representing or describing some situation. It can be useful to transform one to the other, and this technique seems to work. But relations are not entities.

Figures 5.13 through 5.17 illustrate some basic transformations.

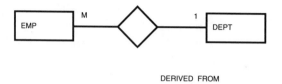

DERIVED FROM

Figure 5.13 **Many to one derived**

In Figure 5.13 we derive a many to one relationship from a many to many. Suppose this to be the situation wherein one use of the data leads to the conclusion that an employee can be related to but one department. This would no doubt reflect the employee's current assignment. An opposing many to many view might result from the desire to retain a history of all assignments ever given the employee.

Given

EMPLOYEE(EMP_ID,...)

ASSIGN(EMP_ID, DEPT_ID, START_DATE, END_DATE,...)

DEPT(DEPT_ID,...)

We might write

SELECT EMPLOYEE.EMP_ID,..., DEPT_ID

FROM EMPLOYEE, ASSIGN

WHERE EMPLOYEE.EMP_ID = ASSIGN.EMP_ID

AND END_DATE IS NULL;

That is, we ignore all but one occurrence of the many to many relationship.

In Figure 5.14 we illustrate that a many to many relationship can be derived from two one to many relationships to a common entity. Suppose a view calling for a many to many relation-

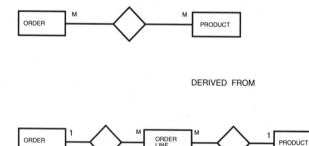

DERIVED FROM

Figure 5.14 **Many to many derived**

ship between orders and products to be in conflict with a view which relates specific order items or "lines" to orders and products.

Given

ORDER(ORDER_#,...)

ORDER_LINE(ORDER_#, LINE_#, PRODUCT_#, QTY,...)

PRODUCT(PRODUCT_#,...)

We might write

SELECT ORDER_#, PRODUCT_#

FROM ORDER_LINE;

thereby converting the entity to a relationship.

In Figure 5.15 we illustrate that we might view related items as a single entity.

Given

EMPLOYEE(EMPLOYEE_ID,..., DEPT_ID)

DEPT(DEPT_ID, DEPT_NAME,...)

We might write

SELECT EMPLOYEE_ID,..., EMPLOYEE.DEPT_ID, DEPT_NAME

FROM EMPLOYEE, DEPT

WHERE EMPLOYEE.DEPT_ID = DEPT.DEPT_ID;

Related entities are combined.

Given the many to many case as described earlier, we might write

SELECT EMPLOYEE.EMPLOYEE_#,..., DEPT.DEPT_#, DEPT_NAME

FROM EMPLOYEE, ASSIGN, DEPT

WHERE EMPLOYEE.EMPLOYEE_ID = ASSIGN.EMPLOYEE_ID

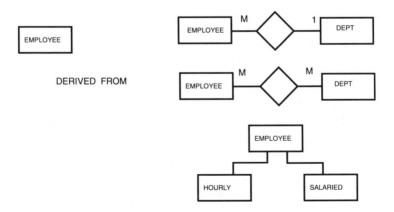

Figure 5.15 Single entity derived

AND ASSIGN.DEPT_ID = DEPT.DEPT_ID

AND END_DATE IS NULL;

Related entities are combined with the relationship.

Given

EMPLOYEE(EMPLOYEE_ID, NAME, EMPLOYEE_TYPE, …)

HOURLY(EMPLOYEE_ID, RATE,…)

SALARIED(EMPLOYEE_ID, SALARY,…)

We might write

SELECT EMPLOYEE.EMPLOYEE.ID, NAME, SALARY,…)

FROM EMPLOYEE, SALARIED

WHERE EMPLOYEE.EMPLOYEE.ID = SALARIED.EMPLOYEE_ID;

/* INNER JOIN */

Or we might write

SELECT EMPLOYEE.EMPLOYEE.ID, NAME, TYPE, RATE, SALARY,…

FROM EMPLOYEE, SALARIED

WHERE EMPLOYEE.EMPLOYEE.ID = SALARIED.EMPLOYEE_ID

UNION

SELECT EMPLOYEE.EMPLOYEE.ID, NAME, TYPE, RATE, SALARY,…

FROM EMPLOYEE, HOURLY

WHERE EMPLOYEE.EMPLOYEE.ID = HOURLY.EMPLOYEE_ID;[14]

Subtypes are combined.

In Figure 5.16 we note that given multiple relationships between two entities, we can ignore all but one or we can combine the relationships via a union.

Given

EMPLOYEE(EMPLOYEE_ID,…)

DEPT(DEPT_ID,…)

ASSIGNED(EMPLOYEE_ID, DEPT_ID,…)

MANAGES(EMPLOYEE_ID, DEPT_ID,…)

PROVIDE_SERVICE(EMPLOYEE_ID, DEPT_ID,…)

We can ignore two of the three relationships

Or we can write

SELECT EMPLOYEE_ID, DEPT_ID FROM ASSIGNED

UNION

SELECT EMPLOYEE_ID, DEPT_ID FROM MANAGES

UNION

SELECT EMPLOYEE_ID, DEPT_ID FROM PROVIDE_SERVICE;

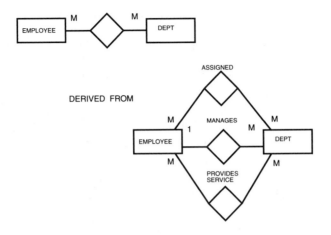

Figure 5.16   Relationships combined

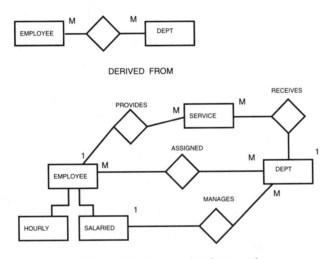

Figure 5.17   A comprehensive example

Figure 5.17 shows a combination of these transformations. Perhaps you'd like to work out the details as a review.

5.7   VIEW INTEGRATION

So far we've adhered to a *top down* approach which involves discovering entities and relationships from the nature of the situation. This approach is often recommended. And it is often possible to proceed in this manner. But it is not always so. There are several reasons for this.

The individual users will usually describe their particular views when asked to help develop a data model.

The situation may be so complex that entities and relationships are not readily apparent. The larger the project, the more likely it is that this is the case.

We really need to make sure that important details are not overlooked.

The alternative is to recognize and document individual views. These will often be embodied in reports and screens. This is often called a *bottom up* approach. Here is a procedure.

- Document each user view. List and define all data elements.
- Look for functional dependencies, multivalued facts, and multivalued dependencies in each view.
- Also, develop an Entity Relationship Model for each view.
- Normalize the content of each view.
- Examine all the views.
- Look for relations or entities *with the same key.* It should usually be possible to combine them into one relation or one entity.
- Look for relations, or entities, or relationships with attributes which are *keys or parts of keys for other relations or entities.* These will usually be *foreign keys* which are indicative of relationships.
- It is necessary to be very careful to *avoid duplication* of entities, relationships, attributes, or relations.
- It is necessary to be careful to *avoid the introduction of multivalued dependencies.*
- It is also necessary to *be careful that lossy joins are not introduced.*

In general, everything we've discussed in the preceding section will apply. Careful attention to definitions and names will greatly facilitate this procedure.

It is easy to describe this. But in practice a lot of work is involved. If there are many different reports and many different users, this may be the only way to proceed. [MARTIN83] refers to this procedure as *canonical synthesis* and provides an extensive example. [PRATT91] also contains an extended example.

Endnotes

1. The ideas expressed here are the author's. The development of these notions was heavily influenced by Hayakawa [HAYAKAWA78] and Kent [KENT78]. But if you disagree with what is presented here, don't blame these sources. Read them for yourself. Make up your own mind. Then blame the author of this work for any shortcomings.

2. Here is an extended example of the "ladder or abstraction" reproduced from [HAYAKAWA78]. "The cow known to science ultimately consists of atoms, electrons, etc... "The cow which we perceive is not the word, but the object of experience... "The word 'Bessie' (a particular cow) is the name we give to the object of perception... "The word 'cow'

stands for the characteristics we have abstracted as common to (all cows)... "When Bessie is referred to as 'livestock,' only those characteristics she has in common with pigs, chickens, goats, etc. are referred to. "When Bessie is included among 'farm assets,' reference is made only to what she has in common with all other salable items on the farm. "When Bessie is referred to as an 'asset,' still more of her characteristics are left out. "The word 'wealth' is at an extremely high level of abstraction, omitting *almost* all reference to the characteristics of Bessie."

3. Peckham and Maryanski [PECKHAM88] provide us with the following definitions.
"*Generalization* is the means by which differences among similar objects are ignored to form a higher order type in which the similarities can be emphasized."
"*Aggregation* is the means by which relationships between low-level types can be considered a higher level type."
"*Classification* is a form of abstraction in which a collection of objects is considered a higher level object class."
"*Association* is a form of abstraction in which a relationship between member objects is considered a higher level set object."

4. Ross [ROSS87] is the exception. He describes numerous entity model extensions, including a means for modeling temporal versions.

5. This is based on an example found in [HAWRYSZKIEWICZ84]. As with most examples, we can't claim it exactly matches anyone's real business requirement. But it does illustrate some things for us.

6. You might note that balance could have been included in this table. At this point the choice to do otherwise appears arbitrary. We are looking ahead. We consider that there will be many occasions to process all checking accounts with balances, all savings accounts with balances, or all credit card accounts with balances. Storing the balance in the base table would require an excessive number of joins. It is also the case that a credit card balance is in some ways a very different thing from a checking account balance. We might argue that because of this there is no common attribute called balance.

7. This is based on an example in [MCFADDEN88]. Again, we are simplifying. Any resemblance to a real hospital, living or dead, is pure dumb luck!

8. Here is an interesting aside. When the hospital staff refers to a bed, they are really referring to a particular place in a particular room. The actual beds are sometimes moved from room to room. If there would be some need to track individual beds for inventory or maintenance, there would be a separate bed identifier and we might care to record the relationship between "bed" in the sense of room number and "bed" in the sense of actual bed.

9. We are very much indebted to Teorey, et al. [TEOREY86] for the basis for this presentation. Once again, don't blame them for everything you read here. But this presentation has been heavily influenced by their work.

10. We say "techniques" rather than "rules" because these are offered as heuristics or "rules of thumb" which must be exercised with some judgment. We make no attempt to "prove" the validity of these rules. We like them because they seem to work. You will do best to understand the thought behind them and decide for yourself.

11. The Oracle system provides a CONNECT operator which simplifies this retrieval. Most SQL systems do not.

12. More detailed programming examples are given in [FERG88] and [INMON89].

13. Once again, we present some "rules of thumb" and demonstrate that they are reasonable, but do not offer any sort of "proof."

14. This could also be accomplished by an outer join.

QUESTIONS AND EXERCISES

1. Why does one develop an entity relationship model? (There may be more than one reason.)

2. List and explain eight or more problems often encountered in data modeling.

3. What are synonyms, homonyms, and aliases?

4. Explain generalization, classification, and association.

5. Explain the difference between the top down and bottom up approaches.

6. Refer to exercise 15 for Chapter 4. Suppose there are Senior Technicians, Certified Technicians, and Junior Technicians. Suppose that some jobs can be performed only by more senior technicians. Thus, when assigning work to technicians, it will be necessary to consult job information to determine the difficulty of the job and then select a technician with an appropriate skill level. Modify your answer accordingly.

7. Refer to exercise 16 for Chapter 4. Suppose there are Business and Private Customers. Work for Business Customers is normally done at night when the business is closed, while work for Private Customers is done during the day. Teams of workers visit the larger Business Customers while individual workers visit Private Customers. Business Customers are also provided with different payment terms. Modify your answer accordingly.

8. The task is to design a database for a multi-level marketing organization. Develop an entity relationship model. Identify dependencies. Develop a set of normalized relations. Discuss the processing which must be done.

   Individuals who become representatives of *Superior Skin Smoothing and Sleaking Stuff, Inc.* have the option of selling Stuff and earning commissions on their own sales. They can also recruit new representatives and earn commissions on sales made by these recruited representatives. One can also earn commissions on the sales made by the representatives recruited by the representatives one has recruited. There is no limit to the length of this commission chain. This process can continue to any depth. The percentage of commission is determined by the level to which the individual who makes the sale is removed from the person earning the commission.

   It is thus necessary to keep track of Actual Sales, Commissions on Actual Sales, Sales by Subordinates, and Commissions on Sales by Subordinates for each representative. It is also necessary to keep track of who has recruited who and when this occurred. And, it is necessary to develop an itemized list of all commissions for each Sale.

Chapter 6

Definitions and Constraints

6.1   CHAPTER SUMMARY

The quality of definitions is a reflection of how well the analyst understands the problem. Poor definitions result in poor communication. This communication might be between analyst and user or between analyst and implementor.[1] Putting ideas down formally forces us to make sure we understand. The documentation often comes in very handy later.

Naming entities, relationships, and data elements seems simple enough. But it isn't. Poorly chosen names can cause a lot of trouble. Selection of appropriate identifiers or keys seems simple too. But it isn't. We need to devote some time to it.

The use of various encoding schemes is quite common, so we need to pay some attention to this.

We must also further discuss security.

Our model must incorporate any constraints that the business rules place on the data. We need to review methods for assuring that constraints are met and implications of doing this.

Most of the issues discussed in this chapter cross several phases of the project life cycle. In some cases the information is not used until the final phases, but it is wise to collect it during the earlier stages.

6.2   DEFINITIONS

We need complete definitions of all entities, relationships, and data elements. If we can't write good definitions, we don't really understand the data or the model. The model isn't complete without definitions which assure that the *next guy* will understand it. A diagram alone is not enough.

Complete definitions are the only vehicle for resolving the differences of opinion which always arise in data modeling.

Why, in a more general sense, are definitions developed?[2]

- Definitions provide the means for communicating new knowledge and terminology.
- Definitions eliminate ambiguity and misunderstanding.
- Definitions clarify meaning.
- Definitions explain theoretical and abstract concepts.
- Definitions sometimes influence attitudes. Explaining what we really mean may bring agreement where there was discord.

What are the basic types of definitions?

- If we have the luxury of coining new terminology, we have the privilege and responsibility of defining what we mean by the new terms. These are called *stipulative definitions*.
- *Lexical definitions* report the meanings which terms already have.
- *Precising definitions* clarify the meaning of vague terms.
- *Theoretical definitions* are attempts to discover a basis for a definition by analyzing the characteristics and behavior of the thing defined.
- *Persuasive definitions* are developed to influence others.
- In everyday speech, words can have different sorts of meanings. Commonly, we can differentiate between *extensional* and *intensional* meanings. The former has to do with the thing or concept represented by a term. The latter has to do with the ideas conjured up by the term. Intensional definitions tend to influence how we feel about a thing, whether we view it in a positive manner or a negative one.

In defining entities, relationships, and attributes for data models, we are primarily concerned to be sure that the definition does describe the thing or concept as we understand it. Generally, we want these definitions to be extensional, lexical, and precising. That is, we want to discover what the members of this organization really mean by a word like *client* and then write a definition which will assure that anyone who reads it will attach the same meaning to the word or at least understand what we mean when we use it.

What are the techniques for defining? We can *define by pointing to examples*. This is sometimes referred to as a form of *denotive definition*. "This is a sample of our famous *pimento stuffer*." "Fred, over there, is about to *rewind a fanster*. Let's watch him." This is a limited technique, since we must have the desired object at hand. It may require a number of examples to convey a precise meaning. It is hard to incorporate this sort of thing in a document or specification.

In a similar manner, we can define by *demonstrating*. "I will now show you what you must do if you are instructed to 'put on the oxygen mask.'" This type of definition is also limited by our ability to provide examples and is difficult to incorporate in documents and specifications.

Many inexpensive dictionaries furnish *connotative definitions* which *consist of one or more synonyms* for the word defined. These can completely fail to convey meaning if chasing the terms takes us in a circle. If we are told that *bashful* means *shy* and *shy* means *bashful* we may not be helped. In general, we try to avoid circular definitions.

Operational definitions explain a term by listing a series of steps. In the "Smythe-Brownne systems development methodology, one performs the following steps..." These can be useful for describing terms that do, in fact, denote operations.

The best approach is to define via *genus and specific difference.* This means we *establish something as a member of a more encompassing class and then specify how it differs from all other members of that class.* "An hourly employee is paid a fixed number of dollars for each hour worked, is docked for arriving late, and participates in benefit plan 'C.'" We've established that the method of calculating wages and the benefit plan differentiate hourly employees from all other employees.

There are some commonly accepted rules.

- Be sure to *include essential or truly significant qualities* of the thing defined. A Stradivarius violin is characterized by having been fabricated by a particular individual. The quality and features of an instrument may help us recognize that a particular instrument is a Stradivarius, but they are not what make it one.
- *Avoid circular definitions* which make use of the term being defined. If we state that an integrated database is one which is integrated, we haven't said a lot.
- *Strike a balance* between a very broad definition and a very narrow one. The very broad definition of database given at the outset of this book would not be suitable in an environment where the more restrictive definition is highly valued. Defining a customer as one who purchases something would be too restrictive if prospects were also referred to as customers.
- *Avoid ambiguous, obscure, or figurative language.* Don't say "the large size is bigger than the small"; say "the large size is 12 ounces." Some of the terms mentioned in this section, including genus and specific difference, probably convey little meaning to the average person. Poetic language can be very pleasant, but it is best omitted from data element definitions.
- *Make positive statements* rather than negative ones. Whenever possible, tell what it is instead of what it is not. In the example above we did not state that "hourly employees are not paid at a fixed weekly rate."

Now, what can we say that's more specific to data modeling?[3]

6.3   ENTITY DEFINITIONS

We will often end up with a single relation or database table which represents an entity. The definition of the entity will be the basis for defining this table. It will also be the basis for deciding whether or not we can, in a given situation, represent a single entity type by a single relation. We will also use the definition of the entity as the basis for physical design and performance tuning decisions. *We are still defining the characteristics of the entity. We are not talking about a relation.*

First of all, an entity definition must describe the thing or concept clearly enough to make it possible to determine whether or not a specific thing or occurrence is an instance of the entity in question. The definition should also show why the entity is of interest to us in the context of this model.

Incorporate any *existence rules*. Can we retain information about an order without retaining information about the customer, for instance? Do we, like some car rental companies, refuse to do business with a customer who has no credit card? Include *deletion rules*. When do we cease to need information about a specific entity occurrence?

For example, it may be necessary to retain information about an employee who has resigned. This might be necessary because of continuing participation in a retirement plan. It might be required by some Occupational Safety and Health Administration or Equal Opportunity Employment Administration rule. It is very likely we must keep the employee's earnings record until we produce earnings reports for employees and the Internal Revenue Service at the end of the year.

Identify various states or statuses that an entity occurrence may progress through and the record keeping requirements associated with each status. In mortgage banking, for example, an individual progresses from applicant to approved applicant to mortgage holder. There are specific data requirements at each stage. Not all applicants become mortgage holders.

We will frequently move data about inactive entity occurrences to an archive or historical file.

- Are there different *versions* of the entity? Do some attribute values change over time? How frequently do they change? Information about a bank account is really specific to a given date and it may be necessary to refer to a history which encompasses a series of dates.
- Is there a requirement for access to historical data about specific attribute values? Is there a need to record dates and times of specific events in the entity's life? How long is it necessary to retain historical information about the entity? Why?
- How many entity occurrences are there in each status at any given time?
- What are normal rates for adding and deleting? Are there sudden changes in number? It is common for banks with branches near colleges and universities to open a very large number of new customer accounts during the first week of the fall semester.
- It is common to purge inactive records at the end of the year.
- Is this a *weak entity* which is included in the model solely because of its relationship to some other entity of primary interest? Spouses and dependents of employees are good examples of this.
- Is this a *subset or superset* of some other entity type? Is it an *is a* or *is a kind of a* situation? In the case of a subset, how does this entity differ from the superset, what qualities and attributes does it inherit from the higher type, and how does it differ from the other subset types?
- Are different names used to identify the same entity type? Are particular names favored by particular users? Are particular names favored in particular circumstances?
- Are there any important naming rules for entity occurrences?

- Who is it within the organization who provides information about entity occurrences, changes this information, makes status determinations, and uses the information? There are often several interested parties. Where is each party located? How frequently does each party add, delete, modify, or reference data about this entity type? Is it possible to identify specific occurrences which are created or referenced by specific parties at specific locations?
- Is there some party who might be thought of as the *owner of data about the entity type*? This would imply the authority to decide who may or may not update or access data about the entity type. It would also imply responsibility for auditing and correcting data about the entity type. In a larger organization there may be parties who own specific subsets of entity occurrences; customers for the western region, for example. There may also be parties who own subsets of the data about the entity type (views). As a classic example of this, there may be a payroll department which controls employee salary data and a training department which controls data about an employee's history of training.
- How does each party identify the entity occurrence(s) of interest? How can we tell one entity occurrence from another? That is, *what are the candidate keys*?
- *What search arguments are commonly used*? In a banking situation, for example, it may be necessary to find individual customer data based on account number, name, part of name, or name and address. It may also be necessary to find all customers who have a certain type of account or combination of account types, all customers who do not have a certain type of account, all customers who meet certain balance criteria, all customers who live in a certain geographic area, and so on.
- Is it necessary to differentiate this entity type from others with similar names or characteristics? How is this done?

6.4 RELATIONSHIP DEFINITIONS

We will usually end up with either a relation or a foreign key for each relationship. The definition of the relationship must provide the basis for intelligent decisions.
- Which entity types are related?
- What is the *degree* of the relationship? Is it between two entity types (binary), three entity types (ternary), or more?
- What is the connectivity? Is the relationship one to one, one to many, many to one, or many to many? In the case of ternary and higher degree relations, identify how many of each entity type can be related to the other types.
- What does the relationship signify? Why does it interest us in the context of this model? "Customers send orders. Acceptance of the order obligates FEAMCO to ship specific goods to the customer in accordance with the terms of the order."
- Does the relationship have a commonly accepted name? Does it have more than one name? It is common to have one name for each direction from which the relationship can be viewed. CUSTOMER_SENDS_ORDER might be the opposing view of ORDER_RECEIVED_FROM_CUSTOMER.

- Are particular names favored by particular users? Are particular names favored in particular situations?
- Are there special rules? "Orders valued at more than $50,000.00 are not accepted from customers with poorer than AA credit rating."
- Is the relationship *mandatory* or *optional*? It may be mandatory for one entity and optional for the other. "An inpatient must be assigned to a bed. A bed may be unoccupied."
- Is the relationship part of a mutually exclusive set? Perhaps an automobile dealer would relate a particular vehicle to either a sales contract or a lease but never to both.
- Are there different versions of the relationship? Do the participating entity occurrences or some of the attribute values vary over time? How frequently do they change?
- How might we differentiate one occurrence from another?
- How many entity occurrences of each type are there in a relationship occurrence at any given time? It is best to examine *average, maximum, and minimum* numbers. One or two significant deviations from the norm may have a dramatic impact.
- What are normal rates for adding and deleting? Are there sudden changes in number?
- Who is it within the organization who provides information about relationships between specific entity occurrences, changes this information, makes status determinations, and uses the information? There are often several interested parties. Where is each party located? How frequently does each party add, delete, modify, or reference data about this relationship type? Is it possible to identify specific occurrences which are created or referenced by specific parties at specific locations?
- Is there some party who might be thought of as *owner of data about the relationship type*? This would imply the authority to decide who may or may not update or access data about the relationship type. It would also imply responsibility for auditing and correcting data about the relationship type. In a larger organization there may be parties who own specific subsets of relationship occurrences. There may also be parties who own subsets of the data about the relationship type (views).
- How does each party identify the entity or relationship occurrence(s) of interest? One individual may be interested only in reviewing or altering order placements based on customer identification, while another might use date or status as the criterion.

6.5   DATA ELEMENT DEFINITIONS—DOMAINS

Some database management systems, programming systems, and data dictionary systems provide for domains. Many do not. Some of the software which provides for domains also provides for recording the description of a domain in such a way that the description is used in software generation. The software might automatically reject invalid input data. It might automatically use standard output formats and column headings. If this is the case, you must determine how this information is accepted and stored by the specific product you intend to use. If this is not the case, you should still collect and retain the information in a text form.

Define each domain as early in the project as possible.

- What is it? What differentiates this domain from all other concepts? Why does it interest us in the context of this model?
- What type of data is this? Is it numeric, alphabetic, or alphanumeric? In the case of numeric, what is the unit of measure? How many characters or digits long is it? In the case of a numeric, how many decimal places are there? Is it an integer?
- Is it a special data type such as date, time, or money?
- What is the acceptable range of values? Is it possible to list all legitimate values? If so, is the list fairly static like the names of the days of the week? Is it likely to change over time as in the case of departments in a company which reorganizes frequently? In the case of a numeric, what are the largest and smallest possible values? Are there any values which are not allowed? Is there some calculation which may be used to validate the value?
- Are there any other special rules? (For example, the third character must be a letter.)
- Do specific character or digit positions have special meaning? (For example, the fourth and fifth digits identify the county.)
- Is this a group item like date, or, a possible component of a group like day of the month?
- Is the item calculated or derived from some other item or items? If so, how? What is the formula? Is there the possibility of a table of matching values as in the case of department numbers and names? We are really asking if there is a known functional dependency, such as

    department number $\rightarrow$ department name
  aren't we?
- Don't confuse the issue of whether or not to store a calculated value with the issue of normalization, by the way.[4]
- Is there a standard format for output? In the case of a monetary value, we might always prefix with a dollar sign, suppress leading zeros, and insert commas. We might always insert blanks at certain places in an identifier as in *123 45 6789*.
- Is there a standard column heading for use in reporting?
- Is there a standard label for use in constructing video displays?

If domains are well defined and the same domain definitions are applied everywhere, exchange of data will be greatly facilitated. If this is not the case, information exchange will, at best, require extensive data conversion and may not be possible.

6.6 DATA ELEMENT DEFINITIONS—ATTRIBUTES OF ENTITIES AND RELATIONSHIPS

Some software products provide for the derivation of attributes from domains. Some do not. Likewise, some products utilize parts of attribute definitions such as validation criteria and standard format in generating programs or output. Some do not.

There are several possibilities.

- If the software does not provide for domains, keep an independent record of domains.
- If the software does provide for domains, enter the information in the format the software requires. If the software does not provide for everything, keep an independent record of the additional data.
- If the software provides for use of attribute definitions derived from domain definitions, you are all set. As of this writing, this is the exception rather than the rule. Most software which does provide for the derivation of attribute definitions from domain definitions provides this for attributes of tables, reports, and screens, not for attributes of entities and relationships.
- If the software does not provide for domains but does provide for the use of attribute definitions, enter the information with the attributes in the appropriate format.

As noted above, the software might provide for use of definitions of attributes of tables, reports, and screens, but not for attributes of entities and relationships. Again, record the domain and attribute information, then enter it in the appropriate format when defining tables, reports, and screens. Otherwise, just note which domain the attribute derives from and record any differences.

- If an attribute is defined by reference to a domain, it may not be necessary to provide any additional information. You can just refer to the domain definition. Otherwise, it is necessary to record all of the information discussed above.
- If the item is not calculated, what is its source? How frequently is it updated?
- Could it be null? Remember, null means there is no known value. It does not mean zero or blank. The real question here is "Are we willing to accept incomplete information into the database?" The converse is that the attribute must have a value. This means that incomplete information is not acceptable.
- A related question is whether or not the attribute participates in an either or relationship with some other. For example, "An employee must have either an hourly rate or an annual salary." In a case like this, there should be some attribute which indicates employee's salary type. It is not a good idea to use the presence or absence of one of these values as an indicator of employee type. It is never a good idea to force one attribute to provide more than one kind of information.
- Is there some *default* value to be used if no other is provided?
- Frequently, there will be some special format, column heading, validation rule, or significance that goes with the use of a value drawn from some domain as an attribute of some entity or relation. In this case, record only the differences as a part of the attribute definition.

6.7 NOW, WHAT'S IN A NAME?

Naming and the selection of naming standards is often very controversial and divisive.[5]
Let's take time out to reflect on what it is that we are naming, and why we are naming it.

We are developing a data model in order to determine what data must be stored in a database and how it might best be organized. Our primary task is to understand the data and how it is used.

It is common practice to assign a unique name to each entity type, relationship type, domain, and attribute. Attributes are best identified by a combination of domain and entity or relationship names. We'll discuss this in more detail shortly.

We use these names to communicate with users and to document the business significance of each entity type, relationship type, domain, and attribute.

Soon, we will define relations, describe them to a database management system, and specify rules for processing in some sort of programming system. This may be one of the traditional procedural languages such as COBOL or one of the newer nonprocedural systems. *Many database management systems and programming systems impose artificial constraints on the names which may be used to identify data items.*There is usually a length restriction. We may be precluded from including special characters and even imbedded blanks in a name. *But we are not yet at that point in the design cycle.* We ordinarily form these names in the next phase.

Many data processing shops make use of automated data dictionary systems. Many of these systems were originally designed to contain descriptions of physical databases and impose the same sort of naming restrictions as database management and programming systems. This is unfortunate. It is usually possible to make use of a description field or the first line of the definition or some form of note to record a meaningful name in spite of the software.

We prefer to use english language names appropriate for human communication to identify the components of a data model. We'll get embroiled in names like *CUST_ACCT_BAL* soon enough. At this point, we prefer *balance of customer's account* or *customer account balance*.

On the other hand, it is beneficial if we follow some rules in naming. The situation will determine how far we must go in enforcing rules. If you are, as an individual, developing a small stand alone system for your own personal use, it may well be possible for you to be very casual. If you are a professional developer, the system you develop will be used *and maintained* by other people. You can't be as casual as in the case above. It may still be the case that you are developing a small stand alone system and can still be relatively informal. This may depend on whether or not your organization enforces standards. If you are part of a team working on a larger project, you can no longer think only of yourself. Your definitions and the names you choose must be merged with and coordinated with the work of others. Some form of standardization and consistency is now very desirable. There may be organizational standards which you are expected to follow. It may be necessary for you to take the initiative and institute some project standards. In this case, it is likely you will have to negotiate with the other team members.

While we all like standards, we greatly prefer those which we personally devise. People really get excited and combative about naming standards! Unless you are supremely confident of your ability to be a dictator, you'd best solicit the views of other team members and negotiate a mutually agreeable approach.

Today, many organizations have Data Administration or Information Resource Management groups, comprehensive data and business models, strategic systems development plans, and the like. In this case there is a need to standardize and coordinate names across systems and projects. You should then become familiar with your standards and do your best to cooperate.

Finally, you may be utilizing some software product to document the data model. The use of Computer Aided Software Engineering (CASE) is becoming very common.[6] The software you use may restrict your choice of naming conventions. It may be possible to customize it to suit your approach. This has to be explored on a case-by-case basis.

Now, we'll review the desirable characteristics for names and make some recommendations. It is most important to create a *conventional name*[7] which is meaningful and looks sensible to the user community. In fact, the name which is commonly used is the best name.

If multiple individuals or projects are involved, it is desirable to always use the same name for the same thing. Otherwise, there are likely to be conflicting inconsistent definitions for the same thing. This can be particularly important in determining whether the thing under consideration is being newly defined or is a new reference to a thing which has already been defined for some other purpose.

Similarly, a consistent technique for forming names is desirable. This facilitates recognition of new references to things which have already been documented. It also facilitates recognition of subsets and supersets.

It is necessary to recognize that there may be multiple names for the same thing and provide for this by means of aliases (in the sense of "also known as").

It is also possible for two different things to be known by the same name. The best resolution is to append some sort of qualifier to one or both in order to differentiate them. It may not be practical to alter a name which has already been recorded. So, it may only be possible to qualify the new name.

It may be necessary to comply with standards and procedures which are already in place. This may temper the application of the recommendations which follow. Or, you may be in the fortunate position of developing new standards. In any event, here are some specific recommendations.

- Develop a list of commonly used words, with definitions. Consult this list in forming new names. It will be necessary to add new terms from time to time. It is not usually practical to alter names which have already been recorded.

- Also develop a list of all names which are in use. Always consult this to see if there already is a name for the item now being defined. It is practical to add to a definition which has already been recorded.

- Entity names can usually be brief; often one or two words will suffice. They will usually be nouns.

- When possible, create subtype names by qualifying the supertype name. Natural English calls for using the qualifier as a prefix. Given the supertype *Customer*, we might define *Cash Customer* and *Credit Customer* as subtypes. Effective use of this technique requires that we be able to search all name fields for any use of a key word. The search should not be case sensitive. That is, *Customer* and *customer* should be equivalent for the purpose of the search. This wouldn't really be that hard to do, but many vendors of dictionaries and CASE tools have not done it yet.

- The same principle applies to the use of qualifiers for differentiating between homonyms.

- Relationship names can usually be formed by placing a descriptor between the two entity names. The descriptor will usually be a verb, as in *customer places order*. It is often useful to define a synonym for the reverse relationship, as in *order is placed by customer*. Do this if it clarifies meaning.

- Domain names can often be brief. They will usually be nouns. Domains which are subsets of other domains are named via qualified forms of the base name. It probably isn't useful to go beyond two or three levels except for special cases.

- Whenever possible, attribute names should be formed by qualifying the domain name with the entity or relationship name, as in *account current balance* or *order requested ship date*.

Let's discuss the names used by the DBMS and the programs here. This will keep the entire discussion of naming in one place.

These names must often be formed according to artificial rules built into the software. It is convenient if the name conveys the nature or meaning of a data element. *It is not necessary, but it is convenient.*

It's also convenient if all programs and database definitions use the same name for the same element. Again, it is not necessary, but it can eliminate a lot of confusion and make life easier for everyone concerned.

With these thoughts in mind, we recommend the following.

- Form mnemonic names by abbreviating English language names.

- Abbreviate only when necessary.

- Use a standard set of abbreviations to assure consistency and simplify name formation.

- If it becomes necessary to differentiate between two occurrences of the same element in one program or system, use short and meaningful descriptive prefixes or suffixes. These too should be standardized.

- A good cross reference between the English name and all the program- oriented names will resolve any questions about what is what and will also facilitate change and impact analysis.

- Be consistent in the use of special symbols such as "#" and "$".

6.8   KEYS AND IDENTIFIERS

It must be possible to differentiate one entity occurrence from another. In the relational model, all information is conveyed solely by data values. We must find an attribute or group of attributes which will uniquely identify each entity occurrence.

Sometimes this is easy. Sometimes it is very difficult. There are many things which do not have unique identifiers. We often tell them apart by pointing or describing. Sometimes we are satisfied if we can identify a thing uniquely within a given context even though we can't differentiate it from all other entity occurrences in the world. "Of course I'm talking about the Henry Stein in this class and no other!"

Many of the identifiers we use for record keeping must be artificially contrived for that specific purpose.

Let's review some characteristics of *good* identifiers.[8] *A good identifier assumes a unique value for each and every entity occurrence.*

It must be possible to assign unique values to every entity occurrence. A four-digit number (which can have values from 0000 to 9999) could not be used as employee identifier by a company with 15,000 employees. It is really necessary to think about possible future growth when selecting an identifier. It can be a difficult proposition to alter the size of an identifier which has been in use for some time. It then is necessary to change the database or file definition, the database or file itself, all the programs, any input files, input screens, input forms, output files, reports, and habits.[9, 10]

It must be possible to assure that a unique value is actually assigned to each entity occurrence. This usually requires some central control over the assignment of identifiers for new entity occurrences.

Perhaps the computer system can assign a new identifier for each new occurrence. It is usually possible for the computer system to at least reject any duplicate identifiers. In fact, we can often assign this task to the database management system.

Perhaps users can be provided with some prenumbered form or document for use in recording new occurrences. Banks, for example, commonly issue new account starter packets containing checks and data entry forms.

The establishment of new identifiers might be the duty of a specific individual or department. This can become political. There might be a power struggle for control of the numbers. Or, it might be that no one wants the responsibility and the bother.

Specific ranges of values might be assigned for use by specific individuals or groups. This can be problematic if one group "uses up" identifiers faster than another. It would also be a mistake to use such an identifier to determine which group is responsible for the entity.

Names are notoriously poor identifiers. A quick review of any metropolitan phone directory will reveal that few, if any, names are unique. Banks, insurance companies, and other organizations which deal with the public have devoted a lot of effort to the search for a customer identifier which provides unique values and is also easy to use.[11]

A good identifier has a definite value for every occurrence. This is not only a requirement of the relational model. It is also a practical necessity. It won't do to have null identifier values for some entity occurrences. There would be no way to identify or retrieve the tuples containing data about those entities.

Whitener [WHITENER89] notes the case of the universal product code which is commonly used to identify products sold in grocery stores. There are products and goods which have no UPC's. Suppose a particular store generates "dummy codes" for these products. Suppose some of these are subsequently assigned to new products.

The use of social security number for student identifier provides another example. Students who are not U.S. citizens may not have social security numbers. Again, it becomes necessary to assign dummy numbers. And these must be controlled to avoid duplicates.

A good identifier provides a known value for each new entity occurrence at the time of data entry. It is just as bad if the entity occurrence does have a unique identifier value but that value is, for some reason, unknown. This can happen if the individual or department which assigns identifier values has a large backlog of work or cannot be reached. In other words, the system for assigning and discovering identifier values must be analyzed.

A good identifier provides a single consistent value for each entity occurrence. Historical analysis is possible only if it is possible to track and compare entity occurrences over time. It is often important to track an entity occurrence across organizational boundaries. If two or more individuals or departments insist on unique schemes of identification, this either can't be done or can only be done if a translation table is maintained (and kept current).

A good identifier has an unchanging value. The corollary to this is that *a good identifier has no changeable imbedded information content.* Some authorities state that an identifier should never contain meaningful data, period. That is a little strong. While this really is not good practice, there may be times when it won't cause harm, and there are likely to be times when users insist on it. But it is important to be aware of the pitfalls.

It is fairly common to incorporate data in an identifier. This is done for a variety of reasons. Meaningful identifiers are considered an aid to memory by some. Identifiers of manufactured items often incorporate descriptive data. AC1047 might represent a ten horsepower alternating current motor. Many banks incorporate a branch identifier in customer account numbers.

There may be a technical reason. Or, there may once have been a technical reason. Imbedding branch identifier in the checking account number made it easier to sort checks by branch. (Some of the older types of check sorting equipment are unable to access any data which is not actually contained on the check.) Canceled checks were returned to the branch, then mailed from the branch to the customer. Today, many banks either do not return the checks or mail them from a central location.

A clever identification scheme can facilitate summarizing and reporting. This is very common in financial accounting. The first portion of the account number identifies a major category such as asset, liability, or expense. The next portion indicates a grouping within the category such as capital expense, sales expense, or salary expense. This is sometimes carried through several levels. Sometimes these account numbers incorporate organizational information to facilitate allocating expense and income items to specific organizational units.[12]

In the past this may have been necessary because of the limitations of computers and information processing equipment. This is no longer the case.

If the entity is represented by a relation, and if the identifier becomes the key of the relation, the result is that a piece of the key is functionally dependent on the entire key. (You can get a headache just thinking about that!)

What happens when data imbedded in an identifier changes? If we change the value of a key, any record of that key value must change. If any user has any record (on a report, on a note pad, in his or her memory) that data value is no longer valid. Will it be possible to find and correct all such instances? In the case of the bank account example noted above, if a customer moves and is adopted by a new branch, and we modify the account number to reflect this, we must issue new checks and induce the customer to discard any which are already in his or her possession. Since the customer probably had to pay for the checks in the first place, this may be a difficult and expensive proposition. If the key value in question appears as a foreign key in any other table, it must be changed there as well. At least, it may be relatively easy to find these and change them in comparison to things which must be altered by manual methods. But the ramifications may be far reaching. If we do not change the value of the key, the data in the database becomes a lie.[13] The branch number in the account number is no longer the branch responsible for the customer's account.

Sometimes we can convert an identifier change to a combination of delete and create. That suggests that the entity occurrence designated by the old identifier has ceased to exist and a new occurrence has come into being. This is sometimes workable, but it can be cumbersome, difficult, and expensive.

There may be cases in which the identifier will never change. A *1/4–20 × 3 inch hex head machine screw* may always be just that. (But as Whitener notes, the net weight of a large size candy bar may very well change.)

There may also be cases where users insist on retaining an informative identifier which has been in use for a long time. It might also be that a user is reluctant to give up his or her brainchild. If, for some reason, it is necessary to use an identifier with information content, it is a good idea to duplicate the data in separate attributes. That is, incorporate a separate attribute for responsible branch or destination, make it possible to change the attribute, and always reference the attribute, not the identifier, in computer programs.

Good identifiers are legally usable. Social Security Number is often used as an identifier. In most cases it is actually very inappropriate. Often an individual may not be compelled to furnish a social security number. In many situations it is illegal to use or to reveal a social security number.

A good identifier is manageable and controllable. Identifiers which are issued by some external agency, such as Social Security Number or Driver's License Number, have been issued with some specific purpose in mind. That purpose may be in conflict with the needs of your organization. Or, the agency may alter the format. (It's almost unthinkable, but suppose the government increases the length of Social Security Number, as they have done in the case of Zip Code. The expense of changing would be incredible.) Identifiers with multiple sources, be they external or internal, can not be guaranteed unique or consistent. We could not use vendor's invoice number as an identifier because nothing precludes two different vendors from using the same series of numbers. If two different departments assign customer identifiers, it is very likely that some customers will have multiple identifiers.[14] Identifiers consisting of arbitrary strings of numbers and letters are error prone. They can be remembered incorrectly. Digits can be transposed when the number is written or typed. Many organizations use self checking numbers.[15] If an invalid number is entered, it can be corrected. Automated data capture via bar code readers, magnetic stripe readers, or optical character readers can also reduce this risk.

A good identifier is known and accessible to those who must use it. The ideal identifier would be in common use outside the database as well as within it.

The identifier is not the only means of access to the data. Key and search argument are two different things. We can query for all coffee shipments whether or not commodity is a component of the key. We can retrieve the records for all students named Joan Smith and then use some other criteria for deciding which data represents the Joan Smith standing at the registration desk. This is why the entity definition should note all arguments which would normally be used as access arguments.

6.9   DATA ENCODING

The use of a variety of data encoding schemes has been common in data processing. In the days of punch cards, encoding was used to reduce the amount of data. *M* or *F* required fewer valuable card columns (and key strokes) than *MALE* or *FEMALE*. Coding schemes are still used to conserve disk storage or memory or data transmission costs even today. Encoding is also used to standardize data values or because the codes are commonly used in the business environment.[16]

Modern software systems can alleviate the need to use encoding as a way to reduce keystrokes (and errors). It has become common to build the ability to select from a list of possible values into data entry programs. It is also possible for the software to suggest values based on the first character(s) of an item.

An encoding system really establishes a specific set of values for a data item and assigns a specific meaning to each. It's similar to a domain, isn't it?

Coding systems also have a lot in common with keys and identifiers. A code is really an identifier for a particular value. You would do well to review any coding scheme, existing or proposed, in light of the principles cited above for identifiers.

It is also true that, as a practical matter, it may not be possible to alter an existing code.

With all that in mind, we will review some principles that may help differentiate a good coding scheme from a bad one. *A coding system should provide for growth.* A single digit code allows exactly ten values. A single character can allow 36 (10 possible digits and 26 possible letters). In practice, it's a good idea to avoid confusing possibilities such as *0* (zero) and "*O*" (oh), *1* (one) *l* (lower case L) and *I* (upper case i), and also *J* and *Q*. It would not be a good idea to intermingle upper- and lowercase letters and it is necessary to remember that most database management software is case sensitive. If *a* and *A* are to be equivalent, it is usually necessary for the programmer or implementor to take special action to assure that this is so. And a coding system which intermingles letters and numbers should probably be avoided whenever possible. There are, of course, situations where growth is not a serious problem. The number of days in a week or states in the union does not change very often.[17, 18]

A coding system must be controlled and unambiguous. The telephone companies must go to great lengths to manage country and area codes and to assure that a customer who wishes to place a local call does not inadvertently make a long distance call. Essentially, certain combinations may not be used for local exchanges in certain areas. This is an extreme case.

A coding system should specifically provide for missing data values. It may be appropriate to use NULL for unknown values. It is often convenient to assign a specific code for *value missing.* This will simplify programming.

Now, we'll review different types of codes.

- *Enumeration encoding* assigns specific representations to specific values. This is probably the most common type of code. It is usually a good idea to organize this sort of code in such a way that data sorted by the code will appear in a reasonable sequence. This is another good reason for not mixing numbers and letters. The hardware designer's choice of representation, ASCII or EBCDIC, will affect the collating sequence.[19, 20]

- *Scale encoding* utilizes a particular measurement system, such as weight in pounds, length in centimeters, dollars and cents, and the like. If different systems or databases use different units of measure, data exchange will require data conversion.

- *Abbreviation encoding* involves the use of abbreviations for codes. These are usually considered easy to remember. But these can result in the use of some very unlikely combinations which may not be so easy to remember.

- *Algorithmic encoding* involves the use of some well-defined transformation or mathematical formula to derive the data representation. The Julian date is an example of this. Many relational systems use a special internal format for storing dates and times. This usually simplifies the process of calculating the number of days between two dates.

- *Hierarchy encoding* utilizes some hierarchical classification scheme as the basis for the code. The Dewey Decimal and Library of Congress systems used by libraries are examples of these. The typical corporate *chart of accounts* [21] is another. The big difficulty here lies in the discovery of a classification scheme which is appropriate and adequate.

The best guiding principle for designing or selecting an encoding scheme is to make sure you really understand the range and nature of the values which must be encoded.

6.10 REFERENTIAL AND ENTITY INTEGRITY[22]

Relational theory provides us with two types of constraints to consider. These are referential integrity and entity integrity. Making sure that these constraints will be enforced is really a part of Physical System and Database Design. But the designer needs to know what the rules are. Thus, we discuss this now because the entity and relationship definitions must provide an adequate basis for informed choices.

Entity integrity requires every entity occurrence to have a complete and known identifier.[23] Since a primary key is the identifier which differentiates one row of a table from all others, it is not reasonable or acceptable for the value, or any part of the value, to be unknown. We will usually specify NOT NULL as a characteristic of any attribute which is a component of a primary key. Since entities are frequently represented by relations, this just reinforces what has already been said about identifiers.

Referential integrity [24] is a little more involved. However, the underlying principle is fairly simple. Do you remember the employee and department example from Chapters 4 and 5? In the simple one to many case, Department Number was included in the Employee table as a foreign key referencing the Department table. This implemented the relationship *Employee is Assigned to Department.* We would expect any Department Number value found in the Employee table to match one of the Department Number values found in the Department table. If this were not the case, there would be some error. Either the wrong data was entered for the employee or data about the department is missing. Certainly it doesn't make sense to assign an employee to a department which doesn't exist.

Thus, *referential Integrity* requires that a foreign key must either contain a value which does occur as a primary key in the table it refers to or it must be completely NULL.[25]

Referential integrity constraints really need to be enforced one way or another. In the example given, we don't want the database to show an employee assigned to a department that doesn't exist.

First, we must understand the constraint. Then we must decide how to enforce it. We could rely on humans to be very careful about entering department numbers. We could incorporate a test for a valid department in any programs which add or modify this data. Or, we can delegate the job to the DBMS. Moving constraint checking into the DBMS is in line with the trend we noted in Chapter 1: get as much as possible out of the application program and into the system software.

There are advantages to this. Constraints will be consistently enforced. We don't need to be concerned that the constraint will be omitted or dealt with incorrectly in one of many programs. There is a time savings. The constraint doesn't have to be repetitively restated by programmer after programmer. If there is a change of policy, we have only one place to make a change. These are the usual benefits of good modular system construction.

There is one disadvantage. When a constraint is enforced by the DBMS, there can be no exceptions. Everyone must live with it. We'd best be very sure that we really do want the constraint enforced in all situations.

There are also limitations to database management constraint enforcement. Typical database management systems can verify that the target of a foreign key does or does not exist. But we do not always delete inactive records. Sometimes we merely set an attribute to a value which designates an inactive status. The level of referential integrity checking provided by most database management systems cannot contend with this.

We will now provide some discussion and illustrations of how things might be done using SQL. We are fleshing out some concepts. *We are not suggesting that you should start thinking in terms of SQL during this phase. The concepts are relevant even if SQL will not be used.*[26] The discussion which follows is more or less based on IBM's DATABASE2 implementation of referential integrity as described in [IBM88-1] and

[IBM88-2]. The latter, a usage guide, contains a complete explanation and numerous examples. Some other vendor may not choose to do things in this exact same way. And it is not convenient as this is written to verify every example on a DATABASE2 system. You can trust the concepts, but you'd better check out the exact language details and syntax on the specific system you intend to use.

Entity integrity is fairly straightforward. We identify the primary key of a table and specify that it may not be NULL. We may also create a unique index on the key to assure that there will be no duplicates. Indexing is discussed in Chapter 7. The primary key designation is also utilized in enforcing referential integrity.

Example 1

CREATE TABLE EMPLOYEE

    (PRIMARY KEY (EMPLOYEE_ID),

    EMPLOYEE_ID   CHAR(9) NOT NULL,

    EMPLOYEE_NAME...,

    etc., etc.,...,

    CURRENT_DEPT   CHAR(5));

CREATE TABLE DEPARTMENT

    (PRIMARY KEY (DEPARTMENT_NUMBER),

    DEPARTMENT_NUMBER   CHAR(5) NOT NULL,

    DEPARTMENT_NAME...,

    etc., etc.,...);

If the key consists of multiple attributes, the idea is the same.

Example 2

CREATE TABLE CITY_STATE

    (PRIMARY KEY (CITY_CODE, STATE_CODE),

    CITY_CODE   CHAR(7) NOT NULL,

    STATE_CODE   CHAR(2) NOT NULL,

    etc., etc.,...);

Referential integrity gets a little more involved. First, we specify the foreign key.

Example 3

CREATE TABLE EMPLOYEE

    (PRIMARY KEY (EMPLOYEE_ID),

    FOREIGN KEY DEPT (CURRENT_DEPT)

    REFERENCES DEPARTMENT,

    EMPLOYEE_ID   CHAR(9) NOT NULL,

    EMPLOYEE_NAME...,

    etc., etc.,...,

    CURRENT_DEPT   CHAR(5));

```
CREATE TABLE DEPARTMENT
        (PRIMARY KEY (DEPARTMENT_NUMBER),
        DEPARTMENT_NUMBER    CHAR(5) NOT NULL,
        DEPARTMENT_NAME...,
        etc., etc.,...);
```

This would instruct the DBMS to check each new value for the foreign key, CUR-RENT_DEPT, against the current values for DEPARTMENT_NUMBER, the PRIMARY KEY of DEPARTMENT. If there is no match for the department number, the new data will be rejected with an appropriate error indication. The specification as shown here will allow a NULL value for CURRENT_DEPT. If the policy is to be that each and every employee must at all times be assigned to a valid department, we will disallow null values for CURRENT_DEPT. Here, *policy* really means our policy for accepting data into the database. It is a very good idea to make sure that this policy matches the business policy.

Example 4

```
CREATE TABLE EMPLOYEE
        (PRIMARY KEY (EMPLOYEE_ID),
        FOREIGN KEY DEPT (CURRENT_DEPT)
        REFERENCES DEPARTMENT,
        EMPLOYEE_ID    CHAR(9) NOT NULL,
        EMPLOYEE_NAME...,
        etc., etc.,...,
        CURRENT_DEPT    CHAR(5) NOT NULL);
CREATE TABLE DEPARTMENT
        (PRIMARY KEY (DEPARTMENT_NUMBER),
        DEPARTMENT_NUMBER    CHAR(5) NOT NULL,
        DEPARTMENT_NAME...,
        etc., etc.,...);
```

Both Example 3 and Example 4 require that any value specified for CUR-RENT_DEPT be found as a value for DEPARTMENT_NUMBER in one of the entries in DEPARTMENT. This precludes entering incorrect department numbers in employee records. *This also means that if someone wants to add new employees to a new department, they must add the department to the department table first, then add the employees to the employee table.* (Actually, given the definition shown in Example 3, they could add the employees with a null value for CURRENT_DEPT, then add the department, then change the employees. Who'd want to do that?) In this particular example, it probably is not a problem. Suppose we were dealing with customers and orders and someone accepts an order from a brand new customer. The design of the system and procedures must provide for the entry of customer data first, then order data.[27]

Example 3 allows the entry of a NULL value to designate that there is no known department number for this employee. It is not, by the way, good practice to use NULL to identify unassigned employees. NULL really means *unknown* or no *value*. If it is important to identify unassigned employees, a separate attribute should be set up. Example 4 does not allow NULLs. Some would follow this example no matter what and create a bogus department named *unassigned employees*. It is necessary to know more about the processing requirement to know if this is a good idea or a bad one. In general, bogus entities are a source of trouble. There is usually a need for too many special exceptions in the processing programs. For example, it would take a special effort to omit a department named *unassigned employees* from a department address and phone number listing.

It is necessary to know the rules for the relationship in order to know which example is correct.

This takes care of changes and additions to the employee table. But what about changes to the department table? Suppose we delete a department entry. There may now be some employee entries with invalid values for the *foreign key*. We don't want that. What do we want?

There are three choices.

- We can disallow the operation. This is called the RESTRICT delete rule. If we specify this, the DBMS will refuse to delete a department which is referenced by any employee records. It would then be necessary for the user to alter all employee data before deleting the department.

- We can specify that if the department is eliminated, all the employees are also eliminated. This is called the CASCADE delete rule. This seems to be the least likely of the choices for this employee and department example. Most situations would call for at least a report of the deleted items. Note that, if the primary key for employee is used as a foreign key in some other table, and that rule is also cascade, there may be three types of records deleted as a result of deleting the department.

- Or, we can specify that the employees of the eliminated department will become unassigned by calling for the SET NULL delete rule. That is, we can specify this if we have allowed NULL values for the foreign key.

```
CREATE TABLE EMPLOYEE
        (PRIMARY KEY (EMPLOYEE_ID),
        FOREIGN KEY DEPT (CURRENT_DEPT)
        REFERENCES DEPARTMENT
        ON DELETE RESTRICT,
        EMPLOYEE_ID   CHAR(9) NOT NULL,
        EMPLOYEE_NAME...,
        etc., etc., ...
        CURRENT_DEPT   CHAR(5) NOT NULL);
```

```
CREATE TABLE EMPLOYEE
        (PRIMARY KEY (EMPLOYEE_ID),
        FOREIGN KEY DEPT (CURRENT_DEPT)
        REFERENCES DEPARTMENT
        ON DELETE CASCADE,
        EMPLOYEE_ID   CHAR(9) NOT NULL,
        EMPLOYEE_NAME...,
        etc., etc., ...,
        CURRENT_DEPT   CHAR(5) NOT NULL);
CREATE TABLE EMPLOYEE
        (PRIMARY KEY (EMPLOYEE_ID),
        FOREIGN KEY DEPT (CURRENT_DEPT)
        REFERENCES DEPARTMENT
        ON DELETE SET NULL,
        EMPLOYEE_ID   CHAR(9) NOT NULL,
        EMPLOYEE_NAME...,
        etc., etc., ...,
        CURRENT_DEPT   CHAR(5));
```

We really can't decide which of these is correct without more information. It depends on how someone wants to run a particular business, or, in a case other than departments and employees, it depends on the rules for the situation.

A change to the primary key of some row of DEPARTMENT would necessitate a similar decision. The difference is that CASCADE would require changing the foreign key values to the new primary key value. It might be necessary to set the foreign key values to NULL, if allowed, then set them to the new value.

We need to be aware of all this whether or not we intend to use the referential integrity feature of SQL, don't we? That's the important point. We must examine each relationship and identify the business rules. We include these in the entity and relationship definitions. During the next design step we decide how to implement the rules. If we are working with a DBMS which provides for these integrity constraints, we will probably want to delegate the work to the DBMS. In this case, you will need to review the capabilities of the DBMS to be used.

We've already noted that some systems provide this feature as this is written, while others do not. It is also likely to be the case that different vendors will provide different levels of support for this feature. As an example, here are the restrictions imposed by a particular version of DATABASE2 as stated in [IBM88-2].[28] The referenced document contains detailed examples to illustrate and justify these restrictions. This is included to illustrate the types of restrictions which may be encountered. You should always check the most current documentation for the software you will be using.

• A primary key may contain no more than 16 columns.

- An update rule can not be specified because the only supported update rule is restrict.
- Within a given table a foreign key may not be part of the primary key. In our example, the primary key for employee could not be employee identifier plus department identifier.
- The foreign key definition must exactly match the referenced primary key definition.
- The SET NULL option can not be specified if NOT NULL is specified for the foreign key.
- If a recursive (BOMP) relationship is defined, the delete rule must be CASCADE.
- If two tables are connected through multiple paths, both must have the same delete rule and that rule must not be SET NULL. (Here's a possible example. Suppose we add a manager table to the employee and department case. Suppose we specify a manager identifier as a second foreign key for employee and the specify department as a foreign key for manager. Employee is now connected to department via two paths, a direct route and a more circuitous one which passes through manager.

What this really means is that we may have to deal with some constraints or situations via programming or procedures. It does not mean that we don't need to identify and address them.

6.11   OTHER CONSTRAINTS

When we considered attribute definitions, we noted that we need to define any rules which determine legitimate values for specific attributes. We saw that these rules may or may not be inherited from domains. It is also possible that there may be rules which involve multiple attributes. Certain classes of employees may be restricted to certain benefit plans. There may be some relationship between wage scale and type of department. There might be an either or situation as in an employee must either participate in the savings plan or the retirement plan. It may be mandatory for certain classes of employees to participate in certain benefit programs.

Thus, we look for rules about domain values, rules about attribute values, rules relating multiple attributes of the same entity type or relationship type, and rules relating attributes of more than one entity type or relationship.

We may find rules which are harder to classify. There may be a limit on the number of occurrences of some entity type. There may be a limit on some function of attribute values for all occurrences of some entity type, a maximum weight perhaps. How about an equal opportunity rule which states that certain percentages of certain categories of employees must belong to certain ethnic groups. We probably would not really want the DBMS to enforce this kind of rule as an integrity constraint, but we would want the system to warn us of noncompliance.

There are often constraints which have never been explicitly stated. Sometimes it is because "everyone knows that." Sometimes they are not publicized intentionally. In any event, the goal is to identify everything that can be identified, incorporate it all in the data model, then decide how to deal with each constraint in another phase.[29]

Some database management systems provide for *triggers*. These are procedures or programs which are invoked when a particular event occurs. You might specify a routine to be performed every time a new row is added to a particular table. This routine could perform a simple integrity check or it could perform a very elaborate test of a variety of conditions. This is a good way to enforce constraints that cannot be handled in other ways. It is really important to document the existence and purpose of triggers because they are usually "hidden" inside the database definition.

6.12 SECURITY

The discussions of entity and relationship definitions include discussions of security and authorization considerations. We've noted that SQL provides capabilities for restricting access to the data based on security considerations. Obviously, we can't specify security restrictions unless we know what they should be.

Many organizations are becoming aware of this issue, but many have not begun to deal with it. Before we had computer databases, data was secured by restricting physical access to it. Those who had physical possession had control more or less by default. The advent of computer systems, shared databases, and networks makes it necessary to deal explicitly with the definition of security policies and rules. *This is really a management issue, not a technical issue.* Conflicts over control of data are often power struggles between organizational rivals. The best advice available is that technicians should try to avoid making political decisions. But it is necessary for a database designer to find out what the rules are.

In general, we begin by noting security requirements in entity and relationship definitions. Can we identify an owner or party responsible for the data? Is the data considered sensitive? Should access be restricted? Should one class of user be able to view but not alter the data? Does a restriction apply to all data about an entity or relationship or only to certain attributes? In the most rigorous circumstances unauthorized users are not even allowed to know that the data exists. How difficult is it to determine who should or should not have access? Who can or should make this decision?

Endnotes

1. Sometimes our purpose is to "communicate with ourselves." Giving credit where it is due, we note that the author first heard this put this way in a talk given by Dick Swenson.

2. The material which follows is largely based on [COPI61] and [HAYAKAWA78].

3. In addition to references already cited, we draw on [SHLAER88] and [ARANOW89] in developing the following.

4. Let's consider a student's grade point average (GPA) as an example. This is really a form of average which can be calculated by examining all course enrollments and grades for that student. We might even go so far as to say that GPA is somehow functionally dependent on the concatena-

tion of all courses and grades for a student. In practice we would never attempt to construct a table containing all possible combinations plus the appropriate GPA. So we tend to more or less ignore this when we consider normalization. We identify that there is a domain of grade point average, that there is a student grade point average attribute drawn from this domain, and that this attribute is functionally dependent on student identifier. Thus, if we elect to store GPA we will store it as an attribute of student. We will, however, have to decide whether or not to store it at all, since we could calculate it when it is needed. Note that this may be expensive since it will be necessary to examine all enrollments in order to calculate it. On the other hand, it will also be expensive to store it. The space required is probably not the big issue. The real difficulty is that we must then recalculate GPA, examining all enrollments in the process, every time a grade is added or altered. We'd also be wise to incorporate some sort of balancing run to assure that all GPA's are, in fact, consistent with the other data. In other words, eliminating GPA from the physical database will eliminate a redundancy which may cause an inconsistency, but we would not ordinarily think of this as a normalization issue. The real reason we mention this here is not to suggest the decision should be made at this point in the process. That's the last thing we want to do. We'll identify that there is such a data item, that there is a unique value for each student, and that it can be calculated. We can then decide whether or not to store it much later on.

5. You probably can't really appreciate this until you've been through a naming war or two!

6. Most CASE tools available today automate one or more of the better known structured analysis methodologies and one or more of the better known entity relationship modeling techniques.

7. This was originally written as "conventional English language name." But the language of choice will not always be English, will it?

8. The organization (and some of the content) of the material which follows is based on [WHITENER89].

9. The author was once called upon to write a program which reviewed a master file, examined all identifiers in use, and produced a listing of those which were no longer active. That is, if 123456789 was followed by 123456791, then 123456790 was no longer active and could be reused.

10. Many companies are still in the process of converting from five-digit zip codes to nine-digit zip codes just because it is such a major undertaking.

11. Name plus complete date of birth works out fairly well in practice.

12. Once again this is an example of a weak entity since a sub account number only has meaning within the context of a major account number. It is also an example of an inherently hierarchical data structure.

13. Sweet [SWEET85] describes the problems which arise when a shipping company imbeds commodity and routing data in a shipping number. In this example, the first two characters of the identifier are a two character commodity code, the next two identify the port of origin, the next two identify the destination, and the final two are a "tie breaker" which differentiates between distinct shipments of the same commodity between the same two locations. Thus, "CF126523" identifies the twenty-third shipment of coffee from Santos to Jacksonville.
A peripheral problem which Sweet identifies here is that some commodity, origin, destination combinations may be used much more than others. The result is that, while ninety-nine tie breakers may be nowhere near adequate for shipments of coffee from Brazil to Florida, there may never be a shipment of coffee from, say, Seattle to San Diego.
And if a shipment is redirected, there is no good solution. If the identifier is changed, all existing documents become invalid. If the identifier is not changed, it becomes a lie. And if some identifiers cannot be trusted as data, the entire scheme falls apart.

14. Identifying individuals and businesses is a particularly difficult problem. We've already noted that financial institutions have a problem identifying customers. It's a problem because there is a desire to recognize multiple relationships with the same customer. The customer may not care to be bothered remembering and furnishing some arbitrary identifier. The customer may even want to deceive the institution. This is really a systems problem. We note it here. But there is no simple solution.

15. Here's an example of a check digit routine drawn from the author's banking experience. Each of the first 8 digits is multiplied by a unique constant. The results are then added. The sum is divided by a prime. The prime minus the remainder becomes the final digit of the number:

Account Number:	7	5	0	7	3	2	6	2
	× 9	× 8	× 7	× 6	× 5	× 4	× 3	× 2
	63 +	40 +	0 +	42 +	15 +	8 +	18 +	4 = 190

$$190 \bmod 11 = 3$$
$$11 - 3 = 8$$

Complete Account Number: 750732628

16. Celko [CELKO89] observes "a bad (encoding) scheme can cripple or kill a database" and "the representation of data in a database is not examined in...database textbooks or training courses." The material which follows draws heavily on this reference.

17. Even though we are not doing physical design here, let's note that it is generally not a good idea to embed a coding system in the instructions of a computer program. At minimum, create a table of values in the data definition section of the program. Better yet, store the table in the database so that it can be changed without recompiling or regenerating the program. Such a table can be brought into memory during the program's initialization phase.

18. Notice that since U.S. Post Office official state abbreviation codes use two letters, it is necessary to use some unlikely representations. "ME" is used for Maine because "MA" is used for Massachusetts. Do you think this has ever resulted in an incorrect address?

19. ASCII, the American Standard Code for Information Interchange, is commonly used in microcomputers, in minicomputers, in Unix systems, and in data communications. EBCDIC, the Extended Binary Coded Decimal Interchange Code, is commonly used in larger (mainframe) computers, especially IBM mainframes.

20. Collating sequence refers to the standard sequencing or sorting of information. "a" always comes before "b." In ASCII, all uppercase letters come before all lowercase letters, but in EBCDIC it is just the opposite.

21. A chart of accounts indicates the organization of expenses, receipts, assets, and liabilities. Expenses may be subdivided into sales expenses, employee expenses, and so on. Employee expenses may then be subdivided into wages, benefits, and the like. It is fairly common to devise elaborate numbering schemes wherein specific digits of the account number relate to specific levels of the hierarchy.

22. This section contains some material on implementation. This might have been deferred to the next chapter. It seems better to deal with concepts and implementation together.

23. "No attribute participating in the primary key of a base relation is allowed to accept null values." [DATE86]

24. At the time this is written (1992), referential integrity is a much discussed topic in relational database. Some vendors have implemented the enforcement of referential integrity. IBM provides it in Version 2 of DATABASE2. ORACLE provides for the definition but does not enforce the constraints. Digital Equipment Corporation has provided it for some time in the RDB database management system for the VAX computer. Earlier versions of RDB utilized a Data Manipulation Language similar to, but not identical with, the QUEL language. QUEL was an alternative to SQL. DEC has since added SQL support to RDB. Cincom provides referential integrity in the SUPRA database management system. (DATABASE2 is a registered trade mark of IBM. RDB and VAX are trademarks of Digital Equipment Corporation. SUPRA is a trademark of Cincom.) The ISO SQL standard [ISO89] defines syntax for specifying referential integrity constraints. The present ANSI SQL standard [ANSI86] does not. There is a separate ANSI document [ANSI89] that does discuss this. Both the ISO committee and the ANSI committee are at work on incorporating more complete integrity specifications in the respective standards. There are other vendors, not mentioned here, who also provide this feature. It is safe to assume that most of those who do not provide it at present will do so in the future.

25. "If base relation R2 includes a foreign key FK matching the primary key PK of some base relation R1, then every value of FK in R2 must either (a) be equal to the value of PK in some tuple of R1 or (b) be wholly null." [DATE86-1]

26. Before discussing referential integrity in SQL, we note that it tended to be more automatic in older database management systems. Network and hierarchical systems relate data in a more direct manner. The related employee and department records would be physically adjacent to each other or linked via address pointers. As a result, it is more or less "built in" that an employee record can only be related to a department record which is actually in the database. Since the relational model implements relationships by means of data values, it is easier to get into trouble.

27. A modern system would provide data entry screens which could accept order information, new customer information, or both.

28. This is included to illustrate the type of thing you may encounter. By the time you read this, some of these restrictions may have been revised.

29. As you might guess, there is quite a variation in what can be done within the DBMS. VAX/RDB and SUPRA, for example, both allow the specification of fairly elaborate constraints on attribute values. Both allow attribute constraints to be inherited from domain constraints. Many other systems do not provide for this at present, but will do so in the future.

QUESTIONS AND EXERCISES

1. Why are definitions important?

2. Explain five different kinds of definitions.

3. Discuss advantages and disadvantages of various techniques for defining.

4. Explain the significance of existence rules and deletion rules.

5. Identify some situations where keeping track of versions may be important.

6. Why would one want to know who is the owner of data about an entity or relationship?

7. What is the difference between a search argument, a key, and a foreign key?

8. Why is it advantageous to relate attributes to domains?

9. How do names used in programs differ from names commonly used by humans?

10. What are the characteristics of a good identifier?

11. Why is a person's name a poor identifier? Why is Social Security Number a poor identifier?

12. Why does the inclusion of meaningful data within an identifier cause problems? Can you give some examples?

13. Is data encoding as necessary today as it was in the past? Why? Why not?

14. Explain entity integrity and referential integrity.

15. What are the advantages and disadvantages of integrity enforcement by the DBMS?

16. Explain a situation where referential integrity is not an adequate solution to the management of data insertion and deletion.

Chapter 7

Physical Considerations and Physical Design

7.1 CHAPTER SUMMARY

This chapter contains a discussion of hardware and physical design. We first discuss storage media and storage concepts. You really need an understanding of these concepts and issues. There is a lot of specialized terminology here and it does vary from vendor to vendor and even varies from one system to another system supplied by the same vendor. We try to stay with commonly used terms. Then we show the relationship to physical database design. We discuss the use of a logical design and a logical access map.[1]

In an ideal world it would not be necessary to worry about many of the topics discussed in this chapter. The relational model is a consistent way of looking at data and specifying manipulations of data.[2] As such, it very correctly does not deal with hardware issues because these are irrelevant to the data relationships and the logic of the data manipulations. Hardware is constantly improving and changing. It is a good idea to differentiate clearly between hardware-related issues and the logic of the data. There are two extremes to avoid.

Some will argue that hardware considerations should not have any influence on a design. It is very likely that hardware will continue to change. Hardware issues will obscure the logic of the system. A design which places undue emphasis on physical considerations will be inflexible, may contain serious logical flaws, and may not even fulfill the requirement.

Others will argue that hardware considerations are all important. An elegant system which consumes too many processor cycles and requires too many disk accesses will be useless because it will not function. Despite all the improvements we've seen, it is still necessary for disk drives to rotate. And, time passes while mechanical movement of access mechanisms takes place.

The prudent course appears to lie between these extremes. The first steps in the design process should result in a clear and precise description of the data and the processing requirement. A normalized relational description augmented by domain, attribute, and constraint definitions is an excellent means of describing everything that is data related. Then it is necessary to look at the specific hardware and software which will be used to implement the design. It is also necessary to look at the nature of the processing, volumes of data, and access patterns. It may be necessary to alter the final design to accommodate physical considerations. Such changes should only be made when it is really necessary, and there must be an awareness of the logical problems which may be introduced in the process.

You need to be aware of the issues discussed in this chapter from the outset of a project in order to appreciate and understand the information that should be collected and documented during analysis. At the same time, *it is important to avoid the temptation to make physical design decisions too soon. It is also important to avoid tying the logical design to physical constraints that may well change.* Decisions made before all the facts are in may be regretted. Physical details may also obscure the logic and business purposes of the system or database.

Many of the details discussed in this chapter are taken care of by hardware and system software. You may never need to deal with them directly. But you will be a better database designer if you are aware that these sorts of things do take place behind the scenes.[3] If you really do need to understand some of these issues in complete detail, you will have to refer to other sources.

Let's pause and review the database design process.

The process is undertaken because some organization or person or activity requires that data be stored in a machine readable form.

We can't be sure we know what data is to be stored unless we understand the activities and the data itself. The main thrust of the first six chapters of this book has been to arrive at a complete understanding of the data and its uses. We've emphasized the data, but we've taken pains to note that we can't really understand the data without understanding its uses.

It is most likely that the data will be the most useful if it is organized in terms of the things of interest and the relationships among those things. We've seen how a combination of careful definition, entity relationship modeling, and normalization produces an appropriate logical organization of the data. We've seen how to define a set of relations or tables which maintain this logical organization.

Our final design steps must assure that the data is stored in a manner suitable for the efficient completion of the necessary tasks. Here, efficient really means at a reasonable cost and in a timely manner. We might break the cost down to include these items; *investment in hardware, investment in software, resources consumed in satisfying a particular request,* and *the length of time required to satisfy the request.*

There are a number of ways efficiency might be defined and measured. You might be primarily interested in *throughput,* the number of transactions which can be processed in a given interval. Or you might want to minimize the *elapsed time* for a single transaction. Cost of *disk storage* or *data transmission* time may be the most important considerations. Number of *cpu cycles* required for a particular operation may be important. Certainly, all of these are important, but different situations will call for measures which emphasize some more than others. There are often trade-offs to evaluate.

Even though we have seen a dramatic reduction in the price of computers and the associated peripheral devices such as disk drives and printers, we still don't want to invest in capacity that would be unneeded if we did things in a more intelligent manner. Software development and the purchase of software are still expensive.

If computing resources are not occupied in performing one task, they will be available for some other. It is expensive and inefficient to require people to wait unnecessarily long for information or for the completion of some data update. There are many cases where an activity must be completed in some given time frame.

There is also a need to protect the data from loss or damage and to assure that it is accurate and correct.

Thus, most physical database design activities have the following motivations.[4]

- *Minimize the amount of space used* to store the data, or at least to make sure that the data can be stored in a given amount of disk space.
- *Minimize the number of disk accesses* involved in processing the data.
- *Provide for data integrity and protect the data from loss*.

7.2   HARDWARE AND MEDIA

If you are already familiar with this material, you will have to decide how much of this section you can safely skip.

Most databases are stored on magnetic disk.[5] There are two main types of media, removable and fixed.

You have probably seen a removable *floppy disk* like the one shown in Figure 7.1. Inside the sleeve is a circular piece coated on both sides with a material which can be magnetized and demagnetized.

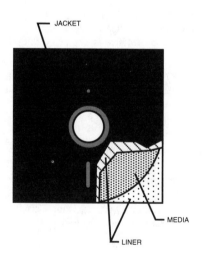

Figure 7.1   Floppy disk

Most floppy disks in use today are either 3 1/2" or 5 1/4" in diameter.[6] Yes, this does mean that it may not be possible to write to a disk on one computer, then read from it on another. The complete personal computer would need three, four, or possibly more, separate floppy disk drives to handle all of the popular formats.

Most of the following discussion applies to fixed disks as well as floppy disks.

Data is stored on (or in) the surface of the disk as a pattern of magnetism. As Figure 7.2 indicates, it is stored in a series of concentric circles called *tracks*. Every track has the same data capacity. The *bits* of magnetism are packed together more closely on the inner tracks.[7] A bit is the smallest recognizable unit of information. An individual bit can assume one of two values. We think of these as one and zero.

Floppy disks are commonly used with microcomputers (personal computers). For a brief period of time these were the primary storage medium for microcomputers. Now they are more often used for transporting data or archival storage.

The capacity of floppy disks in use at the time this is written ranges from 360,000 to 2,880,000 characters of information.[8] Most literature specifies this capacity in terms of *bytes* rather than characters. A byte is usually defined as 8 *bits*. Character information is stored via use of a coding system which assigns a unique eight-bit combination to each character value. Two coding schemes are in wide use today, American Standard Code for Information Interchange (*ASCII*) and Extended Binary Coded Decimal Interchange Code (*EBCDIC*). One character normally occupies one byte. Numeric data may be stored in this form or it may be stored as binary numbers.[9] Relatively large numbers and relatively tiny numbers are sometimes stored as real or floating point numbers.[10] Fortunately, the computer can be programmed to take care of the data translations and conversions.

A related collection of data elements is usually stored as a unit. This unit is commonly called a *record*. It is customary to refer to the individual data elements which form a record as *fields*. Frequently several records are grouped together in a *block* or *page* as shown by Figure 7.3.

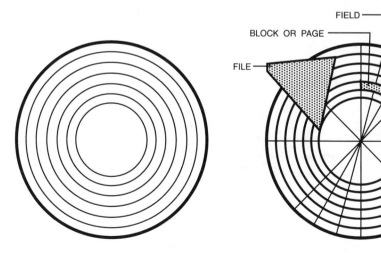

Figure 7.2   Disk tracks   Figure 7.3   Units of storage

Some people use the term *physical record* instead of block or page. It is common to use the term *logical record* to refer to the actual data record. It is possible for a block, page, or physical record to contain several smaller logical records as shown in Figure 7.3. It is also possible for a relatively long logical record to span several blocks. In either case, we usually rely on the system software to sort things out for us. You might visualize a pocket address book. One page of the book is comparable to a block. One name and address entry is comparable to a record. The individual data items are comparable to fields.

A collection of related records is referred to as a *file*. This is comparable to the entire address book. Often, all records in a file have the same layout or design, but this is not absolutely necessary.

Data is stored by altering the magnetic characteristics of a portion of the disk's surface. Data is retrieved by detecting the characteristics of a portion of the surface. We usually use the terms *write* and *read* to describe these processes. The surface must be in motion relative to the *read write head*. The *disk drive* contains a spindle which rotates the disk at a constant velocity. It also contains one or more mechanical arms which position the read write mechanism as shown in Figure 7.4.

Accessing data requires three steps.

- The read write head must be positioned at the proper track. This movement is called a *seek*. This mechanical movement takes place slowly in comparison to the electronic events which take place inside the computer.

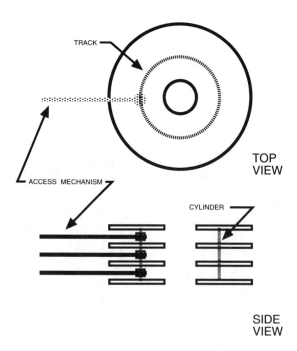

Figure 7.4   Hard disk

- There may be a delay until the desired data rotates to a position beneath the read write head. This is called *rotational delay* or *latency*. This is usually faster than seek time, but is still slow in comparison to electronic speeds.
- The *data transfer* time, like the rotational delay, is determined by the angular velocity of the disk and is slow by electronic standards. It is usually the case that an entire block or page is transferred from the disk unit into memory. A section of memory set aside to receive a block of data is called a *buffer*.

Thus, the average time required to access a single data record will be

> Average_Seek_Time
> + Average_Rotational_Delay
> + Transfer_Rate × Block_Size.[11, 12]

The actual values for these vary from device to device.

The capacity of a floppy disk is limited by the diameter, the number of surfaces, and, most importantly, the manufacturing tolerances involved in the production of inexpensive interchangeable media. It is possible to store much more data on a *hard disk*. These are manufactured as units consisting of spindle, disk surfaces, read write heads, and arm mechanism. Figure 7.4 illustrates that it is common to incorporate more than one surface or platter in a single unit. A set of tracks which are more or less stacked one above another and can be accessed together without arm movement is called a *cylinder*. Hard disks can be manufactured more precisely because they are usually made as complete units. The platters are rigid. The read write mechanism does not touch the surface. The assembly rotates constantly. At the time this is written, units manufactured for microcomputers have capacities from 10 Mbytes to over 300 Mbytes. Units manufactured for mainframe computers can have capacities well in excess of 500 Mbytes per spindle and frequently contain multiple spindles in one cabinet.[13]

Disk units are referred to as *direct access storage devices* or *DASD*. (Some people pronounce DASD as *daz-dee*.)

Characteristics including the size of the unit, number of surfaces per unit, number of tracks per unit, recording density, data encoding technique, and data transfer rate vary from manufacturer to manufacturer and from model to model. These must be determined by examining the technical documentation for the specific device.

Earlier systems utilized magnetic tapes for data storage. These are still used for certain types of systems, especially when large amounts of data are involved. The big disadvantage of tape is that it is essentially linear. It is necessary to pass an entire tape to get to the data at the end. You will notice the same thing with cassettes of recorded music and videotapes.

The advantage of disk is that it is possible, by seeking the appropriate cylinder, selecting the appropriate surface, and accessing the appropriate part of the track, to read or write any of the data in a relatively short time interval. Addressing schemes vary from unit to unit. Addresses almost always consist of a cylinder number plus a track or head number plus an identifier for some portion of the track. One of the most commonly used techniques is to divide each track into a fixed number of fixed size *sectors* as shown in Figure 7.5. Sector sizes in common use today range from 512 bytes to 4096 bytes.[14]

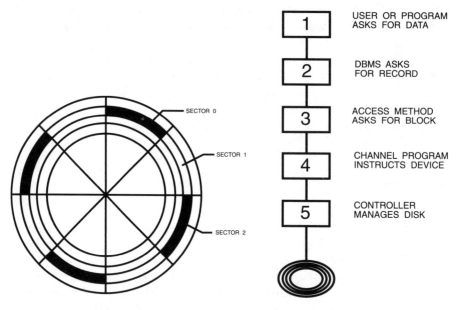

Figure 7.5 Disk sectors

Figure 7.6 Accessing process

You can probably see what the problem is. We want to retrieve data about a particular entity occurrence, let's say customer 1876523. We can access it quickly if we know the correct disk address. If we don't know the address, it will be necessary to search the entire disk. This could, in the case of a high capacity unit (or a relatively slow one), take as much as a half hour. And, we really don't want to get directly involved with addresses if we can avoid it. Remember, the addressing scheme can vary from one unit to another. We'd have a lot of trouble migrating to new hardware if we depended too much on actual addresses. In fact, we'd even have a lot of trouble moving data from one place on a disk to another. Part of the solution lies in relying on some combination of system software and database management system to take care of this.

The portions of the system software concerned with data storage and retrieval are sometimes called *access methods*. Sometimes this term is used to designate the software modules. Sometimes it is used to designate the particular technique used by the software. *Device driver* is another common term. This refers to a software module which is designed to work with and manipulate a specific device or class of devices. Figure 7.6 illustrates that several components are typically involved in any data accessing operation. An end user may interact with an application program which may interact with a database management system which may interact with an access method which may interact with a device driver which accesses the disk. In a particular situation, some of these pieces may be missing or several pieces may be combined into a single module or program.

There is a comparable division of labor on the hardware side. One or more disk units are likely to be connected to one *controller*. Controllers may be connected to *channels* [15]

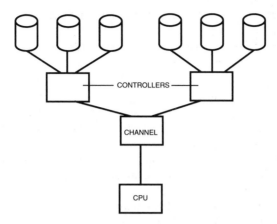

Figure 7.7 Multiple controllers

or *input-output processors* which are then connected to the *central processing unit (CPU)*. Controllers and channels may be thought of as specialized computers which are designed specifically to deal with input-output processing. This is illustrated by Figure 7.7. When performance or capacity is a significant issue, it is necessary to study the operation of the various components in detail. A large scale mainframe environment may be quite complex and may consist of hundreds of disk drives connected to dozens of controllers and channels.

IBM [IBM88-3] considers it valuable to make the following recommendations.

- "Avoid sharing work volumes (for temporary data sets) among multiple systems."[16, 17]

- "Avoid sharing system volumes among multiple systems."[18]

- "If you share high-activity data sets, be sure to place them on the highest-performance devices in your installation."

Some of the recent models of controllers for larger systems are very sophisticated.

Digital Equipment Corporation's Hierarchical Storage Controller [LARY89], for example, provides a number of features intended to optimize disk access.[19, 20]

Many modern systems reduce the number of disk accesses by retaining data in a special memory referred to as a *cache*. This can eliminate repetitive disk access for data which is frequently reused.

Many contemporary systems also provide *volume shadowing (or mirroring)* which performs all operations in tandem on two separate disk drives. This is done to minimize the possibility of losing data due to a hardware failure.

Some of the newest hardware provides for storage of data across multiple surfaces. The content of a single record or even a single character might be distributed across several disk surfaces. The hardware will automatically decompose and reassemble the data. This is sometimes referred to as *disk striping*. Since the data is stored across an array of disks, some systems are described as *redundant arrays of independent (or inexpensive) disks (RAID)*. These frequently incorporate error correcting schemes which make it possible to recover data in the event of a media failure. These devices are said to be faster, more reliable, and less expensive.

A microcomputer system is usually much simpler. We won't go any deeper into this here. But if you are designing a performance-oriented system for a complex environment, you will want to explore further. Be sure you have up-to-date information about the specific equipment you intend to use.

We normally rely on system software to keep track of the beginning and end of each file on disk. Some systems require the user (or the programmer or someone) to specify the amount of space required prior to creating a file. Some systems will just go ahead and find space dynamically as it is needed. Some of the latter will allow reservation of sufficient contiguous space at the beginning. Contiguous means physically adjacent or all in one group. If a file is spread all over, performance can be affected because longer seeks will be required. Some relational DBMS systems allow you to control this. Some do not. This is discussed in the section on file size and placement.

There will usually be a systemwide *catalog* or *directory* containing entries that define the storage locations of files. A particular file may be stored as one contiguous unit or it may be broken up into segments. These are sometimes referred to as *extents*.

- This may be because the file is too big for one device.
- It may be because the data was acquired over a period of time and new space was allocated as needed.
- The designer(s) may have made a conscious decision to spread the data across several devices. This can make it possible for several operations on several different records to take place concurrently. A single read write head can only do one thing at a time. Multiple devices will provide multiple read write heads which will in turn allow concurrency of data access operations.

There may be a hierarchy of catalogs or directories as shown in Figure 7.8. This can speed up the search for a particular record by eliminating the need to search all catalog entries. It can also provide a way to deal with groups of files. Microcomputer systems

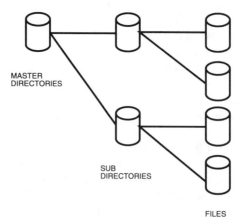

MASTER
DIRECTORIES

SUB
DIRECTORIES

FILES

Figure 7.8   Sub Directories

generally provide a separate catalog for each disk and require the user or operator to know which catalog or device contains the desired data. Mainframe systems usually provide a master catalog with linkages to other catalogs. Individual hard disk units and floppy disks are frequently referred to as *volumes*. The entries which describe the files on a specific volume are sometimes combined into a *volume table of contents (VTOC)* for that volume. If a file consists of several extents, the catalog or volume table of contents must contain the location of each extent. In the MS-DOS operating system for personal computers, this information is contained in a *file allocation table (FAT)*.

This approach makes it possible for a user (or a program) to specify a filename or a directory plus filename combination and rely on the system to locate a specific file. Some microcomputer systems limit file and directory names to eight characters. Some mainframe systems allow them to be virtually unlimited in length. Many systems allow both kinds of names to be built up from a series of components. The series of directories which leads to a particular file is often called a *path*.[21]

In general, one strives for meaningful names which will provide clues to file content, and, at the same time strives for relatively short and easy to type names.

A directory is only a collection of file names. Collecting the names in a directory has no effect on the physical locations of the files.

In a production environment there may be hundreds (and often thousands) of distinct files with distinct purposes. Given this, *it becomes very worthwhile to devise naming rules and naming schemes which make it easy to identify and manipulate files and groups of related files. It also becomes worthwhile to design catalog structures carefully and retain documentation about files and file groupings.*

That solves part of the problem. We still need to locate the required record or records within the file. It is not a good idea to work with actual disk addresses consisting of cylinder, head, sector, and the like. The most commonly used technique for circumventing this necessity is referred to as *relative addressing*. Each record might be assigned a *relative record number*. The *first* record in the file is record number 0, the *next* is record number 1, and so on. Or we might deal with *relative byte addresses* which identify specific displacements, in bytes, from the *beginning* of the file. The records might be physically sequential as in Figure 7.9. However, a disk is normally shared by any number of files. And these are continually being created, deleted, and modified. If the system makes efficient use of space, the pieces of the various files may become intermingled and the parts of a given file may even be in some physical sequence which differs from its logical sequence. This is called *disk fragmentation* and is illustrated by Figure 7.10. This can have a negative effect on performance. We rely on the system to produce a specific record or sequence of records on request. A relative address might refer to a specific data record or logical record. Or, it might refer to a specific block or physical record.

Thus, we don't have to know that data about customer 1876523 is at cylinder 153, track 9, sector 12. We just have to know that it is 203,326 bytes from the beginning of a file named CUSTOMER_DATA. Does that make it easy enough? We are getting closer, but we aren't quite there. How do we know that is the address of the record we want? We could just search the entire file. Sometimes that can't be avoided. But if there are hun-

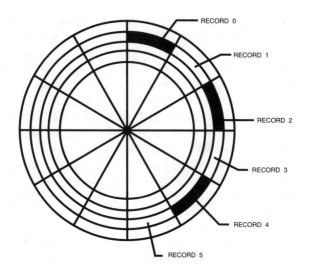

Figure 7.9   Relative addressing

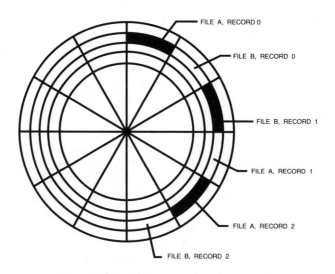

Figure 7.10   Disk fragmentation

dreds, or thousands, or millions of customers, that isn't a good idea. We need some way to relate the identifier to a relative address.

7.3   HASHING FUNCTIONS

Once in a great while, one encounters an extremely well-behaved identifier. Given identifiers that run 0, 1, 2, 3,... with no gaps, one could use the identifier for a relative record number or use (identifier × record_length) for a relative byte address. If the identifiers were to run 10000001, 10000002, 10000003,... it would be possible to subtract 10000000 from the identifier and use the result as the relative record number. This sort of happy coincidence is rare. Any attempt to use most identifiers in this manner would just waste too much space because there will be too many missing numbers.[22] We need a more elaborate function for producing addresses from keys.

One commonly used technique involves performing a simple mathematical transformation on the key. This is sometimes called *hashing* or *randomizing*. One of the simpler methods is to divide the key value by an appropriate prime number[23] and use the remainder for a record number.[24]

Here is an example. Suppose the identifier is a six-digit number but approximately 10,000 records are to be stored.

One might select the prime number 12,983.

12,983 relative addresses would then be reserved for the data.

Records would be assigned to relative addresses in the following manner.

IDENTIFIER	DIVIDE BY 12983	RELATIVE ADDRESS
100000	7	9119
100100	7	9219
120000	9	3153
129830	10	0
200000	15	5255
220010	16	12282
230030	17	9319
233695	18	1
268979	20	9319

The characteristics of this technique are:
- The records will generally be distributed evenly across the file space.
- Often, the data will not be stored in key sequence. It is necessary to sort the data in order to produce a report in sequence by identifier.
- There is the possibility that two different keys will randomize to the same disk address. The software must deal with this possibility.
- Since a record can only be at one disk address, there can only be one key. Randomizing does not help in locating data via alternate or secondary keys.

- Performance is sensitive to the amount of free space provided. More free space will reduce the likelihood of duplicate addresses. It is common to allow 30–40 percent free space.
- If the database management system makes use of this technique, most of the details will be hidden inside. But it is valuable to understand a little about how it works.
- If this is available, it will be an option which the database administrator can select for a particular file or database. In this situation it would be necessary to estimate the size of the database and preallocate the space.[25]
- If use of this technique is not a feature of the database management system, it is not usually practical to think about adding it.[26]

7.4   INDEXED ACCESS

Providing for data access via an index is much more common. This technique is employed by most relational database management systems. The concept is fairly simple. The software establishes a separate area which is populated with short entries consisting of identifier and disk address. The card catalog found in most libraries is a good example of this idea.[27] See Figure 7.11.

You might ask why searching an index is more efficient than searching the data.

- The index is relatively compact and can therefore be examined more rapidly. Frequently, the entire index can be retained in electronic memory. This eliminates time-consuming accesses to disk.
- A lot of effort has gone into the development of highly efficient indexing techniques. Indexes are often built up in layers as shown in Figure 7.12. This makes it possible to locate the desired data record with relatively few index accesses.[28, 29]

The significant characteristics of this technique are:

- The details will be hidden inside the database management system.[30]
- All relational database management systems make use of this technique.

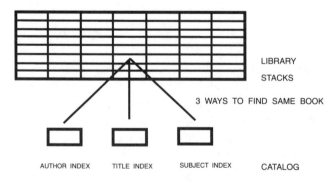

LIBRARY

STACKS

3 WAYS TO FIND SAME BOOK

AUTHOR INDEX   TITLE INDEX   SUBJECT INDEX   CATALOG

Figure 7.11   Multiple indexes

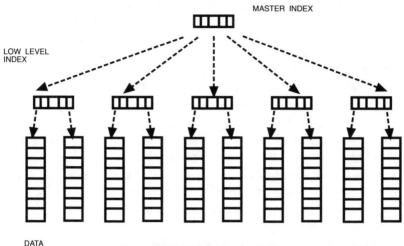

Figure 7.12 Multiple levels of index

- It is possible to create more than one index. Thus, we can utilize indexing to access data via secondary keys as well as primary keys.
- It is not practical to index on columns which are infrequently used as search arguments.
- Indexes take up space.
- Indexes must be changed whenever the data is changed. Each index must be updated every time a row is added or deleted.
- An index can be used to access the data in key sequence even if it is not stored this way. The index can be traversed in key sequence to obtain the actual storage location of each data record. Since the data is not in key sequence, processing in this manner may require an inordinate number of disk seeks.
- In the technique commonly referred to as *indexed sequential*, the data is maintained more or less in key sequence. Some systems provide this capability. Some do not. In IBM's DATABASE2 [31] System these are referred to as *clustering indexes*. Indexed sequential access methods are able to take advantage of the data sequence to increase efficiency and reduce the size of the index. Since the data can only be in one sequence, secondary indexes can not take advantage of the data sequence and may be less efficient and occupy more disk space.
- The DBMS can use an index to detect records with duplicate keys. In SQL, the specification of a UNIQUE index instructs the DBMS to disallow duplicate values. A combination of UNIQUE and NOT NULL will assure entity integrity. This is really just a trick that works. It will be better if the key can be defined as a key to the DBMS.
- An index may be a separate file or it may be imbedded within the same file as the data.
- *Selection and specification of indexes is the most significant performance tuning device available to the users of most relational systems.* If no index is provided, most systems will search the entire database to satisfy an inquiry.

- In a relational database environment, the Database Administrator or database designer determines the need for and specifies indexes. SQL statements will produce the same result whether or not indexes are present, but appropriate indexes can dramatically improve response time. Here are some guidelines which may be used in making decisions about indexes.

1 Index the primary key of a table. Consider a UNIQUE index to prevent duplicates.

2 Index any heavily used secondary key.

3 Index a foreign key if there is frequent access based on it. An example would be the department number in the employee table. We may frequently wish to select the employees who work in a particular department.

4 Index any attribute which is frequently used as a search argument or access path. This is especially important if data is regularly accessed on-line.

5 Avoid indexing an attribute which is frequently updated. The index must be updated every time a value changes.

6 Avoid indexing long character valued attributes.

7 Avoid indexing an attribute for which many duplicate values are likely. Most indexing techniques will be less efficient in this situation. Also, if a query will retrieve a really significant percentage of the rows in a table, it may be just as efficient to search the entire table.

8 Be very stingy with indexes to a table which is frequently updated via adding and deleting rows. Be generous with indexes to a table which is rarely updated.

9 Indexes are unnecessary overhead for very small tables. These can be searched in memory.

A sophisticated system may make use of indexes in satisfying complex queries without accessing the actual data. Suppose there are indexes on employee identifier, department identifier, and skill identifier. It is possible to resolve queries regarding which employees in which departments have which skills solely from data in the indexes.

7.5   ACCESS MAP

An access map such as that shown in Figure 7.13 is very useful in performing the next tasks. This is an annotated diagram of the normalized database design. Depending on which authority you consult, you will find this referred to as an *access map*, a *logical access map*, a *logical database design*, a *conceptual data model*, or possibly something else. You may also encounter a variety of different diagramming techniques. But you will find that the essential idea is always the same.

Each normalized relation is represented by a rectangle. Lines connecting the rectangles represent relationships implemented via foreign keys. These connections between relations will always be one to many or one to one. In Figure 7.13, a student may have many enrollments but the converse is not true. Student identifier appears as a foreign key in enrollment. An arrowhead may be used to indicate the *many* side of a one to many relationship.

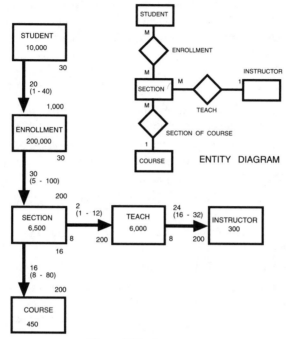

Figure 7.13 Access map

Intersection tables will have been created for many to many relationships. In Figure 7.13, enrollment is an example of this.

The numbers inside each rectangle indicate the number of occurrences or number of rows for each relation. It's a good idea to also include an anticipated growth rate for each. Special notations can be used to describe unusual or difficult to categorize growth patterns.

The numbers which are more or less centered on each line indicate how many rows of the *many* are likely to be associated with the *one*. It is best to identify an average, a maximum, and a minimum, and also to note any exceptional cases (in Figure 7.13, maxima and minima are shown in parentheses). The mode or most commonly occurring value is more useful than the average. Averages can be extremely deceiving. If the owner of a business pays herself $220,000.00 per year while paying each of two employees $10,000.00 per year, the average salary paid will be $80,000.00 per year.

The numbers at the end of each line indicate the expected rate of access via that "path." These are derived by studying each individual transaction and summing the results. The best way to do this is to make as many copies of the diagram as are needed, then annotate one copy for each known activity.

Here's how the numbers on this particular diagram were developed. (All this was done to produce numbers that at least make sense and to illustrate the impact of retaining history. In practice one would discover actual volumes for each relation.)

•   10,000 students was taken as a starting point.

- It was assumed that the average student will enroll in 40 courses before graduation. It was also assumed that the average student is halfway through college.
- It was assumed that the average section size is 30 students.
- It was assumed that the average course has 4 sections and that enrollments remain in the database for the 8 semesters it takes for a student to graduate.
- It was assumed that most courses have one instructor.
- It was assumed that the average instructor teaches 3 courses per semester and that these records are also retained for 8 semesters.

Figure 7.14 indicates that a request to retrieve current enrollments with course name and instructor name for a given student requires these accesses:

- One access to STUDENT for the desired student record.
- Twenty accesses to ENROLLMENT, one for each enrollment on the average student's record.
- Four accesses to SECTION, one for each current semester ENROLLMENT on each student's record.
- Four accesses each to COURSE, TEACH, and INSTRUCTOR, one for each of the enrollments.
- Given an expectation of 50 such queries per hour, these numbers would be converted to 50, 1,000, and 200 for addition to the master diagram of accesses per hour.

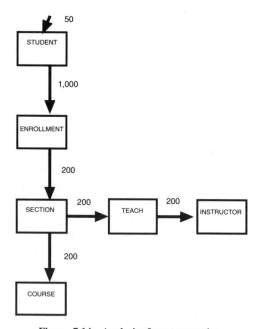

Figure 7.14   Analysis of one transaction

Some of the information may be difficult or even impossible to acquire. That's right. Sometimes no one is sure how many customers or orders there will be. In this case, all you can do is make your best estimate and add in an error factor. The more uncertain the estimate is, the larger the error factor must be. A system or database must be designed to meet a specific requirement. It is true that the newer relational database management systems can reduce the impact of an error by simplifying the process of database modification. It is not true that it is a good idea to create a database with no concept of the requirement which must be met.

In the case of a large system, a detailed analysis of the accessing patterns for every transaction and report can become extremely tedious. This is usually a group activity that can take weeks. The whole group may become really silly or really bored by the time the activity is complete. If it is possible, plan on doing this only a few hours per day and incorporate appropriate breaks in the schedule.

Some authorities suggest that it is appropriate to analyze only *important* transactions or only on-line transactions. It may not be possible to define all reports and queries in advance.

It is often a good idea to weight the needs of on-line or *mission critical* transactions more heavily than the others. One might do this by multiplying this number by two (or ten). It can be useful to make two diagrams, one for on-line transactions and another for batch processing and reporting.

In addition to accumulating a performance requirement, you will be *validating the logical design* by assuring that there are accessing patterns that make each transaction and report possible. (Then it is necessary to examine every transaction, isn't it?)

This is one of many areas where the exercise of good judgment is important. The only way to be certain you understand the whole requirement is to be sure that you have all of these numbers and that they are all accurate. If some data is very difficult to obtain, one must decide what constitutes a good enough estimate. One must decide if and how to weight different requirements. One must decide whether or not to subject every activity to the same rigorous analysis.

7.6   WHAT DOES THE OPTIMIZER DO?

Query optimization is an important feature of any relational database management system. A lengthy and somewhat detailed discussion of query processing and optimization follows. This material will also help you understand some of the important issues in relational database design and the use of relational systems.

To eliminate repetition of the department name, we broke employee and department into two separate relations like this.

EMPLOYEE(EMPLOYEE_ID, EMPLOYEE_NAME, DEPARTMENT_ID)

DEPARTMENT(DEPARTMENT_ID, DEPARTMENT_NAME)

The data looked like this.

EMPLOYEE_ID	EMPLOYEE_NAME	DEPARTMENT_ID
123	Harry	ABC
231	Mary	ABC
312	Larry	BAC

DEPARTMENT_ID	DEPARTMENT_NAME
ABC	Alpha Beta
BAC	Beta Alpha

Now, suppose that there is a need to produce a report listing all employees, in employee number sequence, with the correct department name for each employee. Remember, the data in a relational database is not usually stored in any particular sequence.[32] More often than not, it will be in the order in which the data happened to be stored in the first place.

We are going to review the procedures that the database management system might use to satisfy our request. We don't really have to think about this procedure to write the query. We will just specify the nature of the output. The optimizer routine will evaluate the possibilities and select a strategy. But it is valuable to have some insight into what must be done. Since this is not a tutorial on query optimization, the explanation is a simplification of what really happens.

We would probably write an SQL statement about like this:

SELECT EMPLOYEE_ID, EMPLOYEE_NAME, DEPARTMENT_NAME

FROM EMPLOYEE, DEPARTMENT

WHERE EMPLOYEE.DEPARTMENT_ID = DEPARTMENT.DEPARTMENT_ID

ORDER BY EMPLOYEE_ID

What does the DBMS have to do to accomplish what we've asked? There are a number of possibilities.

Here is possibility one.

- Get the first employee row.
- Search for the matching department row.
- Save the result.
- Repeat for every employee.
- Sort the intermediate result by employee number.

This appears to call for a large number of disk accesses. It is reasonable to assume that the average number of accesses required to locate a department is equal to one half the number of departments. We will also assume there is some form of integrity checking and we can be sure that there is one but only one row for each department. (But note that the DBMS will only know that there is but one row per department if we have defined an integrity rule for this. Otherwise it would be necessary to search the entire department table to make sure there were no more matching rows.) Thus, the total number of accesses will be

NUMBER_OF_EMPLOYEES

+ (NUMBER_OF_EMPLOYEES

× NUMBER_OF_DEPARTMENTS × 1/2)

+ COST_OF_SORT.

If there would be more than one employee row per page (or block), the number of actual accesses for obtaining all employees would be reduced accordingly and the number of accesses will be

(NUMBER_OF_EMPLOYEES / EMPLOYEES_PER_PAGE)

+ (NUMBER_OF_EMPLOYEES

× NUMBER_OF_DEPARTMENTS × 1/2)

+ COST_OF_SORT.[33]

The accesses for employee rows do not necessarily require a disk seek for every access. It may only be necessary to move the arm when all employee rows in a cylinder have been accessed. But if the employee and department tables are both on the same device, there is likely to be a seek for every access.

If the department table is small or there is a lot of free memory, it will be possible to reduce the number of disk accesses dramatically by doing all department searching in memory.

The sort may not be as expensive as you might think. If enough electronic memory is available, most of the work can be done without any disk access. If the sort does write work files to disk, a large number of records can be written to one block and sequential processing of these files can minimize the number of seeks.

Here's possibility two.

• Get the first department row.

• Search for all matching employee rows.

• Save the result.

• Repeat for every department.

• Sort the intermediate result by employee number.

Since we can't be sure how many employees, if any, there are for a given department, we'll have to search the entire employee table for every department. The cost will be

(NUMBER_OF_DEPARTMENTS / DEPARTMENTS_PER_PAGE)

+ (NUMBER_OF_DEPARTMENTS × NUMBER_OF_EMPLOYEES)

+ COST_OF_SORT.

Since there are likely to be many more employees than departments, this is nearly certain to be more expensive than possibility one.

Here's possibility three.

• Sort employee data by department number.

• Sort department data by department number.

• Match and merge the results on department number.

• Sort by employee number.

Given an efficient sort, this may well involve fewer disk accesses than either possibility one or possibility two.

Suppose the department table has an index on department number. *Possibility four* looks just like possibility one.

- Get the first employee row.
- Search for the matching department row.
- Save the result.
- Repeat for every employee.
- Sort the intermediate result by employee number.

There will only be one disk access plus one index search for each department access. The result will be

NUMBER_OF_EMPLOYEES

+ NUMBER_OF_EMPLOYEES

+ COST_OF_SORT.

This seems to be a big improvement over possibility one. The comparison to possibility three will depend on table sizes and the efficiency of the sort.

Suppose the employee table has an index on employee number. *Possibility five* looks just like possibility two.

- Get the first department row.
- Search for all matching employee rows.
- Save the result.
- Repeat for every department.
- Sort the intermediate result by employee number.

Now, the cost of each employee search will be determined by the number of employees per department, giving

(NUMBER_OF_DEPARTMENTS / DEPARTMENTS_PER_PAGE)

+ (NUMBER_OF_DEPARTMENTS

× EMPLOYEES_PER_DEPARTMENT)

+ COST_OF_SORT.

This looks like an improvement over possibility two, but it doesn't appear to be better than possibility three.

Suppose we use the index on employee number to eliminate the final sort. Here's *possibility six*.

- Get the first employee row.
- Search for the matching department row.
- Save the result.
- Repeat for every employee.

There is a pitfall here. The index allows the retrieval of employee rows in employee number sequence. Suppose they are not stored in employee number sequence. Each successive disk access is likely to involve a seek. There will be one disk access for every employee because successive employee records will not be in the same page. This is probably the most expensive of all the alternatives.

Fortunately, one doesn't have to go through all the analysis every time there is an SQL query to be written. (If it were necessary to write a conventional program, it would be necessary to think all this through.) It is, however, necessary for the DBMS to select a strategy. The better systems have elaborate *optimizer* routines which subject the alternatives to a thorough analysis. In our example, we'd expect either possibility three or possibility four to be selected. The determination would be based on the sizes of the tables and the efficiency of the sort. This can vary from system to system and situation to situation. So, we can't give the right answer without assuming specific values.

It is the optimizer's function to find the approach which will consume the least resources. The basic techniques we've just reviewed for join processing are lookup and sort/merge [INGRESXX]. The lookup is better when relatively few values are extracted from one relation and used to locate corresponding data in another. The sort/merge seems better for large and relatively equal numbers of rows from both relations. The optimizer must also determine when and how to apply any restrictions specified in the WHERE clauses. It will often make sense to eliminate rows before the lookup or sort. The optimizer must also make assumptions regarding the numbers of rows which will be selected by the conditions. Systems such as DATABASE2 make choices based on extensive data distribution statistics which are kept in the catalog. Maintaining these statistics could produce a significant overhead. DATABASE2 resolves this by providing for a batch update at installation specified intervals.

There are sometimes a variety of ways in which a particular query may be phrased in SQL. The ideal optimizer would select the same *best* strategy no matter which form were specified. In practice, it is a good idea to try out several possibilities for a complex time-critical query. If a really unusual approach is taken to achieve a performance goal, the statement should be annotated with an explanation. *A different product, or even a new release of the same product, may evaluate the statement differently.* Some products, such as DATABASE2, provide an *EXPLAIN* utility which will reveal the systems' strategy for a particular query or update. This can be very useful in resolving design issues and in finding the optimal form for a query. It will be important to study your vendor's documentation and learn as much as you can about the optimizer.

7.7   TO NORMALIZE OR NOT

This controversial issue is frequently discussed in the literature.[34] Normalization eliminates redundancy and arranges a collection of data according to its inherent logical structure. As a general rule, this is highly desirable. The normalized form reflects an understanding of the data. *Developing a normalized design should always be a step in the design process.*

It seems to be possible to produce nearly any desirable unnormalized arrangement from a normalized database by applying the relational operators.[35] *A fully normalized form is likely to be the most flexible.*

The problem is that, as we've just seen, significant overhead may be incurred in joining relations. If the example data were stored in the original unnormalized form with a department name in every employee row, the matching would not be necessary, the optimization problem would be simpler, and this particular query could be processed much more efficiently. *The cost of storing the data in an unnormalized form would be wasted disk storage space, the possibilities of update, insert, and delete anomalies, and possibly less efficiency in processing other queries and updates. A department name change, for example, would be much more expensive.*

We are certainly not suggesting that the unnormalized form is better in this case. Unless the uses of this data were really unusual, the normalized form is surely better. The point is that there is a potential cost and it is necessary to evaluate it at this stage of the design process.

Let's review some guidelines. If the database will be used for a variety of unpredictable queries,[36] implementation of a fully normalized design is usually best. If this is done, the following considerations apply.

- It is often a good idea to define views which facilitate and simplify specific queries or types of queries. This is not the only reason for defining views. They will also insulate programs from changes to the structure of the database.

- It is sometimes beneficial to create a separate extract database which is designed to facilitate particular queries. We discuss this later in this chapter.

- If there are specific queries or updates which occur frequently and/or have a strict performance requirement, there may be no choice but to denormalize in their favor. This is likely to be true only for extremely demanding performance requirements.

- If you denormalize for performance, you do want to be sure that the denormalization is truly beneficial and that there is no better alternative. You also want to be sure that some other important transaction is not severely degraded or rendered impossible.

- Joins tend to be expensive. It may be necessary to denormalize in order to eliminate repetitive joins, especially those involving very large tables and those involving more than three or four tables. Many subqueries are equivalent to joins.

- Any query involving SELECT DISTINCT, UNION, INTERSECT, OR DIFFERENCE calls for eliminating all duplicate rows.[37] Since this can be expensive, these may be worth eliminating.

- Some queries, especially those involving a combination of totals or averages, can be extremely complex to formulate. It may be necessary to denormalize and/or create an extract database to facilitate these.

- Denormalized tables will almost always be created by combining two or more normalized tables. The rows will thus be longer. Each access to a row of a denormalized table will require that more data be transmitted. This will take longer. More memory will be required for any in memory processing. The more queries or processes which can be satisfied without combining data, the more additional expense the denormalization introduces.

- Denormalized tables must be more expensive to update. Data which is frequently updated should not be replicated without good reason.

- In a subsequent section, we discuss record locking and the management of concurrent updates. Denormalizing may, by reducing the number of records accessed, reduce the overhead associated with concurrency control. It may also, by increasing the number of accesses to specific records, increase this overhead.

Is there a procedure for deciding?

It is possible to imagine a procedure for calculating the costs of processing alternative designs. It would be necessary to develop access maps for the normalized design and for each alternative. It would then be possible to calculate, or at least estimate, the number of disk accesses and the volume of data transmission involved in processing a given workload against each design. Then one would select the optimum. That sounds like a lot of work, doesn't it? If there is a lot of data, if there are a lot of transactions, if performance is an important issue, or if the system is *mission critical*, it may be worth it.

Perhaps there is an alternative. Inmon [INMON87] [INMON89] suggests developing a matrix of tables to business processes as illustrated in Figure 7.15. Each column of this table represents a normalized relation. Each row represents a process.

- Processes might be queries or on-line updates. In this case, one then determines how frequently the process occurs, which tables it must reference, and how many times each is referenced. This sounds like the work we did to construct the access map, doesn't it? Notice that we might need to make more than one matrix. The peak hour mix of transactions might be altogether different from the average for a day. There might be peak days or days with unusual mixtures of activity.

- Processes might also be batch updates, batch reports, or batch extract runs. In this case we'd have to determine how many rows of each table are accessed via a given run. And this might vary from day to day.

At any rate, the matrix or matrices will summarize, in a fairly visual manner, the accessing patterns of the processes which must be performed. It might be wise to indicate the number of accesses for some time interval in each cell of the matrix. We then

PROCESSES	RELATIONS					
	STUDENT	ENROLLMENT	SECTION	COURSE	TEACH	INSTRUCTOR
ENROLL NEW STUDENT	X					
ENROLL STUDENT IN COURSE	X	X	X	X		
ESTABLISH SECTION			X	X	X	X
ESTABLISH NEW COURSE				X		
PRINT ROSTER	X	X	X		X	X
PRINT GRADE REPORT	X	X	X	X		

Figure 7.15   Matrix of relations and processes

suggest placing three numbers into each cell of each matrix, read only, update, and total number of accesses. One then looks for two kinds of situations.

- If tables which can sensibly be joined into one are frequently accessed together, there is an argument in favor of combining them. It might be that many different processes use a given combination. Or, it might it might that a single high volume or critical process does.
- If a table is often used by processes which access no other table, it is a poor candidate for combining.
- If a table is frequently updated and combining would involve replicating the data, it is a poor candidate for combining.

Creating this matrix via a spreadsheet program is very useful. This will facilitate rearranging rows and columns. Doing this will often make some of the patterns easier to discern.

There is another alternative to consider. It might make sense to split a table vertically. Suppose there were a strong argument for replicating department name in every employee record. And, it is probably the usual case that department names rarely change. But suppose the department table has other attributes which are dynamic. Perhaps, for example, there is a daily performance rating. We might retain the department table with the dynamic attributes but move only department name to the employee table. This example is provided to illustrate the concept, but it doesn't sound like a very good idea for two reasons. First, there will probably be a relatively small number of departments, and repetitive processing of a small table is less of a problem than repetitive processing of a large one. Second, can you imagine yourself instructing everyone that an inquiry to determine department name must be processed against the employee table? Maybe department name could be kept in both places. Fine, but make sure that any change of a department name does change all occurrences.

The biggest pitfall of denormalization is that it makes the database less general. One of the highly advertised advantages of relational database is that it can make it relatively easy to satisfy requirements which were not known at the time of the original design. This is more likely to be true if the database design is fully normalized.[38] Denormalization will also tend to make the result of applying relational operators less predictable, confuse or disable the optimizer, and introduce anomalies. We'll close this section by agreeing with [DATE86-2]:

"Denormalization is a slippery slope, however. It smacks very heavily of letting physical performance considerations influence the logical database design, which historically has always led to trouble in the long run. As a general rule, we would advocate normalizing 'all the way'..., and then denormalizing only when there is a very clear advantage to doing so, and *documenting carefully* the reason for each such departure from the fully normalized position."

7.8   FILE SIZE AND PLACEMENT

When we request data from the DBMS, we generally refer to tables (relations) by name. The DBMS will, in turn, request the data from the operating system or from some access

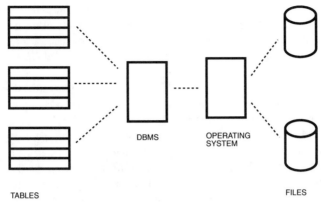

Figure 7.16 Tables versus files

method. The DBMS must frame the request in terms of files and records because the operating system is blissfully ignorant of tables and relations. Figure 7.16 illustrates this idea. Sometimes we need to understand a little about how this works.

It is a little difficult to discuss this in a general book because different DBMS vendors have different ways of dealing with the issue. In fact, the vendors who market to users of several different brands of computer and operating system sometimes find it necessary to use different approaches for different environments. The best we can do is discuss some commonly used approaches.

One approach is to create one file for each table and another for each index, as illustrated in Figure 7.17. Many of the simpler microcomputer-based database management systems do this. The actual table name or index name is usually used for the first part of the name.

The MS-DOS[39] operating system used on IBM personal computers (and the *clones* of the IBM computers) restricts file names to an eight-character name plus a three-charac-

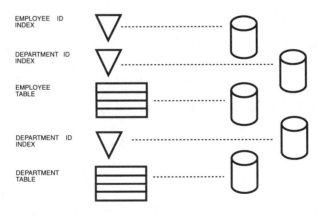

Figure 7.17 One file for each table

ter suffix. This means that the first eight characters of any table or index name will become the filename. This means that the first eight characters of each name must be unique even if the name is longer. Several of these systems restrict the name to eight characters for this reason. There are usually suffixes like.*DBF* and.*NDX* to indicate the type of data.

In a personal computer system such as this, files are usually organized via a directory structure. Left to its own devices, the DBMS is likely to place a newly created table or index in the same directory with the DBMS software. This will happen more or less automatically. MS-DOS and VAX VMS, along with some other operating systems, use the concept of a current or *default* directory. The usual manner of starting any program is to specify the directory which contains reference to the program as the default, then specify the program. MS-DOS then assumes that any file references are to files referenced by that directory. It is possible to reference files via other directories by prefixing the file name with the directory name.

- Some systems allow the user to specify a directory name along with the table name. In this case, one could work with files in two different directories at the same time.

- Many systems provide a CREATE DATABASE command which allows the establishment of a particular directory for all files associated with all tables and indexes for that database. You may encounter CREATE SCHEMA instead of CREATE DATABASE.[40] These systems then provide some means for specifying a current database to be used for all subsequent commands. When this is the case, it is usually necessary for all tables and indexes used in a particular SQL statement or program to be addressed via the same directory.

- It is possible to create more than one database with the same structure. The data content will be different for each database. Judicious use of subdirectories will allow the same suite of programs to access different databases at different times.

In a microcomputer environment, files are often allocated dynamically. This means that the operating system obtains the needed space as it is requested. In some ways, this approach makes things really simple. But there are some things to watch out for.

- First, it is sometimes not possible for a database to reside on multiple devices. Thus, it is necessary to be sure that there will in fact be room on the disk for all the data. Otherwise, one may encounter some error message indicating that the disk is full and no more data may be added. This is the type of thing that will happen at the worst possible time. So it is necessary to estimate the size of the database before it is created and make sure that the device used does in fact contain enough free space. If, as is often the case, the device contains other data, it is necessary to manage the space and make sure that one collection of data does not use up all of the space to the detriment of others.

- Second, because disk space is acquired as needed, it is often acquired in small pieces. The result is that the data for different files may become intermingled as shown in Figure 7.10. This is often referred to as *fragmentation*. Intermingling data in this manner can increase the number of disk seeks required for a particular process. And seek time is more or less proportional to the distance traveled.[41] This can cause a given query or report to take significantly longer. The solution to this problem is that one must periodically reorganize the disk, which can be accomplished by use of standard operating system utilities or by use of programs which are marketed specifically for this purpose.[42]

Many of the more sophisticated database management systems provide correspondingly more sophisticated space management techniques. A database or schema will be organized in terms of some other unit which then relates to files.

Version 5 of the ORACLE System,[43] for example, organizes the data in PARTITIONS.[44] One or more tables and indexes are stored in a partition. The partition name may be specified in the CREATE TABLE or CREATE INDEX statement. If no partition is specified, the data is placed in a default or SYSTEM partition. A partition, in turn, may consist of one or more operating system files. ORACLE runs in a variety of operating system and hardware environments. If the operating system allows it, it may be possible to preallocate a contiguous file of a desired size and even to control the location of that file. It may be directed to a specific device or possibly even to a specific location on a device. ORACLE will then manage the allocation of data within the partition. If a table has all of a contiguous partition to itself, the table will be contiguous. If several tables share a partition, they will be intermingled. It may be desirable to periodically reorganize the data.

Version 6 of the ORACLE System provides a similar arrangement, but the term TABLESPACE is used instead of partition.[45]

ORACLE also provides a CLUSTERING feature which allows the Database Administrator to specify that two tables are to share the same disk pages. This can facilitate access to related data. Thus, we might specify that order data is to be stored with customer data. *If the data entry is done carefully*, the orders for a particular customer will be stored on the same page (or at least the same cylinder) as the customer data.

DATABASE2 provides extensive capabilities for data management.[46] Data is organized in terms of STORAGE GROUPS, TABLESPACES, and PARTITIONS. It is possible for the Database Administrator to exercise a great amount of control over the placement of data and allocation of space. It is also possible to let the system do most of the work.

As you can see, there are a variety of possibilities. The specific DBMS and computing environment will determine the exact terminology and capabilities. The more sophisticated systems provide a somewhat bewildering selection of options. If you get involved with storage management aspects of one of these systems, it will be necessary to study the vendor's documentation carefully and possibly attend some product specific training.

There really can't be one set of rules for all environments. Here are the *guiding principles*.

- It's almost always necessary to calculate the amount of space required. (We discuss this shortly.) Then it's necessary to make sure that the requisite space is available. There may, by the way, be a lead time of many months involved if additional disk units must be purchased in a mainframe environment.
- Someone should monitor disk usage and database sizes on a continuing basis to eliminate surprises. Running out of space for an important database at a critical time

can cause a lot of excitement. And it can take hours, sometimes days, to rearrange things and get back in business. In a large centralized shop, there are likely to be specific technicians assigned to this task. In a personal computer or network environment, the responsibility may not be so clear.

- A disk seek is the most time-consuming operation.
- Periodic data reorganization can reduce the number of seeks required to scan a table.
- Data placement can also reduce the number or length of seeks by assuring that data which is frequently used together is adjacent.
- In a multi-user environment there is a benefit to spreading a table across several devices. This allows multiple accesses to different parts of the table to occur concurrently.
- Combining related tables in one operating system file can simplify backup and recovery.

The possibilities and techniques for control of data placement vary considerably from one environment to the next. We'd hope to find some skilled technicians at an installation with a complex environment. For these reasons, we won't go beyond general principles.

However, closer examination of the space requirement is possible and worthwhile.

7.9   CALCULATING SPACE REQUIRED

Calculation of the amount of space required involves multiplying the number of rows by the size of a row. *The size of a row is the sum of the column sizes plus any overhead introduced by the system.*

The size of a column is partly determined by the size and type of the data element or attribute.

- If a column must contain dollar amounts up to $1,000.00, there must be provision for six digits. If a column must contain names as long as *Franklin Delano Roosevelt*, there must be provision for 25 characters. The data encoding technique is also a factor in determining column width.
- If a numeric data item is stored as a binary number, storage will normally be allocated in terms of the *word size* of the specific computer. Some systems provide for halfwords, double words, and even quad words in addition to full words. Suppose a particular machine provides 16-bit halfwords, 32-bit full words, and 64-bit double words. Integer numbers up to 32,767 will require a half word or 2 bytes.[47] Integer numbers up to 2,147,647 will require a full word or 4 bytes.[48] Integer numbers up to 2^{63} will require a double word or 8 bytes. If a floating point format is used, the number of significant digits will determine the amount of space required.
- Numbers are sometimes stored in a *packed decimal* form which utilizes one byte for each two digits. This form always requires space allocation in full bytes and also requires an additional 1/2 byte for a sign representation.

- The decimal point does not normally take a location. It is assumed in the definition. The number 2,237.87 might be stored as 223787 with two decimal places taken for granted.
- Character data generally requires one byte per character.
- Some systems store character and packed decimal data in a variable length format, suppressing either trailing spaces or leading zeros. Some will do this for all character data. Others will provide variable length data as an option. In either case, a one byte length indicator will be associated with each column. Space calculations involving variable length columns require the determination of an average column size. This will be average data length plus column overhead.
- Most systems require an additional byte for each column which may contain a NULL value.
- Some systems which provide variable length columns do not require any space for null columns at the end of a row.

For still more detail, on this see note[49].

There may also be a row overhead. Systems which allow variable length data commonly place a row length indicator at the beginning of each row. Some systems place all row length indicators at the beginning or end of a page instead of attaching them to the individual rows. In either case, this will usually be one or two bytes per row.

So you can see that calculating row length requires knowledge of the specific hardware and software in use. Lacking this knowledge, one might use number of characters and digits as an estimate of row length.

The next step is to determine the number of data records per block.

Block or page size is generally fixed. There is an overhead associated with each page. The system keeps track of such things as amount of space available in each page. This also varies from one system to another. It might be two to four bytes.

As illustrated by Figure 7.18, the amount of space available in a block may not be evenly divisible by row length. This may result in wasted space. Some software will only store a row as a contiguous unit. Some will split a row and store portions of it in multiple pages. There will be a record keeping overhead and an extra disk access if this is the case.

Finally, it is necessary to determine the number of pages per track or cylinder.

If the disk is addressed in sectors, the page size is likely to be a fixed multiple of sector size. If this is not the case, it is possible that allocation of pages to a track may also result in wasted space. This is similar to the record and page situation explained above.

Also, as indicated by Figure 7.18, there are usually gaps between pages. These are required by the hardware. There may also be hardware control information on each track.

Vendor documentation for disk units for large scale systems will usually provide charts or formulas which can be used to determine the number of pages of a given size which will fit on a track.

In the case of a microcomputer system, it is usually necessary to determine the sector size and work with that. It is common to specify a *cluster* or *allocation unit* size when performing the original low level formatting for a microcomputer's hard disk. This will

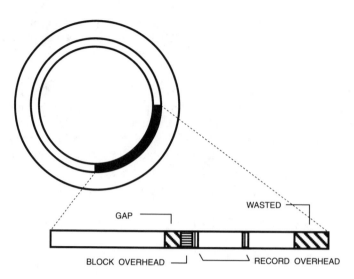

Figure 7.18 Disk space utilization

be some multiple of sector size. A mismatch between page and cluster size can result in an inordinate waste of space. If space is an important consideration, and you are enough of a hardware and systems software wizard, it will be worthwhile to look into this.

As you can see, it is usually the case that a 500 Mbyte disk does not really hold 500 Mbytes of data. *Here is a sample of a space calculation.*

Average Row Length = 180 bytes

(This would be determined by summing columns and adding row overhead.)

Rows Per Page = 5

(Suppose page size to be 1024. Also suppose that rows are always stored as contiguous units. Since 5 times 180 is 900, 100 or more bytes per page will be wasted.)

Pages Per Track = 10

(This would depend on the nature of the device. We've selected an even number for the sake of a simple example.)

Rows Per Track = Rows Per Page × Pages Per Track = 500

(Now, suppose that 100,000 rows are expected. Don't forget that this must include the expected growth for some reasonable time frame. What's a reasonable time frame? How long do you expect the system to be used? How sure are you of your estimates for size and growth? Given your hardware and software environment, how difficult will it be to add space if and when it is needed? There's no choice but to exercise informed judgment here.)

Tracks Required = Rows ÷ Rows Per Track = 100,000 ÷ 500 = 200

It is also necessary to estimate the amount of space required for indexes.

There is likely to be one index entry per row. Each is likely to consist of a key value plus the relative address of the page containing the data row. It is possible to estimate index entries per page and calculate an index space requirement in a manner similar to the calculation of the data space requirement.

If multiple level indexing (see Figure 7.12) is used by the software, there is likely to be one entry in the higher level index for each page of lower level index. Given several levels, the calculation must be repeated for each level.

The documentation for the more sophisticated software packages will often explain this calculation in detail.

The final steps depend on the nature of the DBMS and the environment. It may just be necessary to make sure that there will be enough room for the data. It may be necessary to preallocate space. It may be necessary to define the space requirement to the DBMS. It may be necessary to define the space requirement to the operating system.

The DBMS will also require some fixed amount of space for the catalog or dictionary description of the database. This will be determined by the number of columns, tables, and indexes, not by the amount of data. Some systems will store this in the same space with the data. Some will maintain a separate dictionary in a special area. The documentation may tell how to calculate this. It may be necessary to create a definition and see how much space it occupies.

Once this has been done, it is certainly necessary for someone to monitor the amount of data in the database, the space used, the space used by any other data stored on the same device, and the space available for expansion. Failure to provide for this can result in very unpleasant surprises.

7.10 BACKUP, JOURNALING, RECOVERY, CONCURRENCY

Many microcomputer DBMS systems were originally designed as single user systems. That is, there could be but one user at any given time. This is a relatively simple environment to manage. The assumption which is more or less built into a system like this is that the user will be wise enough to make backup copies of all database files at appropriate times. This might be done with the DBMS or it might be done using an operating system copy or backup command. The backup copy should not be kept on the same physical device as the actual data.

Recovery from device or media failure then involves repair or replacement of the device and recreation of the database from the backup. In this situation, it is necessary for the user to redo any data entry work which had been done after the backup.

It is also possible to erase or undo a batch of work which has been done in error by reverting to a copy made before the work was entered. If a copy was not made at just the right time, it will then be necessary to add or delete data.

Appropriate timing and management of backup copies can be very important.

It can sometimes be very difficult to convince an unsophisticated user that data backup is a necessary and important task. It's a good idea to build it into the system if possible.

Many database management systems provide for a *journal* or *log* of database changes. This does include the more sophisticated single user systems. The journal is a separate file containing a record of each change. A common technique involves placing two types of records on the journal, before images and after images.[50] These are snapshots of data records before and after each change. The after images can be merged with a backup copy to recreate an up-to-date copy of the database. This is sometimes referred to as *roll forward* and sometimes as *redo*. The number of journal records which must be processed will determine how long this takes. This, in turn, will be determined by the time since the previous backup. The before images can be used to restore the database to a prior state. This process is sometimes referred to as *roll back* and sometimes as *undo*. The number of journal records which must be processed will be determined by the size of the unit of work which must be undone. If the journal can not be on a different device from the database, it may not be any more usable than the database in the event of a media failure.

The amount of time necessary to restart the system after a problem has occurred will depend on whether or not it is necessary to restore the database from a backup, the size of the database, and the size of the journal. The designer must weigh the cost of frequent backup against the cost of a long recovery. Obviously it's necessary to know something about transaction and data volumes in order to decide rationally.

In the case of an on-line system, it is also necessary to think about an appropriate time for backup. If the system must be shut down during the backup procedure, the time must be selected with care. Some software will take an *incremental backup* without shutting down. But it still may not be a good idea to schedule this during a busy time.

The before and after images are also associated with the concepts of logical unit of work, commit, and roll back.

A *logical unit of work* or *transaction* is a set of actions which logically form a single operation. For example, a transfer of funds from a savings account to a checking account involves three actions; subtract from savings, add to checking, and keep a record for audit and control purposes. The transfer cannot be considered complete unless all three actions have taken place. In fact, if only the first action occurs, the database is inconsistent.

A database management system can assure that a transaction such as this is either complete or not done at all. A logical unit of work is defined to be completed by a COMMIT on the part of the user. SQL does incorporate a COMMIT statement. This can be issued by the user or by a program using embedded SQL. Each COMMIT marks the beginning of a new unit of work.

The user or program can also ask for a ROLLBACK. This is a request for the DBMS to return the database to its status as of the last commit point. Judicious use of commits and rollbacks can greatly simplify data entry work.

Many systems will also, at startup, test for and roll back any incomplete transactions. These are presumed to be the result of some previous system failure.

Omission of appropriate COMMITs and ROLLBACKs can result in unnecessarily long recovery times. There can also be a performance issue if the number of locks held grows large. (Locking is the next topic we'll discuss.) There will be an overhead in processing the locks. Other transactions may be blocked.

Many systems are designed for multiple concurrent users. This is a must for a shared database in a mainframe or networked environment.

The journal file for a multi-user system will contain intermingled records of updates performed by concurrent tasks. The start transaction record, all before and after images, and the commit record will contain some form of transaction identifier. These will often be time stamped as well. This makes it possible for database utilities to restore or roll back as of a particular date and time.[51]

Concurrent access by multiple users introduces the possibility that two or more users may attempt to access the same data at the same time. As an example, two different ticket agents may request seat reservations on the same airline flight on behalf of two different customers. In a situation like this, it is likely that there will be two different work areas in computer memory, one for each transaction. There is, therefore, the likelihood that each transaction could observe the seat as available and claim it unbeknownst to the other. Multi-user database management systems generally provide *locks* to prevent this. The specification of SELECT FOR UPDATE or UPDATE notifies the DBMS that it is necessary to deny others access to that data until the transaction in question completes and issues either a COMMIT or ROLLBACK.

In an on-line system, most transactions finish very quickly and end users are often unaware of the wait.

A long running batch job which fails to issue frequent commits could have a severe impact on on-line work. Thus, establishing appropriate commit points is an important issue in batch program design.

Granularity of locks is another important issue. A system which supports individual row locks is likely to allow a much higher degree of concurrency than one which locks entire tables or databases. Some systems will lock pages rather than rows. Note that it may also be necessary for the system to lock index entries or pages if these are affected by an update. Some systems allow the selection of a locking option. Others have the option built in. Some systems will begin by locking rows or pages, but will, if a particular transaction acquires ownership of a large number of rows, escalate to a table level lock. There may be considerable overhead involved in managing a large number of locks.

Any number of read-only tasks may have shared access to the same data at the same time. It may also be appropriate for one or more read-only tasks to share data with one update task. This depends on the nature of the application, the data, and the transactions. It is necessary to consider this carefully in the design of a large on-line system. Different vendors have different techniques for dealing with this. It will be necessary to consult the documentation for your system.[52]

The design of a database or application which requires all or many transactions to update one single row occurrence, perhaps some sort of total, can reduce concurrency since each transaction must wait its turn for the data in question. This can have a significant effect on performance.

The possibility of conflicting locks can cause another problem. Suppose transaction A locks record 1 then requests record 2 while transaction B locks record 2 then requests record 1. Each must wait for the other to complete, but neither can complete. This is often referred to as a *deadlock*. The more poetic refer to it as a *deadly embrace*. It is necessary for the DBMS to recognize that this has occurred, then force a roll back for one transaction so the other can proceed. In a single vendor environment this will be handled automatically by the DBMS. There will be overhead and possibly noticeable delay but no special programming is required. In a multi-vendor environment, it may be necessary for the programmer to recognize and deal with this possibility. This problem cannot be completely eliminated, but it can be minimized by judicious database and program design.

- Denormalizing may eliminate the necessity for multi-table updates.
- Sequence constraints can reduce the likelihood of deadlock. For example, always obtain the savings account before the checking account or always obtain the lower part number first.
- Avoid total or summary records which must be updated by many different transactions. Or, if this is not possible, provide several; one total for each region instead of a single grand total, for example.

7.11   EXTRACT DATABASES

The popular notion of *database systems* is that sharing of data is promoted. This is generally considered desirable. There are, however, situations where sharing of a single database is not feasible.

- The design of an existing system or database may preclude sharing. This may be because of the particular way data is represented or encoded, because of the processing techniques used, because of the geographic location of the data, because of hardware capacity, or *just because.*
- Performance issues may preclude sharing. This is very likely given a heavy on-line transaction processing load plus a requirement for extensive batch processing or the existence of many long running queries.
- There may be applications which require static data for analysis, that is, data which does not change until the analysis is complete.
- There may be stringent data security requirements.
- Sharing mainframe-based data with a large number of microcomputer users can be particularly problematic.

In cases like these it is common to perform periodic *extracts* which produce copies of the data for specific uses. These may occur at regularly scheduled times. They may occur on an *as needed* basis. The extract does not have to be in the same format as the original data. Nor does it have to contain all of the data. Sometimes this is the only way to resolve conflicting requirements or performance issues. There is an obvious overhead in creating and storing the extracts.

Management and control can become serious issues. It is beneficial but difficult to keep track of all uses of the data, to make sure that data updates are propagated correctly, to maintain consistency between different copies of the same data, to consider the existence of extracts when evaluating changes, to control security, and even to assure that users understand the nature and source of the data they are using.

Endnotes

10. The topics in this chapter are all interrelated. As we've noted on other occasions, this makes it difficult to separate them and select a "best" sequence for presenting them. Keep in mind that the material in this chapter is a review of concepts and issues and that a step by step design procedure is provided in Chapter 9.

11. In this author's view the relational model is a tremendous intellectual achievement. The consistency of thought reflected by [CODD90] and the coherency of the complete theory are marvelous.

12. In fact, we often illustrate just one or two of several possible ways a thing might be done.

13. In accomplishing these things it is necessary to keep a proper perspective on the nature of the particular tasks to be automated, the importance of these tasks, the scale of the activity, and the cost of recovering from a problem. Let's consider some extremes. The author makes use of a simple relational database for tracking personal and business expenditures and income. This is maintained on a personal computer. In setting this up there was a need for an understanding of the types of data to be stored. It was necessary to give consideration to useful ways of classifying expenses, income, assets, and liabilities given the particular nature of the author's circumstances and activities. But it really wasn't necessary to spend days or weeks developing an elaborate entity relationship model. By the end of the year, the file of data reaches 1,200 to 1,500 records. This can be searched and listed in minutes no matter how it is arranged. Well, maybe there are ways that are extremely inappropriate and would make it take too long. However, if a given activity takes just a little longer, it is annoying, but it isn't a critical problem. If all the data were lost, it could be reconstructed from listings in a few days. In fact, the purpose of the whole business is to produce the appropriate listings, and once this has been done there is little need to access the data which has been listed. Thus, the primary objective was to get the database set up and get on with it. Some analysis and design took place, but it was minimal. However, all the effort would be wasted if all of the necessary data were not stored or if it were stored in some manner that precluded the desired processing. Don't take this discussion to mean that there are cases where no design whatsoever is necessary. And it is still wise to maintain backup copies, taken at appropriate intervals. Contrast this with, say, a major airline's reservation system, to choose an equally extreme alternative case. There is a lot of data. There are hundreds of flights per day with hundreds of seats on each flight. Reservations can be made weeks ahead of time. Schedule changes and changes in travel plans are frequent. Hundreds of agents all over the country are entering transactions all day long. Small fractions of a second count. The consequences of loss of the data are almost unthinkable. The design of a system like this is a major undertaking. Everything must be considered. Performance in terms of response time and transaction volume is critical. Time spent in making sure everything is as right as it can be is really a necessary business investment. Obviously, most activities lie somewhere between these extremes. It is usually important to make sure the analysis and design are thorough enough. But it is important to weigh the benefit against the investment. When doing this, don't forget that many business data processing systems are used for five or ten or even twenty years. A small inefficiency multiplied by thousands and thousands of transactions over a period of years can cost an organization a lot of money. It has probably been more common to err in the direction of too little analysis.

14. We are beginning to see some use of optical storage media. Some systems are also beginning to make extensive run time use of data stored in the computer's electronic memory. Most of the principles we discuss do also apply to these.

15. A system using a 2" diameter was introduced in 1989 but has failed to become popular so far (1992).

16. At least, this is the usual case. There are some devices which do store more data on the outer tracks. Some of the floppy disks used in the Apple Macintosh computer contain more data on the outer tracks.

17. Instead of saying 360,000 characters, one says 360K (three hundred and sixty "kay") bytes. The K is derived from Kilo for thousand. The K is really 1,024, a power of 2 (2^{10}). And, 1,440,000 is referred to as 1.44 M (one point four four "em") bytes. The M comes from mega or million. And, a million bytes is really 2^{20} or 1,048,576.

18. The numbers used in everyday life are decimal or base ten numbers. 1,327 is really $(7 \times 1) + (2 \times 10) + (3 \times 100) + (1 \times 1000)$. Base two or binary numbers are based on powers of two instead of powers of ten. 1101 is $(1 \times 1) + (0 \times 2) + (1 \times 4) + (1 \times 8)$ or 13. This is convenient because it is only necessary to differentiate between two possible states for each bit. Much computerized data is stored in this manner.

19. These are formed by combining a significant value with a scaling factor. 127,000 might be thought of as $1.27 \times 100,000$. This can save space because it is only necessary to store the 1.27 and a 6 indicating 6 places or 10 raised to the 6th power.

20. It isn't always this simple. It is possible to just miss catching the physical record as it goes by. A multiprogrammed system will go on to do other things and subsequently try again. And, there can be another missed rotation. The result is that a more precise calculation of disk access time involves an infinite series based on the probability of a missed rotation. We're getting a little ahead of ourselves here because we haven't discussed all of the components of a complex system. But the following conveys the flavor of what is involved. This material is extracted from an IBM internal document (ZZ05 - 0038 - 00) which discusses the characteristics of the IBM 3350 storage device. This information is probably about 15 years old at this time (1992). We do not claim that the exact same calculations would apply to any other device. But this illustrates the nature of the factors involved.   "At the time you initiate an IO operation, you may be delayed because somewhere in the path to the device, something is busy. If this does happen you should expect to be delayed half the length of time of the average busy operation... The probability that you will be blocked is the busy percentage divide by 100... So you can allocate a time for path delay at (Start IO) of D/2 * B/100 where D is the average length of time of a busy operation on the path and B is the path's busy percentage." ['*' is used for multiplication, '/' for division.] "Finally we break through and set the arm in motion. Now we must wait for the arm to get close and stop moving. This is the seek time....After the arm settles down an attempt as made to reconnect with the CPU. This is just like a start IO operation. The time... is the same, namely D/2 * B/100." "After you reconnect, the set sector causes a latency of half a revolution...What happens when the proper sector comes up and you try to reconnect with the channel? You may get delayed again. Only this time the average delay is one rotation... (and) A set sector has a probability of additional delay... The... formula (that) represents the time that can be allocated to set sector operations is R * ((B/100) + (B/100 ** 2) + (B/100 ** 3) +...+ (B/100 ** N))" (R represents the rotation time of the device. "**" is used for exponentiation) "It turns out that a very simple formula can be used to evaluate this: R * (B/100 – B)" "(The resulting path delay time is) D * B/100 + R * (B / (100 – B))"

21. Some devices incorporate logic to sequence a series of IO operations for optimal performance and disk cache memory can further cloud the issue. The result of all this is that the sim-

ple calculation is really just an estimate and it can be worthwhile to do some experimenting if precise performance data is needed.

22. And, these hard disk units for a large-scale mainframe environment cost hundreds of thousands of dollars.

23. Numbers used by computer systems are almost always powers of two.

24. This term is commonly used with regard to IBM mainframe computers.

25. In IBM parlance, a volume is a specific disk or tape.

26. Work volumes are used for sorting and for storing intermediate results.

27. System volumes contain operating system routines and files.

28. We are not suggesting that devices manufactured by others are not equally sophisticated.

29. "Overlapped Seeks" allow the controller to search for data on one disk drive while transferring data from another. "Optimized Seeks" provide for servicing multiple requests to the same disk in a sequence which minimizes arm movement. "Multiple Simultaneous Transfers" provides for data transfer from several disks at the same time. "Interdrive Rotational Optimization" allows the controller to optimize its activities based on the rotation of several disks. "Intradrive Rotational Optimization" selects a data access sequence which optimizes transfer based on the rotation of a single disk. "Intrarequest Rotational Optimization" minimizes the number of disk revolutions required to service a series of requests.

30. Here are two illustrative examples. The author currently makes use of a Digital Equipment Corporation VAX computer. On this system, at this time, all faculty directories are situated on a device which has been named DISK$FACULTY. Thus, DISK$FACULTY:[WERTZCJ] is the directory containing all subdirectories and files created by C. J. Wertz. The system maintains a master directory which leads here. It seemed convenient to create subdirectories named.STU for student and.SQL for sql. The students in a programming class may be instructed to access a file named DISK$FACULTY:[WERTZCJ.STU]PROBLEM1A.PAS which contains a Pascal program for problem 1. On the author's *personal* personal computer the directory D:\WP51\WRITING contains references to a series of files, including D:\WP51\WRITING\CH-7.WP which is the text of this chapter. WP and WP51, by the way, stand for WordPerfect 5.1 and WordPerfect, respectively. (The name "WordPerfect" is the property of WordPerfect Corporation as are all rights to the word processing program by that name.) '/', '\', and '.' are often used as separators between components of file and directory names. Filenames are often made up of at least two components, a basic name portion plus an extension indicating a file type. Using another VAX based example, PROBLEM1A.PAS would be Pascal source code, PROBLEM1A.OBJ would be object code produced by the compiler, and PROBLEM1A.EXE would be executable code produced by the linkage editor. If one types "DELETE PROBLEM1A.*" all three are gone.

31. In many cases, bank account identifiers for example, numbers can not be reused immediately. Each number that is not reused will cause one record worth of disk space to be wasted. In the case of a self-checking number, only one of every ten possible numbers will be used. The use of Social Security number as an identifier provides an extremely bad example. It will be necessary to allocate disk space for 1,000,000,000 records no matter how few are actually used.

32. A prime number is not evenly divisible by anything but one and itself.

33. If you are interested in more detail on this topic, see almost any standard textbook, [FRANK88] or [MACFADDEN88], for example.

34. Some research has been done in the area of dynamic hashing schemes. See [FRANK88], Chapter 3. But few, if any, commercial products use them.

35. There could be very special situations which would warrant this. But these would be cases where there are significant performance constraints, and a fair degree of programming expertise would be required.

36. Of course, the most modern libraries are replacing card catalogs with on-line databases. Soon we'll need a new example.

37. Once again, all the detail is not relevant here. The reader is again referred to a text such as [FRANK88] or [MACFADDEN88] for more detail.

38. This type of structure is sometimes referred to as a B+ Tree.

39. There are also indexed access methods which can be used directly from a program. Many programs which have been developed without a database management system use these.

40. DATABASE2 is a registered trademark of the IBM Corporation.

41. If a clustering index is provided, the data will be in key sequence or close to it.

42. We've used '/' as the symbol for divide. This notation is used in SQL as well as in many programming languages.

43. See, for example, [CHOUINARD89], [INMON87], and [INMON89].

44. To say that it is always possible to get any arrangement would be a very broad statement. We don't want to be that rash. It would only take one counter example to disprove such a claim! We are satisfied to say that, in our experience, it has been possible to produce just about any desired arrangement from the normalized form.

45. These are often referred to as "ad hoc" queries. In common usage, this term means "for this purpose only." It is often incorporated in the designation of a committee which will accomplish a specific purpose and then disband. Thus, it has been adopted to identify "one of a kind" spontaneous database queries.

46. By the definition of a relation, the result can not contain duplicate rows. The database management system must make sure that none are introduced when these operations are performed.

47. This is another statement that we can't really prove. But it seems reasonable. The examples in Chapter 6 illustrate derivations of combinations from normalized tables.

48. MS-DOS is a registered trademark of Microsoft Corporation.

49. Strictly speaking, a schema and a database are not really the same thing at all. The schema is a description of the database. Whether one is creating the database or its description may be a subtle distinction right here.

50. There is the need for the arm to accelerate, then decelerate. So this isn't exactly true.

51. The Norton Utilities family of products marketed by Symantec is one of several products with this capability. This is mentioned as an example. We make no claim that it is better or worse than any other product.

52. A beta-test Version 7 of ORACLE began shipping on June 15, 1992. There are, however, shops that are still using Version 5.

53. This discussion is based on information contained in [ORACLE86]. We've mentioned before that ORACLE is a registered trademark of Oracle Corporation.

54. See [ORACLE88].

55. This discussion is based on [IBM88-3] and [WIORKOWSKI88]. And, as mentioned, DATA-BASE2 is a registered trademark of IBM.

56. The largest integer that can be stored in n bits is $2^n - 1$. 2 bytes is 16 bits. One bit is used for the sign. $2^{15} - 1$ is 32,767. Some machines also provide an unsigned integer format which uses all 16 bits. In this case, the maximum will be 65,535.

57. $2^{31} - 1$ is 2,147,483,647.

58. Here are some examples. The intent is to indicate the nature of this, not to provide the last word. Be sure to refer to documentation for your system.
DATABASE2 Version 2.1 [IBM88-1] provides these SQL data types: INTEGER is a System/370 binary integer which can range from -2147483648 to $+2147483647$ and occupies 4 bytes.
SMALLINT is a System/370 binary integer which can range from -32768 to $+32767$ and occupies 2 bytes.
FLOAT is a System/370 floating point number consisting of exponent and characteristic. Single precision floating point numbers occupy 4 bytes and range from 5.4×10^{-79} to 7.2×10^{75}. Double precision floating point numbers occupy 8 bytes and provide more significant digits.
DECIMAL is a System/370 packed decimal number. Each byte contains two decimal digits. An additional 1/2 byte is required for the sign.
CHAR is a fixed length character field.
VARCHAR is a variable length character field with a length up to 254 characters. There is a length indicator.
LONG VARCHAR is used for strings longer than 254.
GRAPHIC, VARGRAPHIC, and LONG VARGRAPHIC are used for storing double byte characters representing graphics.
DATE is used to store dates consisting of year, month, and day in a 4-byte format.
TIME is used to store times consisting of hour, minute, and second in a 3-byte format.
TIMESTAMP is used to store date and time in a 7-byte format.
ORACLE Version 6.0 [ORACLE88] provides these SQL datatypes: CHAR and VARCHAR are equivalent and are used to store character data in a variable-length format— a "length byte" (i.e., one byte containing the length), followed by the data stored, one character per byte, up to a 255 character maximum.
NUMBER is used to store numbers. One may specify NUMBER or NUMBER (precision, scale) with *precision* indicating the number of digits and *scale* indicating the number of digits to the right of the decimal point. (A negative *scale* indicates a rounding to eliminate insignificant digits.) ORACLE uses its own proprietary internal numeric format to achieve portability from one hardware "platform" to another and to assure precision. A NUMBER as stored consists of a length byte, followed by a byte containing the sign and an exponent (used for scaling), followed by up to 20 data bytes (each containing two digits). The digits are actually binary numbers representing base 100 digits; each can represent a number from 0 to 99.
DATE is used to store dates consisting of year, month, day, hour, minute, and second in a special 7-byte fixed-length field.
LONG is used to store variable-length character data up to 65,5356 characters long.

59. Of course, this is not the only way. It is beyond our scope to evaluate all of the possibilities. Comparable performance issues will apply to all techniques.

60. This is the case for most systems. There are other ways to do this. Some systems retain multiple copies of data in the database itself.

61. IBM's DATABASE2 product provides a *repeatable read* option which, if invoked, assures that no other user will alter data that has been read until the "reader" commits. ORACLE version 6.0 will retain an "original copy" of data that is read by one user and changed by another to assure that the first user has a consistent view of the data until commit.

QUESTIONS AND EXERCISES

1. Why is it important to know something about hardware?

2. What are the motives for most physical database design activities?

3. Define bit, byte, field, record, file, track, cylinder, and sector.

4. What are ASCII and EBCDIC?

5. Explain seek time, rotational delay, and data transfer time?

6. What are the significant similarities and differences between hashing and indexing?

7. Why are indexes particularly important in relational systems?

8. Why is optimization important? Why does a designer need to be aware of this issue?

9. How can one decide whether or not to implement the normalized design?

10. What are the pitfalls of denormalization?

11. Why is it that space calculation is not straightforward?

12. What is fragmentation? Why is it an issue?

13. Discuss the relationship between locking and database design.

14. What is the journal used for?

Chapter 8

Distributed Systems

8.1 CHAPTER SUMMARY

In this chapter, we discuss the nature of distributed systems and review the elements of distributed database design. There is one new aspect. *We have to decide where the data should be kept.*

There has been a lot of discussion of distributed systems, distributed database, and distributed database management in the literature and the trade press. It seems common to discuss principles and theories in a manner which makes it seem that software implementations are available today.[1] Distributed database systems is an evolving and relatively immature technology. It is necessary to check the precise capabilities of specific software products very carefully before designing a distributed database or system.

We can still say quite a few useful things about distributed database systems and their design. Possibilities for distribution should be evaluated in the design of new systems and also if extensive modifications to existing systems are contemplated. It may be necessary to take a *roll your own* implementation approach and incorporate management of the distributed data in your programs. Or, it may be advisable to limit the approach to distribution in order to stay within the current capabilities of your software. Or, you may even decide to hold off for a while. In any event, the content of this chapter will help you understand the concepts and issues, evaluate the choices, select an approach, and design a database.

8.2 WHAT IS A DISTRIBUTED SYSTEM?

In a *distributed system*, separate components work together. This is usually taken to mean separate machines at separate locations linked together by some form of communications network. A *distributed database* has been divided into separate parts stored at separate locations. Each part can be referenced independently of the others or they may be viewed as a whole and accessed together. A *distributed database management system* does everything any other database management system does and also manages the details of processing the distributed data.[2] The ideal distributed database management system conceals the distribution and its details from the user.

If the DBMS does take over the details of managing the distributed data, the tasks of programmers and implementors will be simplified. It's another example of the trend to move details into system software. *The task of the designer may not be simplified. Someone must still decide how to allocate data and processing to locations.*

A historical perspective is useful.

The first computer systems were single-user systems capable of working on one problem at a time. Originally the user or programmer interacted directly with the machine by setting switches or possibly typing at a console. Soon printing capabilities were added. More computing was obtained by acquiring either a larger computer or additional computers. The economics of computer manufacture and use seemed to dictate larger, more powerful computers as the best means of growth. *Grosch's Law* [3] stated that computing power could be obtained according to the square of the cost of the equipment—three times the cost would provide nine times the power. Additional systems would also mean additional overhead, additional operators, and additional space (in the days when a computer was the size of a large room). Since additional systems would be completely independent, there would be little sharing of data.

This environment led to *batch processing*. Users submitted data on special forms. The data was then converted to a machine readable form by trained key punch operators. The resulting punch cards, paper tape, or magnetic media was fed to the machine by computer operators. Eventually printed output was produced and distributed to the users, often a day or two later. If there were errors in the input, it was necessary to correct them and go through another cycle. Most large enterprises developed a sizable infrastructure concerned with the management of this process, the collection of input, and the distribution of output. Systems and procedures were developed in a manner suitable to this environment. The users were often awed, intimidated, and frustrated in their dealings with the centralized technocracy. Remnants of this environment and this design philosophy are frequently found today.

With the development of *multiprogramming* it became possible for a computer system to work on several different jobs concurrently. This is advantageous because internal processing speeds are so much faster than most input-output devices. One task can proceed while others wait for data transfer operations. This does introduce additional complexities; for example, the need for locking and concurrency control.

At first, this had no effect on the general approach to computing. Then, coupling the advent of multiprogramming with data communications technology made it possible for many users at remote terminals to interact directly with the central computer system. This gave rise to completely different concepts of system and program design. It became possible for a user to enter data directly and receive an immediate response. If it was necessary to correct an error, it could now be done immediately. Many organizations and many system designers were slow to appreciate the full implications of this possibility. Even when the implications were appreciated, it was still time-consuming and expensive to redesign, reprogram, and retrain. The transition from batch to on-line has been gradual and most organizations still have a mixture. Certain operations which require access to or update of large volumes of data are still done best in a batch mode.

The new style of computing was still marked by large central computer centers, staffs of professional operators and programmers, and a continued life for the organizational technocracy. In fact, as an organization's network of terminals became more extensive, it usually became necessary for the computer center and support staff to grow correspondingly. With increasing loads it became necessary to acquire ever larger and more powerful computers and frequently to install multiple computers at the center. The term *multiprocessor* describes a complex of several computers which share memory and storage, perhaps under the control of a single operating system.[4]

Some time in the 1970s or 1980s, the economics of computing changed. We might say that the electronics industry repealed Grosch's law. It became possible to obtain relatively powerful minicomputers and microcomputers at very low prices. This made it reasonable for corporate divisions and departments and even individual end users to obtain separate computers. We began to hear of *departmental computing* and *personal computers*.[5]

Most *departmental systems* tend to be scaled down mainframe systems. While they usually do not require such extensive support staffs, programs must still come from somewhere. The use of smaller systems by smaller businesses has provided vendors of standardized software packages with many marketing opportunities.

Until very recently, personal computers have been single user systems. Since one video screen and one keyboard are associated with one computer it is not easy for more than one person to make use of the system at any given time. As a result, microcomputer software has been less complicated than software for mainframe systems. Newer microcomputer systems do provide for multiprogramming, but this normally means that an individual user can manage multiple concurrent activities. Most users of personal computers purchase general purpose spreadsheet, word processing, and database programs.

There are limitations to what can be accomplished with separate independent systems. Each stand-alone system becomes *an island of information*. Cooperation and exchange of data become difficult or impossible. The next step is the interconnection of geographically separated computers and the development of software and database systems which *distribute* the data and the processing. This really means we'd like the processors and data at the various locations to cooperate and form a coherent whole.

It is very likely that part of the motivation for the move to departmental and personal computers has been the desire to take advantage of new technology and part of it has been the desire to be free of a perceived tyranny of the central data processing organization.

Figure 8.1 illustrates the contrast between the different types of systems.

IBM [IBM88-4] [IBM88-6] suggests several possible "levels of distributed relational processing."

- "Remote *requests* enable a user to read and update data at a remote system." Individual queries or updates sent to the remote system become separate *units of work*. It is not possible to COMMIT or ROLLBACK a series of requests. It may be necessary for the program or the user to specify the location of the data.

- "Remote *unit of work*... allows for transactions that encompass a number of relational database requests." The remote site retains information about the requestor

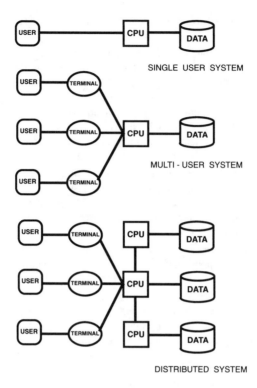

SINGLE USER SYSTEM

MULTI - USER SYSTEM

DISTRIBUTED SYSTEM

Figure 8.1 **Possible arrangements**

until a series of requests has been completed. Again, it may be necessary for the program or the user to specify the location of the data.

- "Distributed *unit of work* enables a user or application program to read or update data at multiple locations within a unit of work." It is necessary to issue a separate request for each action at each location. Involving several sites in a single transaction makes it necessary to coordinate COMMIT or ROLLBACK processing so that all systems do the same thing at the same time. Reading data from multiple sites is much simpler than performing update which involve multiple sites.

- *Distributed request* differs from distributed unit of work by allowing a single request to affect multiple sites. This requires the greatest sophistication on the part of the DBMS. Given the best implementation of this concept, neither the program nor the user will need to be aware of the location(s) of the data and the program will not change no matter how the data is divided or assigned to locations.

Date [DATE90] states "each site is a database system in its own right" and observes that "enterprises normally *are* distributed already, at least logically (into divisions, departments, projects, etc.), and very likely physically as well (into plants, factories, laboratories, etc.)—from which it follows that data normally is already distributed as well." We agree that a systems architecture which matches the structure of the enterprise seems highly desirable. We'd like to adopt as a guiding principle the notion that *it makes sense to distribute data if the organization and the processing are distributed.* The more detailed design recommendations found later in this chapter will support this assertion.

Date provides some rules for distributed database systems. These are much like Codd's rules for relational database systems.

Rule Zero, the fundamental principle: "To the user, a distributed system should look exactly like a non-distributed system."

The user should not need to be aware of the distribution of the data. True and complete data independence should allow the database administrators and designers to relocate and rearrange data with no impact on users or programs.

Rule 1, Local autonomy: "The sites in a distributed system should be autonomous."

The data should be locally owned and managed. Users at each location should maintain control of their data. However, local autonomy does not mean each site can do whatever it wants. There must be some management and standardization of the distributed system as a whole to ensure that the components can and do work together in a harmonious manner.

Rule 2, No reliance on a central site: "There must not be any reliance on a central or master site."

If the failure of a central site could render the entire system inoperable, one of the big advantages of distributed systems would be negated.

Rule 3, Continuous operation: "There should never be any need for a planned system shutdown."

The ability to create backup copies of the data and make changes to the system without halting operations is essential for continuous operation. A distributed approach *may* make it possible to shut down one site for backup or modifications without affecting the others. Coordination of backups and changes across sites will still be a significant problem.

Rule 4, Location independence: "Users should not have to know where data is physically stored."

Obviously the system must have some way of locating the data. If the distributed DBMS is to take care of this, the system catalog must be extended to deal with data stored at several sites.[6] If this is not the case, the programs will have to deal with this issue. In the latter case, the system may be distributed, but the DBMS is not.

Rule 5, Fragmentation independence: "Data can be stored at the location where it is most frequently used."

It must then be possible to divide, fragment, or partition the data in just about any manner imaginable. And, the system must be able to reassemble it as required.

Rule 6, Replication independence: "a relation... can be represented by many distinct stored copies."

This may be necessary for performance reasons. It is then necessary to make sure that the copies do remain identical.

Rule 7, Distributed query processing: "Optimization is... clearly crucial."

We've discussed optimization in Chapter 7. Multiple sites must complicate this problem. Decisions regarding strategy must consider where the data is located and select appropriate locations for performing intermediate activities. The optimizer can do its job best if it has access to statistics about data values, data volumes, and data locations. The optimizer may need to query other locations to obtain the information it needs in order to decide how to handle a transaction.

Rule 8, Distributed transaction management: "There are two major aspects to transaction management, recovery control and concurrency control."

Distribution makes these much more complex. Where are locks maintained? How are they coordinated? Recovery must also be coordinated across locations. Suppose a transaction involves several locations and there is a failure at one. Transaction management across locations generally involves extra messages which coordinate activities.

Rule 9, Hardware independence: "It is desirable to be able to run the same DBMS on different hardware systems."

An organization may have different hardware at different locations. This may result from the preferences of the staff at the sites. It may be a question of economics. Different hardware may just be more suitable at different places.

Distributed systems are classified as *homogeneous* (the same or essentially the same hardware and software at all sites) or *heterogeneous* (different hardware and/or software at different sites). One can also discuss homogeneity at a database design level (given the same hardware and software environment at all sites, there could still be different database designs at different sites) or at a semantic level (data encodings and meanings may or may not be consistent across sites). Sheth and Larsen [SHETH90] discuss *federated systems* which cooperate without forming a coherent whole. They provide an extensive taxonomy of possibilities. Suffice to say that one can imagine and label numerous possibilities, some fairly practical, some quite esoteric.

Rule 10, Operating system independence: "It is desirable... also to be able to run (the same DBMS) on different operating systems."

Rule 11, Network independence: "It is... desirable to support a variety of disparate communication networks also."

Rule 12, DBMS independence: "All that is needed is that the DBMSs at different sites *all support the same interface.*" Many have anticipated that widespread use of SQL will make this a reality.

As is the case with Codd's rules for relational database, these provide an ambitious set of goals which are yet to be fully realized.

Stonebraker[7] provides an equally demanding set of seven rules calling for Retrieval Transparency, Update Transparency, Scheme Transparency (it should be possible to update data definitions from any site), Performance Transparency (the same command should perform the same entered from any site), Transaction Transparency (includes multi-site updating and multi-site transaction management), Copy Transparency (multiple copies of the same data), and Tool Transparency (all software should work at all locations).

Several observations follow.

The processing of one transaction or query at multiple sites must generally be more complex than it would be if all processing took place at one site.

Optimization must be more difficult. Optimization requires knowledge of data characteristics, locations, and volumes. For example, it is necessary to know how many rows of each table are stored at each site. If the relevant information for each site is retained at the site, it will be necessary for the optimizer to query all sites before selecting a strategy for processing the transaction. If the information is retained at the central site, there will be more overhead in keeping it current, the overall system will be vulnerable to failure of the central site, and it will be necessary for transactions initiated and processed at remote sites to query the central site. (There doesn't really have to be a central site, by the way.) If the information is duplicated there will also be problems.[8]

It is also necessary as a part of optimization to decide what processing will take place at what location(s), what data will be moved from one location to another, and where any intermediate results will be developed.

Concurrency control and recovery from system failure must be more difficult.

It is necessary to decide whether all locks will be kept at a central site or whether each site will keep its own locks. Reliance on the central site will introduce additional traffic and vulnerability to failure of the central site. The same is true for journals and recovery processing.

The most common solution is called the *two-phase commit*. One site, not necessarily the central site, accepts responsibility for managing a unit of work. When this location determines that all processing should be complete, it queries all of the locations involved in the transaction. Each location will then respond that it is or is not ready to commit. Each site that signals it is ready to commit must now maintain enough information to either commit or rollback. If all locations respond affirmative, the coordinating site advises them to proceed. If any location responds in the negative or does not respond within an appropriate time interval, the coordinating site advises all locations to roll back.

Recovery at several sites will also be more complex.

There are additional complexities and alternatives to locking and journaling that we won't go into here.

Enforcement of constraints, resolution of problems, and maintenance of security must be more difficult. Constraint checking, for example, may involve querying other sites.

Systems which operate with the same or similar hardware and software at all sites must generally be easier to implement and manage than those which do not.

Relational systems lend themselves better to distributed processing because it is possible for a single request to a remote site to initiate extensive processing which produces a single result. In comparison, older style (record-at-a-time) systems must entail significant overhead. The use of SQL as a standard interface simplifies communication in mixed systems.

Many software systems which have been available provide support for distributed query processing but place restrictions on updating. Some systems will not allow a single transaction to perform updates at several remote locations. Others allow data at multiple sites to be updated but require special programming to deal with this situation.[9, 10] The designer is well advised to be very sure of the capabilities and limitations of the specific software at hand. Remote access to data is one thing and distributed database is another. Most vendors have been doing a lot of work in this area with the result that restrictions present when this is written (1992) may not be present when you read it.[11] You must also realize that it takes time to transmit data from one location to another and there is overhead associated with coordinating activities whether or not the database management system handles it all automatically.

Design and planning must be at least as important to a distributed system as to a centralized system; and it certainly seems they must be more important in the former case. A collection of disparate systems which can communicate but do not share any common data formats or rules doesn't form a distributed system.

The conceptual and logical design process for a distributed system need not be substantially different from that for a nondistributed system. The most significant difference is the addition of a requirement that information be gathered about the geographic locations of the users of the data. Processing patterns and volumes as well as data volume patterns become more important.

Physical design will, of course, be affected. Whether or not distribution and data location is transparent to the user or the programmer, *an injudicious allocation of data to sites will result in additional, possibly intolerable, overhead and delay.* The data must still be moved from one place to another even if it does happen automatically. The distinction between logical design and physical design can be very apparent here.

Since distribution introduces additional complexities and pitfalls, *there should be a good reason for embarking on this course*; for the same reason, a simpler solution involving less distribution or a less complex distribution should be favored.

The first question, then, is whether or not to distribute.

8.3   SHOULD THE DATA BE DISTRIBUTED?

Section 8.4 presents some techniques for finding the best allocation of data to sites. Since placing all the data in one place is a choice, these techniques could be used to decide whether or not a particular database should be distributed. There are some more general issues that can be examined first. It may be that the most significant issues are not technical and do not involve costs versus benefits.

King [KING83] observes "A behavioral assessment suggests that the driving issues in the debate are politics of organization and resources, centering on the issue of control. The economics of computing deployment decisions are presented as an important issue, but one that often serves as a field of argument in which political concerns are dealt with."

Ideally, we'd determine whether or not a distributed approach is appropriate to the structure of the organization.

King discusses centralization versus decentralization in three perspectives: control, physical location, and function.

Centralization of *control* favors decision making by either top management or a central MIS group. This will promote consistency. It may also promote mindless bureaucracy. Decentralization favors decision making by lower level managers and local groups. These may be closer to the problem and have a better understanding. This approach will foster diversity and creativity. There can be too much diversity and creativity.

Centralization of *physical location* realizes any potential economies of scale and may result in the deployment of more sophisticated technologies.

Centralization of *function* provides more standardization and tighter management. Decentralization allows greater individual discretion.

The decision would involve analysis of the nature of the organization and its management style. In practice, these decisions may be made by management based on organizational politics, and the database designer may have to do his or her best within the constraints set in this manner.[12]

[GUIDE81] identifies factors which might influence the decision.

- *Central host saturation* may result from an increase in business volume, development of new applications, the need for voluminous local processing prior to update of the database, extensive processing which does not require access to the central database.
- *User control of data* may be desirable to align authority with responsibility, to allow local access with *user friendly* software, to allow users to schedule their own work, or to establish local accountability.
- *Security* may be enhanced by centralization. Decentralization may allow different security levels for different databases. Lack of secure data communications facilities may negate any advantage of distribution. Distribution may facilitate tailoring security to local schedules.
- *Backup and recovery* may be more difficult in a distributed environment. Planned redundancy may provide a painless form of backup.
- *Tuning* for performance of individual systems may be easier because the loads on individual processors will be less complex. Tuning the overall environment will be more difficult.
- Individual sites will be less affected by *failures at other sites*.
- *Incremental growth* may be cost effective.
- There may be a need to deploy *more technical expertise at remote sites*.

Distributing data and processing across multiple sites can provide benefits if the distribution matches the business.

- Transmission of data can be reduced.
- Sites can become relatively autonomous and independent of each other.
- System outages and other problems at one site will not affect other sites.

Ozsu and Valduriez cite these *advantages* for distributed systems: local autonomy, improved performance, improved reliability/availability, economics, expandability, and shareability.

They enumerate these *disadvantages*: lack of experience, complexity, cost, distribution of control, security, and difficulty of change.

They note these *problem areas*: distributed database design, distributed query processing, distributed directory management, distributed concurrency control, distributed deadlock management, and reliability.

The introduction of distributed processing may profoundly affect the way an organization operates. This can be an advantage if the transition is planned and the new ways are beneficial. It can be wrenching and devastating if the changes are neither foreseen nor managed.

There are many computing tasks which can best be accomplished through the use of smaller stand alone systems. There are also some things which require users at multiple locations to share information or work together.

An uncontrolled and unmanaged proliferation of independent systems may lead to just the sort of data duplication and inconsistency that we'd like to avoid if at all possible.

In the next section we begin the discussion of design decisions. We will, as much as possible, leave internal details of distributed DBMS's to the designers and implementors of those systems and concentrate on database design topics.

8.4 WHAT ARE THE PHYSICAL DESIGN ISSUES FOR DISTRIBUTED SYSTEMS?

All of the design criteria discussed in the preceding chapter are relevant here. The optimal design for a distributed system will meet two additional requirements:

- There is a need to *minimize transmission of data from one location to another.*
- There is a need to *minimize cost of managing the database system.*

The former is, of course, a primary reason for developing distributed systems. We might say that in a centralized system the transaction is sent to the data while in a distributed system the data is sent to the transaction. We can observe that data which is created and used at one location tends to be best stored at that location, while data which is created and used at many locations tends to be best stored at a central location. Our attention will therefore focus on data placement or allocation. Figure 8.2 illustrates the main possibilities.

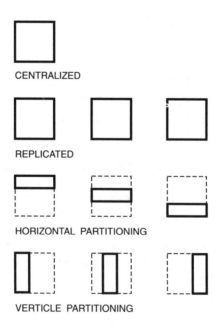

Figure 8.2 Distribution choices

All the data may be stored in one place. We've already called this *centralized*. This makes it necessary for all data access to take place at the central site.

Each site or node may retain a copy of all data. This is known as a *replicated* system. For the right application, this is a good choice. Since all references to data are made locally, communication costs are minimized. If a large amount of data must be duplicated, the cost of storage may render this an unwise choice. An even greater cost can be incurred when the data must be altered since all copies must be changed. This could be a very expensive proposition and it is necessary to make sure that all copies are in fact altered in a consistent and timely manner. Thus we can state that, in general, *replication is a good choice for applications which query static data.*

Suppose, for example, that an order entry application must query a database of part description information and that these descriptions are altered infrequently. Given that the descriptions can be stored economically, all preliminary order preparation and validation might be done locally. It would of course be necessary to provide a mechanism for distributing revisions to this information. Possibly an entire new file would be sent during off hours. But it would not be practical to keep track of the inventory available at a central location in a similar manner. Each new order might require that the records at all locations be altered.

The remaining alternative is to divide the data somehow. This approach is called *partitioned* or *fragmented*. The objective to be achieved in allocating fragments to sites is of course to assure, if possible, that the data to be used by a particular transaction is stored at the site where the transaction is to be processed.

In *horizontal partitioning*, identically formatted records are distributed across sites.

For example, all static data about customers serviced by a particular sales office might be stored at that sales office.

In *vertical partitioning*, portions of data describing a single entity are allocated to different sites.

Customer sales history might be retained by the marketing department, while credit history for the same customers might be retained by the accounting department.

There is no reason that the strategies cannot be combined.

Figure 8.3 illustrates the example we've been constructing in a piecemeal manner here:

- Part Inventory is stored in central site,
- Part Descriptions are replicated,
- Parts Data in its entirety is partitioned vertically between Inventory and Descriptions.
- Customer Static Data (such as name and address) is partitioned horizontally, while
- Customer Accounting Data is partitioned vertically.

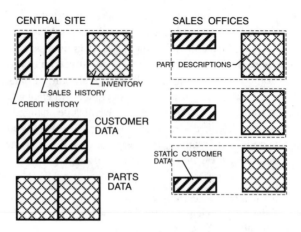

Figure 8.3   Replication and fragmentation

- Customer Data in its entirety is partitioned vertically between the static and dynamic components.

Thus, the primary design decisions involve determining if a distributed database should be implemented and, if so, devising appropriate allocations of data to sites.

8.5   HOW CAN WE DECIDE?

It's easy to describe an idealized approach. Compile access patterns and volumes for all transactions by location along with the costs of storing data at each site and the cost of transmitting data between each pair of sites; then mathematically calculate the least cost, optimal solution. It would also be necessary to assess the impact of possible future changes in patterns, volumes, or costs. This presumes that one can obtain reliable information about the patterns, volumes, and costs. This is the sort of problem which doesn't lend itself to a simple analytic solution and must be solved by a trial and error or heuristic search approach.

In cases such as those we've used for examples so far, the conclusion may be fairly obvious. In other cases, it may be valuable to go through a detailed analysis. In either event, the principles which follow will prove useful. We'll review all of the ideas and suggest some specific ways to perform the analysis.

Teorey [TEOREY90] suggests two approaches to the calculation.[13] "The *nonredundant 'best fit' method* determines the single most likely site to allocate a fragment based on maximum benefit, where benefit is interpreted to mean total query and update references. In particular, place fragment r at site s where the number of local query and update references by all the user transactions is maximized."

"The *redundant 'all beneficial sites' method* selects all sites for a fragment allocation where the benefit is greater than the cost for one additional copy of the fragment."

This means you need a cost of storage. The perfect number to use would be the actual cost associated with storing x bytes of information at site y. This would have to include a percentage of the cost of the device, the cost of maintaining and backing up the data at that site, and possibly a percentage of the overhead (staff, electricity, rent, etc.) for the site. In practice it can be difficult to impossible to obtain this sort of information. It may still be possible to arbitrarily assign a reasonable number. You also need a cost of not storing at the site. This would be the cost associated with communication with some other site. The comment about the availability of the information applies here.

These seem to take the determination of the fragments for granted. But different allocations of attributes to fragments could certainly affect the outcome of these calculations. So the solution of the allocation problem must be preceded by the solution of the fragmentation problem. You might attempt the solution of both problems at once, but this would be quite difficult.

Ozsu and Valduriez [OSZU91] describe some principles and methods for selecting fragments. These provide the basis for the next part of this discussion.

- The fragmentation must be *correct*. This means the set of fragments must be *complete* in that each data item found in the original relation(s) does appear in some fragment.
- It must be possible to *reconstruct* the original relation(s) from the fragments using relational operations.
- And the set of fragments must be *disjoint* (any given element must appear in but one fragment). The fragments do not absolutely have to be disjoint, but if they are not, any update will affect multiple locations. It may, in fact, be very difficult to determine how many locations must be updated, and maintaining consistency and integrity will be *much* more difficult.

In the case of a horizontal fragmentation, item can be taken to mean row or tuple. In the case of vertical fragmentation, item can be taken to mean column or attribute. In the case of vertical fragmentation it is necessary to include the key of the original relation in both fragments to meet the reconstruction requirement.

Horizontal fragments are determined by the queries and updates (or predicates) which will be used.

If, for example, a bank has two regions and a given account must be in one region or the other, region could form the basis for fragmentation as shown in Figure 8.4a.

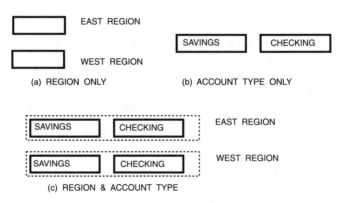

Figure 8.4 Partitioning

There may be additional possibilities. The bank's accounts might also be subdivided by type; for example, any deposit account must be either checking or savings. This is illustrated by Figure 8.4b.

If both schemes are to prevail we can form four fragments as shown by Figure 8.4c, subdividing each account type by region (or each region by account type) because any given account must still fall into but one of the four fragments. Note the implications of this.

- If we know account type and region, we can direct the query or update against one fragment.

- If we only know account type, it will be necessary to direct the query or update against the union of the two region fragments. In the case of a query, it will be necessary to query both locations or form the union by bringing data from one location to another. In the case of an update, it is necessary to determine which fragment contains the data to be updated.

- If we only know region it will be necessary to direct the query against the union of the two account type fragments. This is similar to the preceding.

- And, if either of the latter two cases is common, this four-way partitioning will be much less desirable.

If some activities involve a join of two or more tables, one table might be partitioned on the basis of the value of a foreign key which references another. A join between fragments stored at different locations must introduce additional overhead because there must be some transfer of data between the locations.

Suppose the bank we've been discussing maintains customer data separately from account data. Then there would be but one copy of the customer data no matter how many accounts, and some form of customer identifier would appear as foreign key in each account relation. Since this would lead us to think of the customer relation as the *owner* of several account relations, we'd like to assign each customer to a region and then assign all accounts for that customer to the same region as shown in Figure 8.5a. This is fine as long as it is not possible for the customer to have accounts in more than one region as shown in Figure 8.5b. We might still make the decision to store the customer data at one location or another, but the entire scheme seems much less workable.

If a relation contains more than one foreign key, it will be necessary to select one of the referenced relations as the owner. This choice can be based on the relative frequency of access. Favor the access path used most frequently. The join characteristics of each access path might also be examined.

An appropriate fragmentation may be quite obvious. If this is not the case we'll need to look more carefully at the predicates or search arguments used by our applications.

We'll identify *predicates* or search arguments used in queries or transactions. They may be *simple predicates* involving single attributes or *complex predicates* involving multiple attributes. We may be able to identify these in terms of discrete values. We may be able to identify them in terms of ranges of values. In doing this we ask if the additional predicates do in fact add new requirements. Suppose that in our banking example all accounts of a given type must be assigned to a given region. Then using type as an additional basis for fragmentation would not add anything.

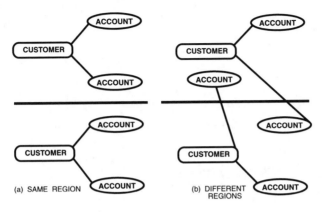

Figure 8.5 Partitioning Sets

Then we can evaluate the possibility of creating fragments based on these predicates. We ask if there are specific values for specific predicates which are only used from specific locations. If so, we can consider assigning the tuples with those values to their appropriate locations.

If this is not the case, we can ask if there are values which are much more likely to be used from one location than any other. If so we can assign a cost to remote data access and calculate total access cost as

> Sum for All Activities
>
> Volume of Activity ×
>
> (percent local access × cost of local access
>
> + percent access from site A × cost site A access
>
> + percent access from site B × cost site B access
>
> +...)

If we can find an allocation which minimizes this cost we have a solution. (If we can determine that for some reason it will be more expensive to store data at one location than another, we must add a sum of number of rows at site A × cost of storage at site A + number of rows at site B × cost of storage at site B +... If there is no difference we can ignore this factor.)

There are a few practical problems here.

- We need a *lot* of information about transactions, queries, predicates, and volumes.
- We need to be able to assign costs to remote data accesses. These can be relative costs if specific costs can not be obtained.
- If there are very many different transactions or very many different locations to consider, this will be a big calculation. But it can be set up as a worksheet or spreadsheet, as shown in Figure 8.6.

PREDICATE:
xxx

VALUE(S):	aaa	bbb	ccc
LOCATION:	SITE A	SITE B	SITE C

Source of Query:

SITE A	cost of % local access	cost B % from A	cost C % from A	sum of (cost × %)
SITE B	cost A % from B	cost of % local access	cost C % from B	sum of (cost × %)
SITE C	cost A % from C	cost B % from C	cost of % local access	sum of (cost × %)
				sum

PREDICATE:
yyy

VALUE(S)	uuu	vvv	www
LOCATION	SITE A	SITE B	SITE C

Source of Query:

SITE A	cost of % local access	cost B % from A	cost C % from A	sum of (cost × %)
SITE B	cost A % from B	cost of % local access	cost C % from B	sum of (cost × %)
SITE C	cost A % from C	cost B % from C	cost of % local access	sum of (cost × %)
				sum
				sum all costs

Figure 8.6   Analysis of predicates and locations

There must be a separate calculation for each predicate (or way of accessing the data).

The columns represent specific values or ranges of values assigned to specific locations. (These are actually pairs of columns, one for a cost and one for a percentage.) Each row represents all queries from a particular site.

The entries across represent the cost factor assigned to an access from the site represented by the row to the site represented by the column and the percentage of the total accesses from that site. The row percentages should add to 100 percent.

Sum (cost × percent) for each row. Then sum these columns. Then sum the sums for all predicates. This could be a linked or three-dimensional spreadsheet (one plane for each predicate).

The advantage of using a spreadsheet is that it is easy to perform a sensitivity analysis. Try different cost factors and percentages to determine how much of a change will alter the result. (This will be facilitated by setting up separate cells or variables to contain these values.) This is an indication of how much margin for error there is.

This is a trial and error or heuristic approach. The amount of work involved will be a motive for keeping the fragmentation scheme fairly simple, which seems like a good thing.

Vertical fragments are determined by establishing the *affinity* of one attribute for another. This is done by tabulating the number of accesses which refer to each attribute pair.

A transaction or query which accesses attributes A, B, C, D, and E can be represented by a matrix like this.

	A	B	C	D	E
A		1	1	1	1
B			1	1	1
C				1	1
D					1

One which accesses A, C, and D can be represented like this.

	A	B	C	D	E
A		0	1	1	0
B			0	0	0
C				1	0
D					0

Replace the 1's with numbers representing the transaction frequency or volume. Develop a matrix for every transaction or query. Calculate the sum for each attribute pair. The numbers which result represent the number of times the pair will be accessed together. Pairs with a high affinity should be stored together. Pairs with low affinity or no affinity may be separated. This analysis could be performed in terms of groups of attributes rather than individual attributes.

We've shown a triangular matrix. The diagonal need not be filled in because it is meaningless. The lower half need not be filled in because it is a mirror image of the upper half. Given a large number of attributes and transactions this will be a lot of work. You'll want to work with groups of attributes if you can.

Once again, use of a spreadsheet will be helpful, and it will be fairly simple to create a three-dimensional or "linked" spreadsheet.

This type of analysis will also help you decide whether or not to store relations in their normalized form (see Section 7.7).

Let's recast this in the form of a procedure.

- *Develop a normalized database design.*

- *Tabulate transactions by location and type of data accessed. Tabulate transaction volumes by the same categories.*

- *Assign costs to local and remote access and to data storage.*

- *Look for an optimal solution.* (This may be very obvious. It may be very difficult to find. Be sure to include centralization as an alternative.)

8.6   WHAT ABOUT CLIENTS AND SERVERS?

Recently, the notion of a CLIENT/SERVER architecture has become very popular. [GOLD90], [OZSU91], [KHOSHAFIAN92] This is driven by many of the same factors which drive the move to distributed systems.

The basic premise involves assigning activities to modules or software components in such a manner that one provides some service to the other as illustrated by Figure 8.7a. We might, using this model, think of our application program as the client and the DBMS as the server.

There is no reason the client and server must be on the same machine. It is common to place one server on a local area network with a number of potential clients as illustrated by Figure 8.7b. It is also possible to place several potential clients and several potential servers on the same network as illustrated by Figure 8.7c.

There are a number of additional issues and possibilities. The application program may or may not *be aware* that the server is on another machine. A true distributed DBMS might consist of several servers but conceal this from the application. There is no need to stop at the boundaries of a local area network. The client and server might be in different cities or countries.

Thus, a client-server architecture may provide distributed database or it may just provide remote database. In either case, the database design considerations will be the same ones we've been considering throughout this book.

[BUZZARD91] itemizes factors for use in discriminating between database server products. These provide a useful summary of issues which must be addressed in the selection and design of both client-server and distributed systems.

Standards. Adherence to standards such as SQL simplifies the use of software from a variety of vendors.

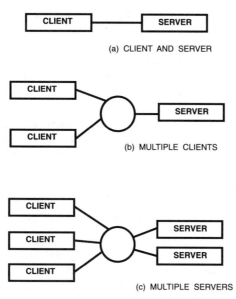

(a) CLIENT AND SERVER

(b) MULTIPLE CLIENTS

(c) MULTIPLE SERVERS

Figure 8.7   Clients and Servers

SQL Extensions. Many vendors have chosen to add non standard SQL extensions. These can be powerful and attractive. They can also negate the value of standards.

Performance. "The most important features for achieving a high level of performance are the abilities to monitor actual performance of an application and to manage performance by altering the configuration and operation of the database server software and the physical layout."

Performance may be improved by altering the placement of data, by use of alternative access methods, by use of better algorithms, and by use of improved query optimization techniques. Benchmarks and simulations may be used to validate a product and a design.

Concurrency. Locking and deadlock resolution must be more complex in a multisystem configuration.

The general rule is that all data which is likely to be accessed and locked by a single transaction is best kept at a single location.

If transaction volumes are high or response time is critically important, it will be worthwhile to examine and evaluate the concurrency management techniques used by the vendor. It may be possible to design the database in a manner which best takes advantage of a particular product.[14]

Communication and connectivity. The capacity of the communications link, the communications protocol used, and the degree of sharing with other users and applications can all have significant impacts on performance.

Products from several different vendors may not work together unless appropriate standards are followed. Even if the vendors do *support the standards*, it may still be necessary to try the configuration to make sure it works.

Scalability and portability. It is necessary to make sure that the software and hardware chosen provide adequately for growth. It will be a serious problem if it is not possible to increase capacity without rewriting for a different environment.

Recovery and transaction recovery. Distributed and client-server systems provide more kinds of failure possibilities. It is necessary to plan for failures at the remote locations. It is more difficult to manage and coordinate backups when multiple sites are involved. The trend is to automate backup, recovery, and diagnosis as much as possible. Monitoring of activity and auditing of data integrity become more important. Again the trend is to automate these activities as much a possible.

Security. Physical security of systems at remote sites is an important issue. Security of communications is another. Encryption of transmitted data may be required.

Distributed system support and server administration. Provision of adequate staff, training of the personnel, assignment of responsibilities, and implementation of appropriate controls should all be addressed as database and system design issues.

Application development support. Management of the development process and the management of software and hardware updates are more complex and require more attention.

The use of CASE for development will be more desirable. However, it may be more difficult to obtain appropriate tools.

What we've shown here are some basic analytical techniques that can be used to design distributed systems. Ozsu and Valduriez [OSZU91] provide a more extensive mathematical explanation. They also note "there are no general heuristic models that take as input a set of fragments and produce a near-optimal allocation subject to the types of constraints discussed here." This leads us to conclude that the best approach is to understand the nature of our application, collect as much data as we can, and exercise informed judgment regarding how far to carry these calculations. It also reinforces our beliefs that *we need a good reason for embarking on the distributed database* course in the first place and that *distribution should be kept as simple as possible.*

Endnotes

1. This is written in 1992. A lot of functionality has become available recently but there are still some limitations. In fact, changes are taking place as these words are being written.

2. Oszu and Valduriez [OZU91] define a *distributed computing system* as "... a number of autonomous distributed computing system processing elements... that are interconnected by a computer network and that cooperate in performing their assigned tasks,"; a *distributed database* as "a collection of multiple, logically distributed database interrelated databases distributed over a computer network"; and a *distributed database management system* as "the software system that permits the management of the [distributed database] and makes the distribution transparent to the users."

3. This formulation is generally credited to Herb Grosch, one of the pioneers of computing.

4. There is an extensive terminology and taxonomy for the different types of multiprocessing systems which are possible. You might see [LIEBOWITZ85] or [KRONENBERG87] for discussions of some of the issues.

5. Trying to establish precise meanings for some of these terms is still a very good way to start arguments. We don't really need to get involved in that here.

6. The catalog or directory for a distributed database must itself be distributed since the locations of all data must be known to all sites. The VAX Distributed Name Service [MARTIN89] is an example of a "directory system for computer networks...The DNS designers utilized such techniques as partitioning of the name space and data replication to assure service reliability and availability." The reference cited here discusses some interesting techniques for assuring that the data at the various locations remains consistent.

7. Michael Stonebraker is another pioneer of relational systems. The rules quoted here were cited in [BORSOOK88].

8. The system catalog itself must be a distributed database. All of the design issues we discuss below will be relevant.

9. A recent Version 2.1 of IBM's DATABASE2, Version 2 [IBM88-5] [IBM91-1], provides remote query capabilities across multiple sites but only allows a unit of work to update at only one site. Version 5.0 of Informix, version 6.4 of Ingres, and Version 4.8 of Sybase provide for update of multiple sites by a single transaction. Oracle announced and began to ship Version 7.0 of Oracle on June 15, 1992. An important feature of this product is the ability to handle distributed updates in a manner which does not require any special programming.

10. It is, of course, possible to design and implement a system which has the capability to update at multiple sites. This can be done by utilizing more sophisticated features of the systems and communications software. Since a preceding note points out that a version of DATABASE2 does not support true distributed update, we'll mention one of several ways this can be done in an IBM environment. CICS/ESA (Customer Information Control System - Extended Systems Architecture) Version 3.2 [IBM90-2] provides the capability for a CICS on one machine to communicate with a CICS on another machine. And, while both machines must be IBM, they need not be members of the same IBM family. However, the programmer must be aware that for certain functions it is necessary to send a message to another system. It may also be necessary to be aware of the communications path to or identity of the other system. It will also be necessary to pay much more attention to transaction synchronization, commit management, and error recovery. Thus, by the definitions we are using, this may be a distributed database, but the DBMS is not distributed. Detailed discussion of this is far beyond the scope of this book. It is not a course for the timid or the uninformed. But the database design procedures discussed here will be appropriate to design of such a system.

11. Several years can pass from the start of work on a book like this to its publication. And, you may not be reading it the day after it has been published. The result is that it is nearly impossible for all of the product details in *any* book to be up to any date.

12. It is sometimes necessary for *someone* to develop a *justification* citing technical and economic factors which support a decision that has been made on the basis of politics.

13. He, in turn, cites [CERI84] as his source.

14. See [BUZZARD91], [CERI84], [LIEBOWITZ85], [ORACLE88], [OZSU91] for detailed discussions of the possibilities.

QUESTIONS AND EXERCISES

1. Explain distributed system, distributed database, distributed database management system, and client server system. Note the differences and similarities.

2. What are the potential benefits of distributed database systems?

3. What are the potential drawbacks of distributed database systems?

4. Explain remote request, remote unit of work, distributed unit of work, and distributed request.

5. Why do relational database systems lend themselves more readily to distribution?

6. What are the organizational considerations for distributed database systems?

7. How does conceptual design of a distributed system differ from conceptual design of a nondistributed system? How is it the same?

8. How does physical design of a distributed system differ from physical design of a nondistributed system? How is it the same?

9. How can you decide whether or not to distribute? What are the issues?

10. Explain centralized data, replicated data, and partitioned data. Is there more than one way to partition?

11. Comment on this statement. *Since the DBMS handles all the details, design of a distributed database is no different from design of a nondistributed database.*

12. Comment on this statement. *Allocating fragments to locations is one problem while selecting fragments in the first place is another.*

Chapter 9

Design Methodology

9.1   CHAPTER SUMMARY

This chapter organizes the material we've discussed. While it is possible to discuss database design as if it were independent from other aspects of systems design, this separation is not really practical. In this chapter, we position the techniques we've discussed in the systems design cycle.

Many life cycles and design methodologies have already been proposed. The marketplace offers the prospective system developer a wide variety of CASE tools which embody the various methodologies. Presentations of these tools and methods frequently are marked by what we might call *one true method syndrome*. The last thing the world needs is another *one true method*. Instead of presenting one, we'd rather review some general systems development concepts and approaches, and discuss the selection of one over another.

While we do provide a step by step approach that you can follow, it is very important for you to realize that *understanding the concepts and their application is more important than memorizing rules and procedures.*

If your organization already has a method in place, your objective should be to integrate the principles and techniques presented in this book with that method.

If you have acquired or are expected to use a particular CASE tool (or tool set), your objective should be to employ these principles in the use of the tool.

If your organization already has specific standards for diagramming or for organizing and presenting information requirements, by all means use them. You will most likely discover that we recommend collecting the same information and that the form of presentation is less important than the information itself.

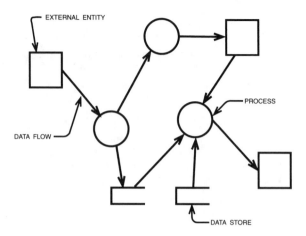

Figure 9.1   Data flow diagram

9.2   STRUCTURED ANALYSIS

For the example in the final chapter of this book, we've adopted *Structured Analysis*. It is widely known and is supported by many CASE tools. A brief review of basic concepts follows. (It is very tempting to include a lot of details about structured analysis. That, however, would take another book. This *very definitely* is not a complete exposition.)[1]

Requirements are analyzed by identifying processes, data stores, external entities, data flows, and data elements. These serve the same purpose as the entities, relationships, and attributes of the entity relationship model. They provide a way to organize and document ideas. It is customary to develop a *Data flow diagram* (DFD) similar to Figure 9.1. The diagram provides a convenient visual reference. It must be supported by detailed documentation.

A *process* manipulates or transforms data. Documentation of processes describes the data processed, the procedural steps, and the decision rules. On the data flow diagram, processes are represented by circles. (Some use rectangles with rounded corners.)

A *data store* retains data for some time interval. A data store is represented by an open ended rectangle. Documentation of data stores describes the data stored and the data volumes.

An *external entity* is something outside the system; some agent that provides data or receives data. It can be a person or organization. It can be another system. An external entity is sometimes called a *source* or a *sink*. An external entity is represented by a square. Descriptions of external entities are usually brief because they are outside the system.

External entity on a data flow diagram and entity on an entity relation diagram are two different concepts. The former is some person, place, or thing that interacts with the system. We retain data about the latter in the system. They may correspond. Customer, for example, would most likely appear in both models. Customers send information to the system. We retain information about customers in the system. They may not correspond. While we retain information about customer orders, the system does not receive information from orders or send information to orders.

The information that the system retains about entities is kept in the data stores.

A *data flow* represents the transfer of data. Data is transferred between an external entity and a process, between two processes, or between a process and a data store. While it is tempting to include other possibilities, these are the only ones that make sense. A data flow represents the movement of information. It does not represent the movement of goods or other material things. A data flow is represented by a line. An arrow at the end of the line indicates the direction of the flow. Documentation of data flows describes the data, frequency, and volume.

A *data element* is an atom of data. Documentation of data elements is similar to documentation of attributes. Data elements are not shown on the diagram.

It is often useful to develop a series of diagrams representing different levels of detail. A *context* diagram represents the complete system as one process and shows the data flows between the system and the external entities. Normally, data stores do not appear on the context diagram because they are inside the system.

The first level data flow diagram represents the major activity groups and communication between them. Subsequent diagrams show more detail about specific activities. For example, process order might be decomposed into receive order, check credit, and schedule shipment.

Structured analysis emphasizes the logical system. The logical data flow diagram shows what is accomplished. It does not show how it is done. If it is necessary to address this, a separate physical data flow diagram is developed.

What is the relationship between the entity relationship model and the data flow diagram? Since they are two different ways of viewing the same system, there must be some connection. This is a topic that has yet to receive a lot of attention.[2]

Formulating either model causes one to ask questions and examine issues that we might have otherwise overlooked. Here are some examples.

- If there are entities on the entity diagram which do not appear on the data flow diagram and vice versa, we might ask why this is so.
- Entities and relationships are represented by data contained in data stores. The same entity or relationship may be represented by entries in more than one data store. We may ask if this is appropriate.
- Data about entities and relationships is also contained in data flows. Data flows to and from external entities are user views of the data.
- Data used by processes often describes entities and relationships.
- Both models must contain the same data elements. We might more correctly state that the elements for each are drawn from the same domains.
- Every element of every data flow and data store and every element used by a process should be an attribute of some entity or relationship; or it should be possible to derive it from these.If this is not so, we must ask why.

- Every attribute of every entity or relationship should be available via some data flow and/or in some data store; or it should be possible to derive it from these. If this is not the case, the design may be unworkable.

We should cross check these carefully and rectify any discrepancies. Correction may require us to add entities, relationships, or attributes to the data model. Or, we may find it necessary to search out additional data flows or data stores and add them to the process model. Or, we may eliminate the unnecessary from one or the other.

Some CASE tools will check many of these details.

Examination of data stores will suggest data entities. The same is true for data flows. We might best think of them as views, normalize the view content, and consider the keys as potential identifiers for possible entities.

We can also review external entities. We must be careful here. There is a corresponding data entity only if we do, in fact, care to store data about the external entity.

These data and process models provide two complementary views of the situation, and neither is really complete without the other.

The example in the next chapter will clarify these ideas.

9.3   DOES ONE SIZE FIT ALL?

There are a multitude of books, articles, courses, and seminars about systems development and database development and corresponding methods. With each there is the assumption, sometimes explicit, sometimes implied, that here, at last, is *the* solution to design and development. Even if the author does not make this claim, there is a tendency for the reader or audience to assume that this may be the case.

Can this be possible? There can only be one correct method if all problems and all organizations are the same. If there are differences from project to project, then the one true method must contain a lot of statements on the order of "if such and such is the case, then proceed in the following manner." Any attempt to produce a comprehensive methodology becomes incredibly detailed and complex because there are so many differences between situations.

Davis [DAVIS82] provides a framework for evaluating projects and selecting an approach. We'll review some of the factors here.

- *Is there a global model?* A proposed system may be viewed as a component of an organizational *information architecture*. To the extent that other components have been developed or even defined, many of the data elements, entities, processes, and rules may already be documented. Or, it may be necessary to coordinate with other project teams. On the other hand, the project and the system may be viewed as completely independent of any other.

Many organizations have defined or are attempting to define an overall information system architecture. Some form of data model is usually an important component of an information architecture. These architectures are developed for a number of reasons.

- The architecture provides the basis for evaluating the existing systems portfolio. New projects are undertaken to remedy defects and fill needs identified by matching the portfolio against the architecture.

- The architecture provides a framework for evaluating new requirements and selecting implementation strategies and approaches.
- The architecture is a vehicle for achieving systems integration and eliminating redundancies and inconsistencies between systems.
- The architecture is used for evaluating new technology, planning for the use of new technology, and migrating systems from one environment to another.
- The architecture is useful for business planning.
- Developing an information architecture is somewhat different from developing a specification for a specific application development project. An information architecture is usually much less detailed. It is necessary to summarize in order to keep the model manageable and comprehensible. Summarizing is also necessary in order to keep the modeling activity manageable and doable.

- If an information architecture does exist, the procedure for developing a new application will refer to the architecture for information about data entities and business processes and update the architecture with information produced by the development project. It will be important to adhere to standards and utilize formats incorporated in the architecture. (Factors bearing on the relationship between an information architecture and an application data model are discussed in Section 5.6— Global Models, Integration, Disparate Views.)

  If there is no architecture there will be no base of existing information to draw on and the initial phases of defining the application's information and processing requirements will be more difficult and time consuming.

- *Is there an existing system?* There may be an existing system which is, for some reason, perceived as inadequate. It may be possible to draw extensively on documentation of the existing system for data and process definitions. Or it may be that documentation is inadequate and it is necessary to devote a lot of energy to the study of the programs, reports, and file definitions in order to extract definitions and ensure consistency between the new and the old. In either case there will be an emphasis on identifying the defects of the old system and the added features and capabilities of the new. If it is possible to use existing definitions, the format of the old definitions may determine the format of the new. It is becoming more common to use *re-engineering* software to analyze existing code and extract data and process definitions. The nature of the tool used may dictate a particular format for documentation and even a particular approach.

- *Is the problem well defined? Are the objectives clear?* The problem and the system requirements may be well understood and well documented. In such a case it will be possible to adopt a very formal and structured approach. It may be that the problem and the requirement are not well understood or documented and not susceptible to a formal and structured approach. Some form of incremental development or even trial and error development may be the only possibility.

  It may be possible to derive the new system from an existing system, manual or automated. It may be necessary to start with a blank sheet of paper.

  It may be possible to ask users or prospective users to explain the requirement. It may not. It may be possible to observe an existing operation. It may not.

- *What is the nature of the requirement?* There are different types of projects which are undertaken for different reasons. The system may serve the needs of a single individual or group. It may have many masters.

  Many projects have very specific *operational* objectives. That is, there are specific and fairly well-defined business activities to be supported by the application. There may, for example, be a need to improve the process of accepting new orders. Process-oriented analysis will be very important to such a project. It is likely to be necessary to develop very detailed specifications of procedures and processing steps. Data definitions are likely to be viewed as by-products of process definitions.

  Some projects are very much *information oriented*. In this case, there is some need for "management" information. This may be high-level summary information for use by higher management as a basis for decision making. Providing summaries of sales by location and product might be an example of this. It may be more detailed information intended to facilitate or automate auditing and control at a more operational level. Perhaps there is a need or desire to eliminate a particular kind of error. Data-oriented analysis will be much more important to this type of project. There should be a considerable emphasis on discovering the nature and structure of the data, understanding the nature of the decisions to be made on the basis of the data, and determining appropriate formats for presenting the data. It will be important to identify and document data relationships, data selection criteria, and the need for summaries and totals.

  Naturally most projects lie somewhere between the two extremes. It is then necessary to determine both data and processing requirements and to make sure that both are identified in a consistent manner.

  In addition, specific projects do have to deal with organization-wide information requirements even if there is no formal architecture in place. The architecture really is there whether or not it is documented. It's just harder to deal with. It is also likely that information-oriented projects will require more investigation into other systems or into the overall architecture.

- *There are different strategies.* It is possible to identify four distinct strategies for requirements determination, asking someone, deriving requirements from an existing system or operation, synthesizing requirements from the characteristics of the using system (the environment), and experimenting with an evolving system. Selection of one or more of these approaches should be based on an understanding of the requirements of the situation. It is necessary to evaluate the uses of the new system, the nature of the requirements, the nature of the users, and the nature of the development team.

  We can summarize Davis' detailed analysis fairly simply.

  Asking someone will be a feasible approach if there is someone to ask. The someone must be knowledgeable, accessible, and willing to participate. Asking can be further subdivided. There can be interviews, questionnaires, or meetings. Interviews and questionnaires may involve specific predetermined questions or open questions. Meetings may be formal with rigid agendas and formats or they may be less formal *brainstorming*[3] sessions. The level of knowledge possessed by users and analysts will be a factor in selecting an approach. It matters if the users are close by or far away, if they work together or are geographically dispersed, if they are a homogenous population or a diverse one. The amount of time and energy the users can or will expend is also a factor. So is the willingness of the users to accept responsibility for the system.

Deriving requirements from an existing system or operation is clearly possible only if there is an existing system. It must be appropriate and accessible. The more the existing system is perceived as inadequate, the less effective this approach will be. This may not be a sound approach if the existing system is poorly documented or understood. There is also the risk that the evils and flaws of the existing system will be perpetuated.

Synthesizing requirements from the characteristics of the using system (the environment) involves studying the environment and deducing the data and processing from the needs of the users. Many of the formal development methodologies consist of specific techniques for observing and documenting a requirement, then deriving a system design from it. This can be a very time consuming procedure. It requires highly skilled analysts.

Experimenting with an evolving system has been popularized as *prototyping*.[4] This approach generally utilizes some form of application generating software which produces reports and screens from relatively high level specifications. The general idea is to relieve the users of the need for answering detailed questions or reviewing voluminous specifications. Screens and reports are developed rapidly and reviewed with the actual users. This technique can be particularly useful when the specific nature of user interaction is not well defined or understood. On the other hand, it seems that there must be some initial analysis to determine general processing or information requirements. (Exploring the possible inputs and outputs to meet a poorly understood requirement could be an endless process. Implementing a poor database design could result in the need for extensive data conversion at a later date.)

Actual projects are likely to incorporate some combination of the characteristics which lead to each of the above approaches. Most traditional systems development methodologies incorporate some combination of the first and third. Thus, it behooves us to understand a variety of techniques and intellectual tools; appreciate some basic concepts of data and process analysis; determine the nature of a particular place, a particular time, and a particular project; and adopt the most appropriate approach.

Different life cycles are possible. Many attempts at the development of life cycle methodologies have centered around the specification of a series of sequential steps. This leads to a so-called *waterfall* model similar to Figure 9.2. This approach is particularly attractive from a project management standpoint. Each step is viewed as a more or less independent activity with a fixed beginning and end. Thus it is possible to establish milestones which can be checked off as they are completed. This really is important, particularly in the case of a large project. It is necessary for a variety of reasons to keep track of progress and make a determination as to whether or not the project will be completed on time and within budget. It is also possible to estimate time and effort required for a project by examining and estimating each step. More sophisticated versions of this approach incorporate a review at the end of each step and an opportunity to reevaluate the estimates for the remaining steps.[5]

There are some problems with this approach. It is sometimes very difficult to decide which steps should come first. Frequently, it seems appropriate for steps to overlap. It is also easy to get mired in the details of step 3.4.7 vs. step 3.4.8. A more significant prob-

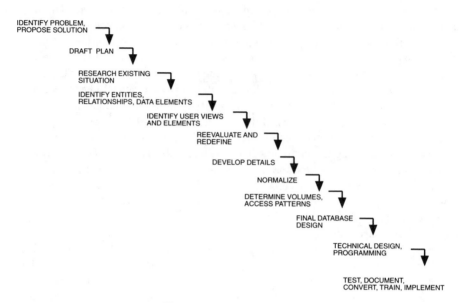

Figure 9.2 Waterfall model

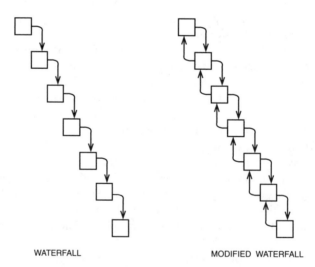

WATERFALL   MODIFIED WATERFALL

Figure 9.3 Modifying the waterfall model

lem with this approach is that it does not provide for requirements changes which occur after the project is under way. A common remedy is to envision a set of bidirectional links as shown in Figure 9.3. This is intended to indicate that, at the conclusion of each step, we may elect to go back and modify the product of a previous step. In practice,

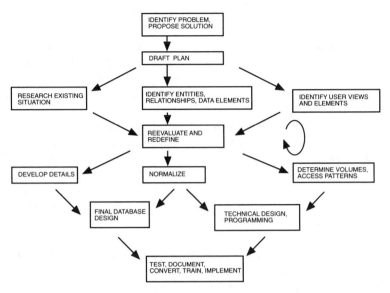

Figure 9.4 Concurrent model

most people don't like to go back and revisit something that is already considered complete. Management also tends to take a dim view of this.

Boehm [BOEHM88] suggests a spiral model consisting of repetitive cycles of requirements determination, risk analysis, prototyping, and validation. This is very realistic because it is reasonable to begin with a fairly high level definition and work through successive stages of refinement.

Analysis of the activities discssed in this book leads to the conclusion that many are best conducted in parallel. The research into the existing situation will lead to some form of process model with data element definitions; some definitions of entities, relationships, and data elements; and some definition of user views and data elements. Refinements to the process model, normalization of the data, and collection of volumes and access patterns also seem to go together. Final database design and specification of programs must also interact and go together. Figure 9.4 illustrates the general idea of this. The "reevaluate and redefine" step in the middle indicates the possibility of several iterations, each adding more detail.

We also note that there should be an element of opportunism here. Suppose the analyst finds himself (or herself) in a good position to accumulate some volumes and access patterns during an early phase. It does not really seem reasonable to say, "No don't tell me that now—I don't want to know it until step 8.7.9!" This is particularly true if it is difficult to get time with the users. The big warning that does go with this, however, is that one must be careful not to get bogged down in too much detail too soon.

9.4 THE RECOMMENDED APPROACH

In Chapters 3 through 8 we've discussed some specific design issues, tools, and techniques. We've also attempted to show that entity relationship analysis forms a basis for normalization and that both form the basis for physical design. We've also shown the relationship between data and process. Chapters 7 and 8 demonstrate the uses of the information collected by following the procedures in Chapters 3 through 6. If we've succeeded, you now appreciate the nature of the information which must be collected, why it must be collected, and how to use it. You will be able to evaluate the requirements of a particular situation and select an appropriate strategy. Given that a particular style of model or documentation or life cycle or tool is called for, whatever the reason, you will see how the information and techniques we've discussed fit into that framework. That's the real key to success—*understanding and intelligent application of that understanding*! It's a lot harder to achieve this than it is to say it, but it's still the only way to be sure of success.

In the remainder of this chapter we review each of the stages we've identified, make reference to the appropriate explanations, and in some cases suggest specific formats for documentation and analysis of the data.

9.5 IDENTIFY A PROBLEM AND PROPOSE A SOLUTION

This could be the most problematic part of the entire process. It is also the part we take the most for granted here. Someone, somewhere will have somehow identified that there is some problem or some need. There will be at least a germ of an idea regarding the nature of the solution. This may be a very general idea on the order of "We'll form a project and study the problem." The project may begin with the proposal of a very specific technical solution. In the latter case, the risk is that the solution has been adopted without really understanding the problem. Project initiation is often a very political process.

At any rate, you should begin with a fairly concise statement which describes the *nature of the problem* or the *expected result* of the project, tells *who is involved*, discusses *risks and anticipated costs*, explains the *most likely possibilities* for solution or implementation, and identifies the *next steps*.

Even if a formal life cycle and methodology is not in place, it is a good idea to document this information, make sure the sponsors of the project find it acceptable, and keep track of any changes which occur during the discovery process.

9.6 DRAFT A PLAN

This is another crucial and difficult step. Here one assesses the nature of the problem and the environment, determines what standards and procedures are in place, identifies or selects *methods and approaches* to be used, identifies *sources of information*, plans *specific activities*, assigns *specific roles* to specific parties, establishes *timetables and milestones*, and in general maps out the plan of attack. The ideally enlightened approach to all this recognizes that things will change and incorporates appropriate points for *review and revision* of the plan.

The form of this may or may not be established by organizational policies and standards. Once again, it's a good idea to spend a little time mapping this out for yourself even if it is not required. You should know what you are doing and how you are progressing even if no one else does. And, it is a good idea to be sure that the sponsor or management (or whoever is paying the bill) understands and agrees to the approach.

9.7   RESEARCH EXISTING SITUATION

This activity consists of taking the initial cut at a process model. It involves analyzing and documenting specific tasks to be performed by the system.

It is often valuable to begin by gaining an understanding of the manner in which things are being done at present. It may be necessary to begin with analysis of the physical system and subsequently extract the logical system from the details of the physical.

One might be told or observe that a clerk performs the following activities.

- Remove an order from the in basket.
- Refer to a 3 × 5 card file to identify the customer.
- Call the credit bureau.
- Refer to a product inventory list for the product, price, and availability.
- Copy all information to a three-part form. Retain the pink copy in the file cabinet. Send the green copy to the shipping dock. Send the white copy to the warehouse.

This is the existing physical system. The existing logical system consists of receiving an order, validating customer identification, verifying customer credit, verifying inventory and price, retaining a record of the order, and notifying both the warehouse and shipping dock.

The purist will maintain that it is valuable and necessary to fully document this in both forms. In practice it may or may not be adequate to document only the logical. (It's also getting rare to encounter a completely manual, paper-based system like this.)

The analysis then focuses on the logic of the activity, what is actually accomplished, the rules to be followed, and the data flows. If a thorough analysis is to be done, the next step will be to determine what, if anything, must change regarding the logic.

Finally, the details of the new physical system will be worked out. Here, as an example, the determination might be made to do away with paper and transmit information electronically. This activity might not take place until much later.

There are two pitfalls to avoid in all this.

- If too much detail is developed too soon, the project may become hopelessly mired in analysis and die on the vine.
- If too little detail is developed too late, irrevocable decisions may be based on inadequate data and the project may be an embarrassing failure.

In the process of documenting processing and developing a process model, one will encounter data.

- Most, if not all, of the data elements consumed and produced by the processes will be the same data elements to be stored in the database.
- These data elements will be drawn from domains.
- Many of them will be destined to become attributes of entities and relationships, and eventually attributes of relations.
- Data stores will generally contain data about entities. They may actually correspond to specific entities or they may contain views.
- Data flows will generally constitute views as well.

Thus, this activity does overlap with the data definition activities we've discussed.The data elements of the process model must be the same data elements incorporated as attributes in the data model. The approach taken to this must assure that the same work is not done twice and that the data element descriptions are collected in a manner that is useful for all activities.

Many systems analysis methodologies and many CASE tools do not acknowledge the existence of domains. You will avoid a lot of duplication of effort and clarify many difficult analysis problems if you begin documenting domains as you document data elements or even before.

General concepts of definition are discussed in Section 6.2.

The concept of domains is explained in Section 2.4.

The definition of domains is discussed in Section 6.5; the formation of names for domains is discussed in Section 6.7.

Here is a summary of the information that should be collected about each DOMAIN.[6]

DOMAIN DEFINITION

NAME

    ALTERNATE NAMES

DEFINITION

DATA TYPE

    TYPE

    LENGTH

    DECIMAL PLACES

ACCEPTABLE VALUES

    RANGE

    LIST OF VALUES

    SPECIAL RULES

METHOD OF CALCULATION

COMPOSED OF

STANDARD OUTPUT FORMAT

STANDARD OUTPUT HEADING

SOURCES

PLACES REFERENCED

At minimum you could use a word processor to keep a running list with definitions and references to all elements and attributes drawn from each domain. You might consider a simple relational database of domain definitions. You might consider using the data element definition capability embodied in your case tool or data dictionary as a vehicle for documenting domains. These usually make it possible to attach some sort of category or type identification to element definitions and subsequently retrieve them all via this identification.

These important points about documenting domains are worth repeating.

- Business-oriented English language names are preferred. (In another country, you might prefer another language.) These definitions will be reviewed with users. If you use software which requires some arcane internal name, make sure that a human-oriented name is also provided.
- Short names are preferred because it will be convenient to form element names by qualifying domain names.
- The definition of the domain and the documentation of acceptable values or ranges will subsequently form the basis for data validation. Constraints are discussed in Section 6.11.
- Security, as discussed in Section 6.12, is an aspect of domain definitions.
- Data encoding is discussed in Section 6.9. An encoding system may be a domain definition in disguise.

The data elements of the process model must overlap with the *attributes* of the entities and relationships and the attributes of relations.

- The nature of attributes of relations is discussed in Section 2.3..
- The nature of attributes of entities and relationships is discussed in Sections 4.4 and 4.7.
- The definition of attributes is discussed in Section 6.6.
- Security, as discussed in Section 6.12, is an aspect of Attribute definitions.
- Data encoding is discussed in Section 6.9.

Some of the calculations and procedures documented in the process model are really definitions of derived or calculated attributes in disguise. Make sure you make these associations.

Here is a list which illustrates the general nature of the information to be collected about attributes.

ATTRIBUTE DEFINITION

NAME

DOMAIN

SPECIAL CHARACTERISTICS

      VALUES

      RULES

      FORMAT

      COLUMN HEADING

SPECIAL RULES

DEFAULT VALUE

NULL ALLOWED

SOURCE

FREQUENCY AND MEANS OF UPDATE

Some of the procedures and validation rules documented in the process model are really disguised *entity and referential integrity constraints*. These are discussed in Section 6.10.

The process definitions will eventually lead to the selection and definition of *keys* and *search arguments*. Keys are discussed in Section 2.5, Sections 3.5 through 3.11, and Section 6.8.

The process definitions will form the basis for the *access map* discussed in Section 7.5 and decisions about distribution as discussed in Section 8.4.

9.8 IDENTIFY ENTITIES, RELATIONSHIPS, AND DATA ELEMENTS

This phase really constitutes the development of the *conceptual data model*.

These activities are well covered by Chapters 4, 5, and 6. Pay particular attention to Sections 6.3, 6.4, and 6.10. Also see Section 1.4, and Section 2.5.

Here are lists which indicate the general form of entity and relationship documentation.

ENTITY DEFINITION

NAME

    ALTERNATE NAMES

DEFINITION

EXISTENCE RULES

DELETION RULES

STATUS INFORMATION (repeat for each status)

    DESCRIPTION

    RECORD KEEPING REQUIREMENTS

    HOW STATUS IS ENTERED

    HOW STATUS DEPARTED

VERSION INFORMATION

NUMBER OF OCCURRENCES

    MAXIMUM

    MINIMUM

    AVERAGE

    RATE OF ADDITION

    RATE OF DELETION

    SPECIAL NOTES

SUBSET OF

SUPERSET OF

NAMING RULES

OWNER

SOURCES OF INFORMATION (repeat for each source)

    ROLE

    LOCATION

CANDIDATE KEYS

ENTITY DEFINITION (Continued)

COMMON SEARCH ARGUMENTS

ATTRIBUTES (list)

SPECIAL NOTES

RELATIONSHIP DEFINITION

NAME

    ALTERNATE NAMES

    INVERSE NAME USED

ENTITY TYPES RELATED

NUMBER OF OCCURRENCES OF EACH

    MAXIMUM

    MINIMUM

    AVERAGE

    RATE OF ADDITION

    RATE OF DELETION

    SPECIAL NOTES

CONNECTIVITY

SIGNIFICANCE

SPECIAL RULES

MANDATORY / OPTIONAL

MUTUALLY EXCLUSIVE WITH

VERSION INFORMATION

CANDIDATE KEYS

COMMON SEARCH ARGUMENTS

OWNER

SOURCES OF INFORMATION (repeat for each source)

    ROLE

RELATIONSHIP DEFINITION (Continued)

LOCATION

ATTRIBUTES (list)

SPECIAL NOTES

9.9 IDENTIFY USER VIEWS AND ELEMENTS CONTAINED IN USER VIEWS

This technique is discussed in Section 5.7. It is also necessary to review Section 5.6. Elements of this approach are also discussed in Section 2.13.

This activity consists of identifying, documenting, and merging user views. Reports, screens, some data stores, and some data flows can be considered user views. One must essentially make a small model for each view, develop a listing of all entities from all views, and examine those with identical keys. This may be the only workable approach for a large project, a project with many reports, or a project with many or disparate users. It is easy to understand but difficult and sometimes tedious to execute. Careful attention to names and definitions is essential because it is necessary to recognize that two elements described by two different users for two different reasons are actually occurrences of the same thing. It is quite easy to err in combining views that should not be combined. It is also quite easy to overlook views that should be combined.

9.10 MODIFY THE ENTITY MODEL AS REQUIRED— REVALUATE AND REDEFINE IF NECESSARY

It may be possible to do the analysis once, review it with the users once, make a few minor changes, and proceed. There may also be a need to review and revise many times. This will depend on the nature of the problem, the quality of the analysis, and the accessibility of knowledgeable users.

It may also be advisable to plan several cycles of modeling and review with each cycle incorporating more detail. Just about everything that has been discussed so far in this chapter will be a factor in making a judicious decision about this.

Each review, especially those which occur early in the cycle, provides an opportunity to reevaluate cost and feasibility and possibly radically alter the scope of the project or even discontinue it.

It is also necessary to appreciate that it may never be possible to define everything precisely in advance and the right approach may be to go ahead with the project and rely on the flexibility of relational database and modern application generating software for dealing with future changes. (The alternative may be to keep defining and redefining forever.) In some cases the nature of the project will lead to a rational decision. In some cases it will be a matter of personal style. The important thing is to recognize that this is an issue, evaluate the factors and risks, and proceed in a knowledgeable manner rather than a haphazard one. Too much analysis can result in the demise of a project. Too little can end in a poor result.

9.11   DEVELOP DETAILS OF PROPOSED SOLUTION

At some point everyone has to agree that there is enough detail or that the problem is as well understood as it's ever going to be and it is time to move on. That realization marks the end of this phase. The product or deliverable of this phase would be the equivalent of a complete and detailed set of data flow diagrams incorporating all rules and input-output formats.

The details of the proposed solution include process definitions, data flow definitions, data store definitions, rule and constraint definitions, domain definitions, data element definitions, and entity and relationship definitions.

9.12   NORMALIZE

Normalization is discussed in detail in Chapter 3 and also in Section 4.9. We recommend that you go to the trouble of spelling out each and every *functional dependency*, *multivalued fact*, and *multivalued dependency* as we do in the example in the next chapter. Remember that the normalized design may or may not be the final design.

The result of normalization is a set of functional and multivalued dependencies and a set of normalized relations. This normalized design is what many refer to as the *logical database design*.

9.13   DETERMINE VOLUMES, ACCESS PATTERNS

The content of Chapters 7 and 8 is relevant here. Specific methods and forms are provided in Section 7.5, in Section 8.4, and in the next chapter.

Complete and accurate information can be surprisingly difficult to come by. Sometimes it is possible to reason and extrapolate from what is known. An example is provided in Section 7.5. This is another case where it is important to exercise judgment. It may not be worth weeks of effort to gain just a little more knowledge. If, on the other hand, performance is critically important or really large amounts of data are involved, all the details may be necessary.

9.14   FINAL DATABASE DESIGN

Here we apply the principles of Chapter 7, paying particular attention to Sections 7.4, 7.5, 7.7, 7.8, and 7.9. Sections 2.13, 6.8, 6.9, and 6.10 are also particularly relevant, along with all of Chapter 8.

Here is the usual sequence of steps.

- Determine any need for *denormalization*.
- Determine any need for *partitioning* and *distribution*.
- Identify *rules regarding NULL values*.
- Identify and evaluate *integrity constraints*.
- Select appropriate *indexes*.
- Establish *data encoding* and *data formats*.
- Identify required *views*.
- Determine *file sizes*.
- Determine *file placements*.

  The normalization and distribution issues are worthy of special comment.

- You need a good reason to denormalize. The normalized form will generally be the most flexible. It is also likely to require the least amount of space.
- You need a good reason to distribute. It must add complexity. If it's not well thought out, it will also introduce additional overhead. Make sure your DBMS will deal with distribution adequately.

Specific details of these activities are provided in the sections referenced. There is considerable variation from one product to another. It will definitely be necessary to *consult vendor documentation for your DBMS*.

This is another place where you can't always go step one, step two, step three. It is very possible, for example, that the consideration of file size and placement will result in a rethinking of the normalization issue.

It is very much the case that *this activity and the technical design of the system will have an effect on each other*.

9.15 TECHNICAL DESIGN, PROGRAMMING

This is a topic that is well covered by other authors ([DEMARCO79], [INMON89], [PAGEJONES88], and [PRESSMAN87] to name but a few). We will not rehash discussions of program design, structured programming, or the like here. There are, however, several observations to be made.

As we just noted above, *this activity and the final database design will have an effect on each other*.

Design and definition of data structures and data variables is a very significant issue in program design and in programming.[7] Data and data definitions are specifically discussed in Sections 1.5, 2.4, 2.5, 6.5, 6.6, 6.8, and 6.9.

The program designer and the programmer must be familiar with the concepts of database systems and relational database systems. These are discussed in Sections 1.2 and 1.3 and Chapter 2.

Constraints are discussed in Sections 6.10 and 6.11. These may be enforced by the DBMS or they may be enforced through programming. There are significant technical design issues here. The same can be said for the material discussed in Section 6.12.

The program designer and the programmer must be familiar with the general modeling issues discussed in Chapters 3, 4, and 5 and also with both the data model for the system and the nature of its transformation into a relational database. Otherwise, very inappropriate programming strategies may be adopted.

It is also the case that programming considerations must be a factor in the design of the database.

The discussion of Section 7.10 is very relevant to program design. This is another issue which can only be resolved by cooperation and negotiation between database and program designer. Some pause for a detailed technical review before programming commences. Some delay many of the activities we've been discussing until programming commences.

Programming is the activity which often seem to be *real systems development*. There are several reasons for this.

- It finally looks like people are really doing something.
- Traditional methods have allowed the activities we've assigned to previous phases to continue during this stage with important design decisions sometimes being made by programmers with tight deadlines to meet.
- Code generation has traditionally seemed to be the easiest thing to automate and has received a lot of attention by software tool vendors.
- Many of the newer tools and methods provide for generation of (some or all of) the code from high-level specifications. To the extent that this is possible, it means that there may be no programmer to make corrections and adjustments and if the specifications are wrong, the result will be wrong.

9.16 TEST, DOCUMENT, CONVERT, TRAIN, IMPLEMENT

Since these activities tend to come at the end, circumstances often force them to be done in a hurried or cursory manner. We make a few observations before we move on.

- If the system has been well designed, testing will consist more of verifying than finding and repairing errors. Human frailty does still result in the need for careful testing. It takes time and effort to develop a good set of test data and procedures. It is time and effort well spent.
- Documentation is often neglected. One might note that all of the information we've recommended collecting is a major component of the documentation and that contemporary CASE and word processing approaches make it relatively easy to keep it up to date.
- Data conversion can be a significant activity. Planning for this should really begin early in the life cycle.
- The same can be said for training and the planning of the actual implementation.

9.17 STRUCTURE CHANGES, CHANGE MANAGEMENT

Suppose it becomes necessary to change the design of the database after it is implemented. Suppose a change is required during development.

Ease of change is one of the advertised benefits of relational technology. It is true that changes are much easier to effect in a relational system than in a more traditional database management system. Many changes can be made without taking the system off line.

Most systems allow the creation or elimination of indexes at any time. This makes it possible to tune (or detune) the database. Don't forget, however, that CREATE INDEX instructs the system to define and populate an index. It is necessary for the DBMS to scan the entire table in order to do this. After extracting the index data, the system may also sort it before loading the index. This could take a while. It is possible the table or even the entire database will be locked while this takes place. Select an appropriate time.

Most systems allow the addition of new columns to an existing table. Usually these must appear at the end of a row. Defining the new column is easy. Acquiring and inserting the actual data may be very difficult and time consuming. Also note that programs which must use or manipulate the new data must be modified. And, any program which uses SELECT * must be modified.

While it is easy to alter the structure of relational data, it is still a good idea to design it right the first time. Database design by trial and error can be expensive and difficult even in a relational environment.

Managing and tracking changes is also be a major issue. Often program changes and database changes must be coordinated. This means that all the changes must occur at a specific time and that it is necessary to be sure all programs which must be changed have been identified.

Once again, it is necessary to select techniques and procedures appropriate to the situation. Large software projects involving many people and many programs call for detailed procedures and rigorous controls. These are sometimes spelled out in procurement contracts for large systems.

Vendors of software packages frequently have different versions for different environments. Vendors must also resolve problems for customers who have not purchased or installed the latest release.

It may be possible to employ simpler, less formal procedures when fewer people are involved. *It is not wise to ignore the problem no matter how small the system or project.*

Most complete life cycle methodologies and many CASE tools do provide means for dealing with all this. Here are some guidelines and suggestions.

- Keep a *library of database definitions.*[8]
- Clearly identify each item in the library.
- An automated library system will provide for a name and description for each item. A single item, such as a table definition or the source code for a particular program, is often called a *member.*
- If there is no automated library system, set up a simple directory containing name, text description, creation date, date of last change, and location. Location should be

the appropriate combination of disk volume, directory, and file name. Use word processing or a spreadsheet program. Or, if you like, design and implement a simple database for this.

- The naming and indexing scheme should provide for *different versions* of the same table definition.
- The naming and indexing scheme should also provide a way of identifying all tables that form a particular database.
- Keep track of *views*. Be sure to identify the base table for each view.
- Keep a *history of changes*. What was changed? When was it changed? Who made the change? Why was it done?
- Maintain a *cross reference* indicating which programs access each table or view. It sometimes proves valuable to identify which versions of the program will work correctly with which versions of the table or view. It is useful to indicate whether the program alters the data or merely makes reference to it. It is also useful to identify *reports and displays* which contain data from particular tables.[9]
- Establish procedures for *checking out* table definitions for changes.
- It is necessary to make sure that changes are applied to the correct version or versions of a table definition.
- It is necessary to know that a particular person is working on changes to a particular definition or collection of definitions. If more than one person makes changes to the same definition, it will be necessary to combine them and resolve any conflicts.
- There must be a mechanism for assuring that the library is updated after the changes have been made.
- Establish procedures for *moving from development to production*. This is usually the mechanism for assuring that changes to multiple system components are coordinated, that libraries and records are updated, and that any required reviews and approvals have been completed.
- A large project may necessitate multiple development versions of the same definition. There may be a *baseline*. This is a relatively fixed version used by everyone for system testing. Then it becomes necessary to have procedures for moving one or more components to baseline status.

This sort of thing seems like a lot of unnecessary bother to many people. It can be very difficult to convince people that the procedures suggested here are important.

In a larger project or organization, people tend to follow the form of the procedures while violating the principles. Approvals tend to be automatic. Reviews tend to be very superficial.

Make sure everyone involved understands the reasons for the procedures. Make sure there is management reinforcement. The price of mismanaging this aspect of the development process can be very high.

Endnotes

1. For more information, see [DEMARCO79] or [GANE79]. Most texts on systems analysis also discuss this technique. These discussions are frequently incomplete. The examples often contain errors. These original sources are still best.

2. Once again, we are about to present some useful and usable ideas but we are not going to attempt to prove them.

3. The term "brainstorming" is often used to describe any open freewheeling discussion. There is also a more formal procedure for brainstorming which involves the use of specific techniques to direct and harness the capabilities of a group. See [PARNES81].

4. You might refer to [BOAR84] for more information on prototyping. This was one of the first books published on this topic. You should note that Boar envisions prototyping as a vehicle for eliciting user requirements and NOT a technique for developing a system by trial and error.

5. There is an extensive literature on development methodologies and life cycles. [ORACLE89] provides a typical example. If you are not familiar with the basic concepts, you might refer to a standard text such as [FITZGERALD87] or [SENN89]. [PRESSMAN87] is another good reference. [BROOKS75] is perhaps the classic discussion of the problems and pitfalls of software development. Many proprietary methodologies are marketed by consulting companies and vendors.

6. It is traditional for books like this to provide samples of forms that could be used for collecting this information. It is becoming less and less likely that anyone will actually use these. Most people will computerize and customize the information. We decided to include a simple list instead.

7. The author has been teaching undergraduate programming courses for a number of years (and also has considerable experience working as a programmer). Misunderstanding of the data, misuse of the data, and just plain use of the wrong name and hence the wrong data are among the most common programming errors.

8. This might be kept in text form. It might be a custom-designed database. A CASE tool might be used. A Data Dictionary might be used.

9. Use of embedded SQL with IBM's DATABASE2 leads to an additional wrinkle. The DATABASE2 precompilation process invokes the optimizer and creates an *application plan* which is stored in the catalog and will be used at run time. If a database change is likely to require an alteration to a plan, it becomes necessary to make sure plan is recreated. The system will automatically recreate a plan which has become unusable. But this may occur at an inconvenient time. Also, plans which are still valid but may no longer be efficient will not be recreated automatically.

QUESTIONS AND EXERCISES

1. Is the following statement true or false? Explain your answer. *The author selected Structured Analysis because it is the* only *way to design correct systems.*

2. Discuss the entity relationship diagrams and dataflow diagrams. What do they have in common? How do they relate to each other?

3. Discuss the factors which influence the selection of an approach to a specific project.

4. What are the elements of a project plan?

5. Discuss the general flow of a project from beginning to end.

6. What is the role of prototyping? What are its advantages and disadvantages?

Chapter 10

Example

10.1 CHAPTER SUMMARY

In this chapter we illustrate the database design process with a simple but complete example. As is true of most examples in most books, this one is unrealistically simple. (It's a little startling that this is true despite all the detail we do provide!) Also, *the business we analyze has some unusual aspects which have been invented to illustrate particular concepts.* The usual disclaimer that any resemblance to real life is coincidental applies here. There is a danger that the reader who has some knowledge of this type of business will spend a lot of time reviewing and correcting the business analysis. Please try to concentrate primarily on the approach and procedure. And, we are concentrating our attention primarily on database design issues. Life cycle and systems analysis topics are discussed, but many details are ignored.

All of the diagrams and lists we show here will, in practice, go through many revisions. They will also be built up over time as more and more detail is added. It's just not practical to try to show that process here.

10.2 THE BUSINESS SITUATION

Montoni's Marketplace sells books, compact discs, and grand pianos.[1] All orders are placed by telephone. The customer specifies the merchandise, the customer service representative determines whether or not the desired item or items are in stock. No back orders are accepted.[2] All merchandise is tracked by a nine-digit Montoni catalog number. If the customer does not know an exact catalog number or product description, the customer service representative will provide some assistance.

A book is identified by Montoni catalog number or by ISBN number.[3] There is a need to search for a desired book by title, partial title, author name, or partial author name. Books are also assigned subject categories. These are not used to locate a desired book, but as an aid in determining that the correct book has been identified. The same is true for copyright date and publisher.

A compact disc is identified by Montoni catalog number or by publisher and publisher catalog number. There is a need to search for a desired compact disc by title, partial title, artist, or partial artist name. As in the case of books, there are categories which are used only as an aid to determining that the correct item has been identified.

A specific grand piano is identified by manufacturer plus model number plus serial number. Each general type of piano identified by manufacturer plus model number combination is assigned a Montoni catalog number.

The customer service representative carries on a dialogue with the customer. Since the customer service representative must be able to verify that the item is on hand and quote a price, a quantity available, manufacturer's list price, and Montoni's bargain price must be available for each book, compact disc, and piano model. Eventually, the items are selected and ordered.

Montoni's maintains a record of customers who have made purchases in the past. This information is reused to eliminate typing and error. Each customer is assigned a Montoni priority customer number. But many customers who call do not remember their numbers. There is a need to search for customer by last name or last name plus zip code.[4] If a customer is calling for the first time, the service representative will establish a new customer record. The customer record contains customer name and address, day time telephone number, and payment method. Most customers are required to provide a credit card number. In this case, it is necessary to know type of card, card number, and card expiration date. The most recently used credit card number is retained. If the customer uses the same card the next time, no typing is required. But it must be possible for a customer to specify that a particular card and number be used for a particular order. Credit availability is verified with the credit card company as a part of the order entry process. There are commercial customers who have a predetermined line of credit with Montoni's and are billed periodically. The customer service representatives are not involved in establishing the line of credit. Assuring that the customer's credit limit is not exceeded is a part of the process. Clearing paid amounts is not a part of this system.[5]

A date of last purchase, dollar amount of last purchase, number and dollar amount of purchases for this year and number and dollar amount of purchases for last year are also retained for each customer. This is used for generating mailing lists and for sales analysis.

A picking slip is then sent to the warehouse. This contains an order identifier and a list of items with warehouse locations. The quantity available is updated when the order is entered. Quantity actually on hand is updated as the items are removed from the warehouse. When the complete order has been picked, a packing list is produced and sent to the customer with the goods. Occasionally actual stock does not match the record. In this case the customer is notified that the items are not available and the billing is adjusted accordingly.

A complete record of every shipped order is sent to the accounting department. These are used for accounting, resolving and reconciling credit card sales, resolving disputes, sending bills to commercial customers, and analyzing sales. These activities are not part of this system.[6]

10.3 CONTEXT DIAGRAM

Figure 10.1 is a *context diagram*. We assume that this diagram has been reviewed with and accepted by the Montoni management team. This implies that several life cycle steps have been completed.

- The *problem* has been *identified*.
- A *solution* has been *proposed* and accepted.
- A *plan* has been *drafted* and accepted.
- At least a partial *investigation of* the *existing situation* is complete.

The diagram reflects the determinations that have been made.

The Order Fulfillment System interacts with customers, credit card companies, the accounting department, and the warehouse. Order information and customer information are accepted from customers.

Customer information consists of customer priority number, customer name and address and telephone information, and customer credit information. In the case of an existing customer, the customer priority number is sufficient. In the case of a new customer, all information must be obtained.

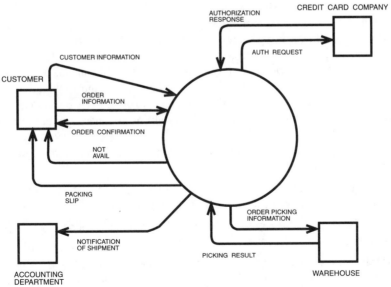

Figure 10.1   Context diagram

Order information consists of a list of order items, each consisting of Montoni catalog number and quantity ordered. The customer may provide some form of product description in lieu of Montoni catalog number.

The customer may provide this information in a very straightforward manner or it may be elicited by means of a dialogue with the customer service representative.

The customer receives an immediate order confirmation. This consists of an order number, an order total price, and a verification that the order has been accepted.

At a later date the customer is sent a packing slip. This consists of a complete duplication of all order information.[7] The customer may also receive a notice of unavailability consisting of the order number, the catalog number, and indicating that the product will not be delivered after all.

The accounting department receives a notification of shipment which is another complete duplication of all order information.

The warehouse receives order picking information, which is another copy of the order information augmented by a warehouse location for each item.

The warehouse provides a picking result consisting of the order number plus a positive or negative result for each order item.

The credit card company[8] receives Montoni's merchant identifier, customer credit card number, credit card expiration date, and order total amount. The credit card company responds with a rejection or with an acceptance plus a confirmation number.

Some comments about this are in order.

The *first cut* description of the system will be about this detailed; there could be more information, there could be less. The purpose is to *clearly define what the system will and will not do*, to *establish a set of boundaries*, and to *provide the basis for the next steps*. It is possible to get into a lot of discussion about just how detailed this should be, about the exact form in which it should be cast, and so on. Our concern in this book is that we must reach a point where we have this much information about the system.

We should really also account for the sources of product descriptions, the updating of quantity on hand and quantity available when new products are received, the establishment of credit lines for commercial customers, and other such details. These will not just happen. They must be provided for. If there is a file that is truly outside the scope of our system, we can consider it an external entity. Otherwise we must include data flows, with sources, and processes for maintaining the data. In order to keep this *short and simple* example from becoming a book in its own right, we intentionally omit many such details.

At this point we have also developed the first cut *entity relationship* diagram shown in Figure 10.2. These are the *entities*:

CUSTOMER. A customer is any individual or company that places an order with Montoni's or establishes a line of credit with Montoni's.

PRODUCT. A product is any book, compact disc, or piano which Montoni's will sell to a customer.

ORDER. An order represents the agreement between Montoni's and a specific customer that specific products will be shipped to the customer for a specific price. It incorporates an agreement regarding method of payment.

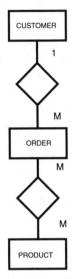

Figure 10.2   First cut entity relationship diagram

These are the *relationships*:

CUSTOMER PLACES ORDER. A particular order will have been placed by one customer. A Customer may place any number of orders.

ORDER FOR PRODUCT. An order may be for any number of products.

We might well go through several reviews and revisions to get this far. Establishing the content and boundaries of the system is an important step. We discuss this diagram in much more detail in Section 10.5.

10.4   DOMAINS

In the process of explaining the context diagram we've made reference to a number of domains. A *domain* is really a definition of a particular data type. For a given project or environment we must identify, name, and define the types of data we will be working with. A given value or attribute or field found in a particular place will be an instance or occurrence of one of these data types. Several things about this are important.

The things we list here are types of data. There will be multiple occurrences of each in the system. By this we mean that Montoni catalog number, for example, will appear in numerous places—relations, screens, reports, data flows, and so on. There will be times when it is necessary to clearly specify that a reference is to the catalog number which appears on the order entry screen as opposed to some other occurrence. This is particularly true in programming. At that time we will need to somehow provide a unique name for a unique occurrence. Right now we are not doing that. We are just identifying kinds of data.

We've included groupings of data which often go together as distinct items. We've been systematic, but not overly meticulous, in selecting names for domains. We do the best we can to make do with the names that people at Montoni's actually use or at least will recognize. Eventually, we may be forced to abbreviate and eliminate spaces. This will be for the convenience of the computer software. In order to provide a cross reference, we've shown the abbreviated names along with the English language names. This is a useful thing to do. *We don't really have to develop these names until later. In this book we have included them here so we don't have to repeat all the definitions. In practice you will most likely add them later.* Some of the items have no abbreviation because we find later that we don't need them.

In fact, you may not develop such a complete list immediately. It is very likely that you will begin with a shorter list and add to it as you develop the next level of detail. Once again it seems to make sense to include the complete list in this book once in order to avoid unnecessary repetition. *It is, however, true that you can't claim to really understand the data or the requirement until you have this much detail.*

Here is the list:

Book Author (BOOK_AUT) identifies the author(s) of a book as identified on the book's title page. It may be the name of one individual or the names of several individuals. It may also be the name of a person who edited a book consisting of a collection of works by several authors. In the case of an individual, it is customary to provide the full name. This is also the case when there are two authors. If there are more than two, the list often contains only first initials and last names.
This is character string information. There is really no limit to the possible length. Montoni's has agreed that 100 characters is adequate.[9]

Book Copyright Date (BOOK_CPY) is the date on which the current edition of the book was registered with the copyright office. This consists only of year. The information is provided by the publisher and appears on the book's title page.

Book Publisher (BOOK_PUB) is the name of the publisher of the book. It is a character string. Montoni's has agreed that 35 characters is adequate.

Book Subject (BOOK_SUB) indicates the primary subject matter of the book. Montoni's uses a standard set of categories. The list is...[10] Subject is a character string. It may be up to 20 characters. It is in the nature of Montoni's set of categories that no book has more than one subject.

Book Title (BOOK_TIT) is a book's descriptive title as shown on the title page. It is a character string. Based on a review of a current edition of *Books In Print*, it is accepted that 40 characters is adequate.[11]

Compact Disc Artist (CD_ART) is the name(s) of the artist(s) or performer(s) as featured on the label of the compact disc. It is free form character information and may be as many as 45 characters.

Compact Disc Category (CD_CAT) indicates the primary style or type of music for a compact disc. Montoni's uses a standard set of categories. The list is... Category is a character string. It may be up to 20 characters. It is in the nature of Montoni's set of categories that no compact disc has more than one category.

Compact Disc Publisher (CD_PUB) is an abbreviation of the record company's name. These are character strings up to 12 characters long. They are drawn from a standard list established by Montoni's. The list is...

Compact Disc Publisher Catalog Number (CD_PNUM) is the catalog number assigned to the compact disc by the record company. It is treated as a character string of up to 12 characters. The original source of this data is the record company.

Compact Disc Title (CD_TIT) is the title of the compact disc as featured on the disc label. It may duplicate or incorporate compact disc artist information. It is a character string of up to 40 characters.

Complete Order Information consists of order number, customer information, order information, and payment method.

Confirmation Number (CONF_NUM) is provided by the credit card company to identify a credit approval. It is necessary to retain this and refer to it if there is a subsequent problem. The information is numeric but is stored as a 10-character string.

Customer Address is the address to which the merchandise will be delivered. It consists of customer street address, customer city, customer state, and zip code. Post office box numbers are not accepted because merchandise is shipped via carriers who cannot make use of post office boxes.[12]

Customer City (CUST_CTY) is the city portion of the customer address. It is provided by the customer.[13]

Customer Credit Information consists of either of the following:

• Customer credit card type, customer credit card number, and customer credit card expiration date as provided by the customer.

• Line of credit established by Montoni's credit department and customer curren balance maintained by the system.

Customer Credit Card Expiration Date (CRED_EXP) is the date the customer's card expires. As part of the credit approval process, it is sent to the credit card company in an MMYY format. It must be a valid date. This is provided by the customer based on information provided to the customer by the credit card company.

Customer Credit Card Number (CRED_NUM) is the number which identifies the customer's credit card account. The information is provided by the customer based on information originally provided to the customer by the credit card company. A credit card company will never issue duplicate numbers. It is unlikely but conceivable that different credit card companies would issue identical numbers. The information is numeric but is stored as a 25-character string.[14]

Customer Credit Card Type (CRED_TYP) identifies the particular credit card company which has issued the customer's card. The name is provided by the customer and translated by the customer service representative to one of the standard identifiers used by Montoni's. These are...[15]

Customer Current Balance (CUST_BAL) is the amount in dollars and cents currently owed by a commercial customer. It is maintained by the system.

Customer Information consists of customer priority number, customer type, customer name and address and telephone information, and customer credit information.

Customer Name is the customer's name, consisting of first and middle name and last name. It is originally provided by the customer. In the case of a commercial customer, last name is used to store the entire name.

Customer Priority Number (CUST_NO) is a 9-digit customer identifier assigned by Montoni's. The normal format is nnn-nnn-nnn.

Customer State (CUST_ST) is the state portion of the customer's address. It is provided by the customer. The standard U.S. state abbreviation is used. These are...[16]

Customer Street Address (CUST_ADD) is the customer's street number and street name stored as a 35-character string. It is provided by the customer.

Customer Telephone (CUST_PH) is the customer's day time telephone number consisting of area code, exchange, number, and extension if any.[17] This is provided by the customer. It is stored as a 13-character string. The normal external format is aaa-eee-nnn-xxxx.

Customer Type (CUST_TYP) "I" indicates an individual who pays by credit card. "C" indicates a commercial customer with a line of credit.

Date Of Last Purchase (DLP) is the year, month, and day[18] on which the customer last purchased something. This is to be recorded by the system. In the case of a brand new customer it is NULL.

Date Of Order (ORD_DATE) is the date on which the order was placed. It consists of year, month, and day.

Date Of Shipment (SHP_DATE) is the date on which a customer's order was shipped. This consists of year, month, and day.

Dollar Amount of Last Purchase (ALP) represents the value in dollars and cents of the customer's most recent purchase. In the case of a brand new customer it is NULL. This is to be recorded by the system.

Dollar Amount Purchased Last Year (ALY) represents the total value of all purchases made by the customer during the previous calendar year. A calendar year runs from January 1 to December 31. If the individual or company was not a customer last year this is NULL. This is updated by a special program at the beginning of the year.[19]

Dollar Amount Purchased This Year (ATY) represents the total value of all purchases made by the customer during the current calendar year. A calendar year runs from January 1 to December 31. In the case of a brand new customer this is zero.[20] This is set to zero by a special program at the beginning of the year and is then maintained by the system.

First and Middle name (CUST_FRS) is the customer's first and middle names stored as a 20-character string.

ISBN is the International Standard Book Number, "used by publishers, distributors, wholesalers, bookstores, and libraries, among others, in 64 countries to expedite such operations as order fulfillment, electronic point-of-sale checkout, inventory control, returns processing, circulation/location control, file maintenance and update, library union lists, and royalty payments." [SIMORA91]

In the United States, the ISBN system is administered by the U.S. ISBN Agency in New York under the auspices of the International ISBN Agency in Berlin.

The system provides a unique 10-digit number to each book. The number consists of a group identifier ("national, geographic, language, or other convenient group") followed by a publisher or producer identifier followed by a title identifier followed by a check digit.[21]

"When an ISBN is written or printed, it should be preceded by the letters ISBN, and each part should be separated by a space or hyphen. In the United States, the hyphen is used for separation..." The number of digits for each component is not constant. It is necessary to store the locations of the 3 hyphens.

Last Name (CUST_LST) is the customer's last name stored as a 20-character string.

Line Of Credit (LOC) is a predetermined credit limit set by Montoni's credit department for a commercial customer. It is recorded in dollars and cents.

Manufacturer's List Price (LIST) is the unit retail price suggested by the publisher, record company, or manufacturer in dollars and cents.

Montoni's Bargain Price (PRICE) is Montoni's selling price in dollars and cents. It is established by the sales department.

Montoni Catalog Number (M_CAT) is Montoni's Identifier for a specific product. It is a 9-digit number assigned by the sales department. The usual external format is nnn-nnnnn-n.

Montoni's Merchant Identifier is the merchant identifier assigned to Montoni's by a credit card company. There is a unique number for each credit card type. Twenty characters is adequate.

Notification of Shipment consists of all complete order information and date of shipment.

Notice Of Unavailability consists of customer information, order number, and one order item, and indicates that the item was omitted from the order.

Number of Purchases Last Year (NLY) represents the total number of purchases made by the customer during the previous calendar year. A calendar year runs from January 1 to December 31. If the individual or company was not a Customer this is NULL. This is updated by a special program at the beginning of the year.

Number of Purchases This Year (NTY) represents the total number of purchases made by the customer during the current calendar year. A calendar year runs from January 1 to December 31. In the case of a brand new Customer this is zero. This is set to zero by a special program at the beginning of the year and is then maintained by the system.

Order Confirmation Information consists of complete order information plus the implied statement that the order has been accepted.

Order Information consists of a list of order items plus order total amount.

Order Item consists of Montoni catalog number, quantity ordered, Montoni's bargain price, and order item value.

Order Item Value (ITEM_VAL) is calculated as quantity ordered $\times$ Montoni's bargain price.

Order Number (ORD_NUM) is assigned by Montoni's to uniquely identify a specific order. This is an 11-digit number and is normally represented as nnn-nnnnn-nnn.

Order Picking Information consists of complete order information augmented by a warehouse location for each order item.

Order Total Amount (TOT_AMT) is the sum of all order item values for a particular order.

Packing Slip Information consists of complete order information and date of shipment.

Payment Method is the method of payment for a specific order. It is included for all individual customers and consists of customer credit card type, customer credit card number, customer credit card expiration date and confirmation number. In the case of a corporate customer, a purchase order number may be included.

Piano Manufacturer (P_MFR) is the name of the piano's manufacturer stored as a 35-character string.

Piano Model Number (P_MOD) is a unique model identifier assigned to a specific type of piano by the manufacturer. There is no guarantee that two different manufacturers will not use the same number. It is stored as a 10-character string.

Piano Serial Number (SERIAL) is the unique serial number assigned to a specific piano by the manufacturer. There is no guarantee that two different manufacturers will not use the same number. It is stored as a 20-character string.

Piano Status (P_STAT) a given piano in the warehouse may be available for sale or reserved for an order.

Picking Result Information is essentially the same as complete order information. It is possible that some items which could not be located in the warehouse are omitted.

Product Type (P_TYPE) does not become evident until much later. It will be used to differentiate books, compact discs, and pianos from each other.

Purchase Order Number (PO) identifies a specific commercial customer purchase order. These numbers are assigned by the customers. There is no guarantee that two different customers will not use the same number. Some customers do not provide PO numbers. Twenty characters is deemed adequate.

Quantity Available (QTY_AVAL) is the quantity of a given product which is available for sale. This is decremented when an order is entered. This is a 6-digit integer number.

Quantity On Hand (QTY_OH) is the quantity of a given product actually in the warehouse. This is decremented when an order is picked. This is a 6-digit integer number.

Quantity Ordered (ORD_QTY) is the number of units of a particular item ordered by a particular customer on a particular order. This is a 4-digit integer number.

Unit Availability (UNIT_AVL) does not become evident until later. It is an indication of whether or not a particular piano has been reserved for an order.

Warehouse Location (WHSE_LOC) identifies the specific bin or shelf in the warehouse which contains the item. This is stored as a 10-character string.

Zip Code (ZIP) is the 9-digit U.S. postal code for the customer. This is provided by the customer. It is originally established by the post office.

More comments are in order here.

We suddenly find we've developed a *lot of detail*. It is again possible to debate about just how soon this much detail should be collected. (It is also possible to debate the precise form of presentation.[22]) *We will not be able to go much further without this information. We also can't be sure we are building the right system if this list is not identified and agreed to.* We could wait a little longer to develop this list, but not much longer.

It may seem foolish to be so careful about definitions. "Everyone knows what these are." It is not foolish. Everyone doesn't know. We avoid a lot of trouble by being very careful about this.

Collecting and recording this much information can be time-consuming, difficult, and tedious.[23] But neither the system nor the database can possibly be correct unless this is all correct!

10.5 ENTITIES AND RELATIONSHIPS—VERSION 1

Figure 10.2 is a very simple *first cut entity relationship diagram*. Soon we will refine and extend this. It is included at this point just to be sure we know what we are working with here. Even this simple diagram can lead us into a lot of detail.

These are the *entities*:

CUSTOMER
A customer is any individual or company that places an order with Montoni's or establishes a line of credit with Montoni's.
The *candidate key* for customer is customer priority number.

It is also necessary to be able to locate customers by the combination of last name and zip code.

Customers are categorized as individual or commercial. Individual customers pay by credit card. Commercial customers have a predetermined line of credit.

New customer records are created by customer service representatives when orders are place by individual customers. They are also created by the credit department when new lines of credit are established for commercial customers.

Customer records are deleted by a special annual program which analyzes customer history data.

There are 50,000 customers. New customers are added at the rate of approximately 100 per week. Approximately 10,000 customers are deleted once a year.

Attributes of customer are:

> Customer Address
> Customer Credit Information
> Customer Name
> Customer Priority Number
> Customer Telephone
> Customer Type
> Date Of Last Purchase
> Dollar Amount Of Last Purchase
> Dollar Amount Purchased Last Year
> Dollar Amount Purchased This Year
> Number of Purchases Last Year
> Number of Purchases This Year

PRODUCT

A product is any book, compact disc, or piano which Montoni's will sell to a customer.

The *candidate keys* for product are:

- Compact disc publisher and catalog number (for compact disc only)
- ISBN (for book only)
- Montoni's catalog number
- Piano model number (for piano only)
- Piano model number and serial number (for individual piano only)

There is also a desire to search for products by book title, partial book title, author name, partial author name, compact disc title, partial compact disc title, compact disc artist name, or partial compact disc artist name.

Product records are created, updated, and deleted by the sales department. Quantities are updated as a part of the sales process and also when new goods are received.

There are 25,000 book titles. This number is relatively constant.

There are 15,000 compact disc titles. This number has been growing rapidly but seems to be stabilizing.

Montoni's normally stocks about 50 units total of 10 different models of piano.

Attributes of product are:

> Book Author
> Book Copyright Date
> Book Publisher
> Book Subject
> Book Title
> Compact Disc Artist
> Compact Disc Category
> Compact Disc Title
> Compact Disc Publisher
> Compact Disc Publisher Catalog Number
> ISBN
> Montoni's Bargain Price
> Montoni's Catalog Number
> Piano Manufacturer
> Piano Model Number
> Piano Serial Number
> Quantity Available
> Quantity On Hand
> Warehouse Location

ORDER

An order represents the agreement between Montoni's and a specific customer that specific products will be shipped to the customer for a specific price. It incorporates an agreement regarding method of payment.

The *candidate key* for order is order number.

It may also be desirable to search for orders by customer priority number, date of order, or Montoni's catalog number.

New orders are entered by customer service representatives. They are also maintained as a part of the shipping process. A record of a shipped order is forwarded to the accounting department. Order history is maintained by the accounting department. The order processing department does not retain a record of an order once it is shipped.

There are normally about 600 new orders per day. Roughly 2,400 orders may be on file at a given time. There is about 10 times as much activity from October through December.

Orders cannot exist without corresponding customers and products.

Attributes of order are:

> Complete Order Information
> Date Of Order
> Date Of Shipment
> Order Confirmation Information
> Order Picking Information
> Packing Slip Information

It is instructive to note several potential entities we omit. We do not include accounting department, credit card company, customer service representative, manufacturer, publisher, record company, or warehouse because we do not think we have information about these to store in the database. (We may change our mind about some of these later.)

These are the *relationships*:

CUSTOMER PLACES ORDER

A particular order will have been placed by one customer. A Customer may place any number of orders.

ORDER FOR PRODUCT

An order may be for any number of products. The average is 3. The minimum is 1. The highest that has ever been recorded is 128. Any number of orders may be placed for a given product.

Completion of the context diagram, the first entity relationship diagram, and the list of domains provides a well-defined review point.[24] We'd solicit as much user comment as we could possibly get, conduct some detailed reviews, and *reevaluate the plan, the schedule, and the cost estimate.*

10.6   DATA FLOW DIAGRAM

Figure 10.3 is a moderately detailed data flow diagram. We'd be even more detailed for a real project.

We've decomposed the system into three major processes.

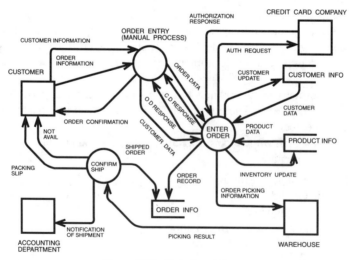

Figure 10.3   Data flow diagram

- ORDER ENTRY
- ENTER ORDER
- CONFIRM SHIP

ORDER ENTRY is a manual process. Here the customer service representative is interacting with the customer and with the automated system. We'd really be concerned to develop a detailed procedure for this. In the process of doing so, we'd be likely to identify more specific data flows. We'd be particularly interested in the data flows between this process and the automated portion of the system because these would then guide the design of the screens used. The process of locating a particular customer already on file is likely to be quite involved. The same is true of the process of locating desired product(s). Both may involve extensive exchanges of information between the customer service representative and the automated system and between the customer service representative and the customer. We avoid this to keep this discussion from getting any more involved than it already is. (Working out these kinds of details is the sort of activity that can readily be approached by prototyping. We understand the data. We know in general what we want to accomplish. But we need to develop a detailed exchange of information.)

Here are the data flows for order entry. We omit detailed discussions of the data elements in the cause of brevity. An asterisk (*) marks a data flow which has already been discussed. Note that the same name is always used for the same thing and different names are used for different things to be consistent and avoid confusion.

Customer Data Entry. This is the customer data provided to the automated system by the customer service representative.

Customer Data Response. This is the customer data provided to the customer service representative by the automated system.

Customer Information*

Order Confirmation*

Order Data. This is the order data provided to the automated system by the customer service representative.

Order Data Response. This is the order data provided to the customer service representative by the automated system.

Order Information*

ENTER ORDER is the automated portion of the order entry process. It consists of the screens and/or programs which process the data entered by the customer service representative. These include searching the customer data, updating the customer data, searching the product data, updating the product data, keeping a record of the order, transmitting an authorization request to the credit card company, accepting an authorization response, and transmitting order picking information to the warehouse. Again, we just list the data flows in the sake of brevity. Again an asterisk (*) indicates a data flow we've already discussed.

Authorization Request*

Authorization Response[*]

Customer Data. This is the customer information extracted from the customer information file.

Customer Data Entry[*]

Customer Data Response[*]

Customer Update. This is the customer information placed in the customer information file.

Inventory Update. This is the update of the quantity for each product ordered. Note that in the case of books and compact discs we merely decrement a quantity while in the case of a piano we assign a particular unit.

Order Data[*]

Order Data Response[*]

Order Picking Data. This is the picking information sent to the warehouse.

Order Record. This is the record of the order which is kept until the merchandise has been shipped. Another complication we can note and then ignore is that we'd need a periodic audit of this data to assure that no orders were overlooked by the warehouse.

Product Data. This is the product information extracted from the product information file.

CONFIRM SHIP is the process of accepting the picking result from the warehouse. We clear the record of the open order, notify the accounting department, and notify the customer.

These are the data flows.

Not Available[*]

Notification of Shipment[*]

Packing Slip[*]

Picking Result[*]

Shipped Order. This is the elimination of shipped merchandise from the open orders record.

Note that while we know the quantity on hand must be updated by the warehouse staff, we've not included it in this system and it doesn't show up here. (We'd probably decide to add this function to this system.)

The data flow diagram also shows three data stores; Customer Info, Order Info, and Product Info which represent the retention of information about customers, orders, and products. Most methodologies and CASE tools will justifiably provide for documentation of the details of these. Again we simplify by omitting this.

Notice that most of the detailed discussion of data flows and data stores will consist of reference to our list of domain definitions. This is also true of the process descriptions.

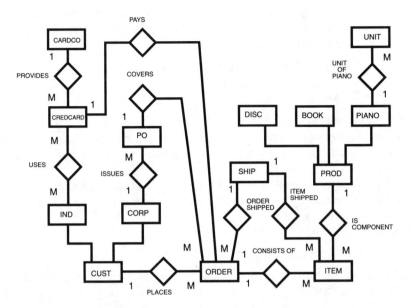

Figure 10.4   Detailed entity relationship diagram

10.7   ENTITIES AND RELATIONSHIPS—VERSION 2

Now it's time to develop a more detailed *entity relationship diagram*. This diagram is illustrated by Figure 10.4. The first diagram we developed (Figure 10.2) was intentionally very simple. It was really intended to go along with the *context diagram.* The unstated philosophy was to omit any details that were not absolutely necessary. The philosophy for this new diagram is just the opposite. Because we want to be sure we don't omit anything important, we use the "if in doubt, make it an entity" approach suggested in Chapters 4 and 5. You should also observe that we could use the techniques described in Section 5.8 to transform one diagram to the other.

It is also time to become more careful about data items which are composed of other data items. Here we use indenting to clarify.

Here are the *entities*:

BOOK is a subtype of PRODuct. We accept that anything a publisher calls a BOOK
   is a BOOK.[25] BOOKs are distinguished from periodicals which have a regular
   publishing schedule.[26]
   There are 25,000 book titles. This number is relatively constant.
   Attributes of BOOK are:
       Book Author
       Book Copyright Date
       Book Publisher
       Book Subject
       Book Title
       ISBN

CREDCARD is an abbreviation for customer credit card. It represents a specific credit card account which may be used by an INDividual CUSTomer.[27]
Attributes of CREDCARD are:

> Customer Credit Card Expiration Date
> Customer Credit Card Number
> Customer Credit Card Type

CARDCO is an abbreviation for credit card company. It represents a specific credit card company or the agent of a credit card company. Montoni's obtains credit authorizations from this entity and subsequently submits charges and receives payments.
There are in the neighborhood of 12 separate credit card companies or agents. A CARDCO is added when Montoni's makes a formal agreement with the credit card company or agent.
Attribute of CARDCO is:[28]

> Customer Credit Card Type

CORP is the subtype of CUST which represents a CORPorate CUSTOMER. CORPorate CUSTOMERs are differentiated from INDividual CUSTOMERs in that they have predetermined lines of credit and are billed for purchases.
There are approximately 1,000 CORPorate CUSTOMERS.
Attributes specific to CORP are:

> Customer Credit Information
>> Customer Current Balance
>> Line Of Credit
> Customer Name
>> Last Name

CUST is an abbreviation for CUSTOMER. A customer is any individual or company which places an order with Montoni's or establishes a line of credit with Montoni's.
The candidate key for customer is customer priority number. It is also necessary to be able to locate customers by the combination of last name and zip code.
CUST is a supertype with IND and CORP as subtypes or kinds of CUSTOMER. Customers are categorized as individual or commercial. Individual customers pay by credit card. Commercial customers have a predetermined line of credit. It is very likely we'd generate one version of the diagram that did not contain this detail and subsequently add it.
New customer records are created by customer service representatives when orders are place by individual customers. They are also created by the credit department when new lines of credit are established for commercial customers.
Customer records are deleted by a special annual program which analyzes customer history data.
There are 50,000 customers. New customers are added at the rate of approximately 100 per week. Approximately 10,000 customers are deleted once a year.

Attributes of CUST (common to all CUSTomers) are:

> Customer Address
>> Customer Street Address
>> Customer City
>> Customer State
>> Zip Code
>
> Customer Credit Information
>> (While all customers have credit information, the type of information varies by customer type.)
>
> Customer Name
>> (While all customers have customer name, the type of information varies by customer type)
>
> Customer Priority Number
> Customer Telephone
> Customer Type
> Date Of Last Purchase
> Dollar Amount Of Last Purchase
> Dollar Amount Purchased Last Year
> Dollar Amount Purchased This Year
> Number of Purchases Last Year
> Number of Purchases This Year

DISC is a compact disc recording.[29] This is a subtype of PRODUCT.

There are 15,000 compact disc titles. This number has been growing rapidly but seems to be stabilizing.

Attributes of DISC are:

> Compact Disc Artist
> Compact Disc Category
> Compact Disc Title
> Compact Disc Publisher
> Compact Disc Publisher Catalog Number

IND is the subtype of CUST which represents an individual CUSTOMER. INDividual CUSTOMERs are differentiated from CORPorate CUSTOMERs in that payments for purchases are made by credit card.

There are approximately 49,000 INDividual CUSTOMERs.

Attributes specific to IND are:

> Customer Credit Information
>> Customer Credit Card Type
>> Customer Credit Card Number
>> Customer Credit Card Expiration Date
>
> Customer Name
>> First and Middle Name
>> Last Name

ITEM represents an individual Line ITEM of an ORDER.

An ITEM cannot exist without a corresponding ORDER and PRODUCT.

An Order may be for any number of products. The average is 3. The minimum is 1. The highest that has ever been recorded is 128. Any number of orders may be placed for a given product.

The *candidate key* for ITEM is order number and item identifier.[30]

Attributes for ITEM are:

> Order Number
> Montoni Catalog Number
> Quantity Ordered
> Montoni's Bargain Price (Derived from Montoni's Catalog Number)
> Order Item Value (Calculated)

Note that it is necessary to include the price used for this order because the price for the item could change after the order has been booked.

ORDER represents the agreement between Montoni's and a specific customer that specific products will be shipped to the customer for a specific price. It incorporates an agreement regarding method of payment.

The *candidate key* for order is order number.

It may also be desirable to search for orders by customer priority number, date of order, or Montoni's catalog number.

New ORDERs are entered by customer service representatives. They are also maintained as a part of the shipping process. A record of a shipped order is forwarded to the Accounting Department. Order history is maintained by the Accounting Department. The order processing department does not retain a record of an order once it is shipped.

There are normally about 600 new Orders per day. Roughly 2,400 Orders may be on file at a given time. There is about 10 times as much activity from October through December.

Orders cannot exist without corresponding customers and products.

Attributes of ORDER are:

> Complete Order Information
> Order Number
> Customer Information[31]
> > Customer Priority Number
> > Customer Type
> > Customer Name
> > > First and Middle Name
> > > Last Name
> > Customer Address
> > Customer Telephone
> > Customer Credit Information
> Order Information
> > Order Items[32]
> > Order Total Amount (Calculated)
> Payment Method

For Individual Customers (A Customer may use different Credit Cards for different Orders.)

> Customer Credit Card Type
> Customer Credit Card Number
> Customer Credit Card Expiration Date
> Confirmation Number

For Corporate Customers

> Purchase Order Number

Date Of Order

Date Of Shipment

Order Confirmation Information (Not really an attribute. It is implied by the acceptance of the order.)

Order Picking Information (Warehouse Location for each Item.)

Packing Slip Information (We need to record that the order has been shipped.)

> Date Of Shipment.

PIANO is a grand piano.[33] This is a subtype of PRODUCT.

Montoni's normally stocks about 50 units total of 10 different models of piano.

Attributes of PIANO are:

> Piano Manufacturer
> Piano Model Number

PO is an abbreviation for customer purchase order. A purchase order is a document issued by a corporate customer. It is the customer's official order for something. Many corporate customers request that an invoice make reference to a specific purchase order number.[34]

Attributes of PO are:

> Purchase Order Number

PROD is an abbreviation for PRODUCT. A PRODuct is any book, compact disc, or piano which Montoni's will sell to a customer.

The *candidate keys* for PRODuct are:

- Compact disc publisher and catalog number (for compact disc only)
- ISBN number (for book only)
- Montoni's catalog number
- Piano model number (for piano only)
- Piano model number and serial number (for individual piano only)

There is also a desire to search for products by book title, partial book title, author name, partial author name, compact disc title, partial compact disc title, compact disc artist name, or partial compact disc artist name.

PROD is a supertype of BOOK, DISC, and PIANO. PRODuct records are created, updated, and deleted by the sales department. Quantities are updated as a part of the sales process and also when new goods are received.

Attributes of PROD (common to all PRODucts) are:

Montoni's Bargain Price
Montoni's Catalog Number
Quantity Available
Quantity On Hand
Warehouse Location

SHIP is an abbreviation for SHIPMENT. SHIPment really represents an ORDER that has been shipped. It is possible that some ITEMs will not be found in the warehouse and will be omitted from the SHIPment.

Information about this entity is NOT stored in the order entry database. It is transmitted to the accounting department.

UNIT represents a specific grand piano. Montoni's normally stocks about 50 units total of 10 different models of piano. A UNIT cannot exist without a corresponding PIANO.

Attributes of UNIT are:

Piano Manufacturer
Piano Model Number
Piano Serial Number
Status (Available or Reserved)

These are the *relationships*:

CONSISTS OF (ORDER CONSISTS OF ITEM)

This relates ONE ORDER to MANY ITEMS. An order may be for any number of PRODucts. The average is 3. The minimum is 1. The highest that has ever been recorded is 128. Any number of orders may be placed for a given PRODuct.

COVERS (PO COVERS ORDER)

ONE CORPorate CUSTomer PO may cover MANY ORDERs.

IS COMPONENT (PRODuct IS COMPONENT OF ORDER)

This relates one PRODuct to MANY ITEMS. A PRODuct may be a component of any number of ORDERs.

ISSUES (CORP ISSUES PO)

This relates ONE CORP to MANY POs.

ITEM SHIPPED

This relates one SHIPment to MANY ITEMs. It is possible that some of the ITEMs ordered are not available and are omitted from the shipment.

ORDER SHIPPED

This is a ONE TO ONE relationship between ORDERs and SHIPments. Montoni's does not back order or make partial shipments.

PAYS (CREDCARD PAYS ORDER)

ONE Credit Card Account may be used to PAY for MANY ORDERs.

PLACES (CUSTomer PLACES ORDER)

This relates ONE CUSTomer to MANY ORDERS. A particular Order will have been placed by one CUSTomer. A CUSTomer may place any number of ORDERs.

PROVIDES (CARDCO PROVIDES CREDCARD)
This relates ONE CARDCO to MANY CREDCARD.

UNIT OF PIANO
This relates ONE PIANO to MANY UNITs.

USES (IND USES CREDCARD)
This is a MANY TO MANY relationship between INDividual CUSTomer and CREDCARD. While a CUSTomer may use different CREDCARDs for different ORDERs, Montoni's only retains a record of one Customer Credit Card Type and Customer Credit Card Number. If the CUSTomer uses the same Card, typing and possible error is eliminated.

Let's review.

This is a fairly detailed version of the *entity relationship diagram*. We have included as entities some things which probably will not be represented as tables in the database. *The purpose of this data model is to clarify and communicate our understanding of the data. It is not the final database design.*

You should note that the data items which appear here can be cross referenced to the detailed data flow diagram. If there are any which appear one place but not the other, the circumstances must be questioned. It is possible that some intermediate result which appears in the process model will be omitted from the data model. But the converse does not seem as reasonable. Some of the data shown in the data model might be *for future use.* But if there is no process to place it in the database, including it here is very questionable. At minimum, we will be sure we have an explanation for every discrepancy. Many CASE tools will provide a way to perform this analysis.

This would without a doubt be an *appropriate time for a detailed and careful review of everything that has been developed so far.* We'd solicit as much user comment as we could possibly get, conduct some detailed reviews, and *reevaluate the plan, the schedule, and the cost estimate.*

10.8 NORMALIZATION

We begin the normalization by formally identifying dependencies.

We should examine each entity and relationship carefully as we make this list. The normalization will follow directly from the list.

In practice, this could be the place to begin introducing abbreviated data names. We retain the full names here because it helps clarify the meaning of each dependency.

Most of these are self-evident from the diagram and the explanation we've gone through. Remember

$$A \rightarrow B$$

means A determines B or there is but ONE B for any given A.

Compact Disc Publisher +
Compact Disc Publisher Catalog Number $\rightarrow$ Compact Disc Artist

Compact Disc Publisher +
Compact Disc Publisher Catalog Number $\rightarrow$ Compact Disc Category

Compact Disc Publisher +
Compact Disc Publisher Catalog Number $\rightarrow$ Compact Disc Title

Compact Disc Publisher +
Compact Disc Publisher Catalog Number $\rightarrow$ Manufacturer's List Price

Compact Disc Publisher +
Compact Disc Publisher Catalog Number $\rightarrow$ Montoni's Bargain Price

Compact Disc Publisher +
Compact Disc Publisher Catalog Number $\rightarrow$ Montoni Catalog Number

Compact Disc Publisher +
Compact Disc Publisher Catalog Number $\rightarrow$ Quantity Available

Compact Disc Publisher +
Compact Disc Publisher Catalog Number $\rightarrow$ Quantity On Hand

Compact Disc Publisher +
Compact Disc Publisher Catalog Number $\rightarrow$ Warehouse Location

Customer Priority Number $\rightarrow$ Customer City

Customer Priority Number $\rightarrow$ Customer Credit Card Expiration Date

Customer Priority Number $\rightarrow$ Customer Credit Card Number

Customer Priority Number $\rightarrow$ Customer Credit Card Type

Customer Priority Number $\rightarrow$ Customer Current Balance

Customer Priority Number $\rightarrow$ Date Of Last Purchase

Customer Priority Number $\rightarrow$ Dollar Amount Of Last Purchase

Customer Priority Number $\rightarrow$ Dollar Amount Purchased Last Year

Customer Priority Number $\rightarrow$ Dollar Amount Purchased This Year

Customer Priority Number $\rightarrow$ Number of Purchases Last Year

Customer Priority Number $\rightarrow$ Number of Purchases This Year

Customer Priority Number $\rightarrow$ Customer State

Customer Priority Number $\rightarrow$ Customer Street Address

Customer Priority Number $\rightarrow$ Customer Type

Customer Priority Number $\rightarrow$ Customer Telephone

Customer Priority Number $\rightarrow$ First and Middle Name

Customer Priority Number $\rightarrow$ Last Name

Customer Priority Number $\rightarrow$ Line Of Credit

Customer Priority Number $\rightarrow$ Zip Code

ISBN $\rightarrow$ Book Author

ISBN → Book Copyright Date

ISBN → Book Publisher

ISBN → Book Subject

ISBN → Book Title

ISBN → Manufacturer's List Price

ISBN → Montoni's Bargain Price

ISBN → Montoni Catalog Number

ISBN → Quantity Available

ISBN → Quantity On Hand

ISBN → Warehouse Location

Montoni Catalog Number → Book Author

Montoni Catalog Number → Book Copyright Date

Montoni Catalog Number → Book Publisher

Montoni Catalog Number → Book Subject

Montoni Catalog Number → Book Title

Montoni Catalog Number → Compact Disc Artist

Montoni Catalog Number → Compact Disc Category

Montoni Catalog Number → Compact Disc Title

Montoni Catalog Number → Compact Disc Publisher

Montoni Catalog Number → Compact Disc Publisher Catalog Number

Montoni Catalog Number → ISBN

Montoni Catalog Number → Manufacturer's List Price

Montoni Catalog Number → Montoni's Bargain Price

Montoni Catalog Number → Piano Manufacturer

Montoni Catalog Number → Piano Model Number

Montoni Catalog Number →→ {Piano Serial Number}

Montoni Catalog Number → Quantity Available

Montoni Catalog Number → Quantity On Hand

Montoni Catalog Number → Warehouse Location
(There is an exception: there will be multiple locations for individual pianos of a given model.)

Order Number → Confirmation Number

Order Number → Customer Credit Card Type

Order Number → Customer Credit Card Number

Order Number → Customer Credit Card Expiration Date

Order Number → Customer Priority Number

Order Number → Date Of Order

Order Number → Date Of Shipment

Order Number → Order Total Amount (Calculated)

Order Number → Purchase Order Number

Order Number ↠ {Order Items}

Order Number +
Montoni Catalog Number → Quantity Ordered

Order Number +
Montoni Catalog Number → Order Item Value (Calculated)

Order Number +
Montoni Catalog Number → Montoni's Bargain Price

Piano Manufacturer +
Piano Model Number → Manufacturer's List Price

Piano Manufacturer +
Piano Model Number → Montoni's Bargain Price

Piano Manufacturer +
Piano Model Number → Montoni Catalog Number

Piano Manufacturer +
Piano Model Number → Quantity Available

Piano Manufacturer +
Piano Model Number → Quantity On Hand

Piano Manufacturer +
Piano Serial Number → Montoni Catalog Number

Piano Manufacturer +
Piano Serial Number → Piano Model Number

Piano Manufacturer +
Piano Serial Number → Status (Available or Reserved)

Piano Manufacturer +
Piano Serial Number → Warehouse Location

The next step is to develop a set of normalized relations based on these dependencies. For the most part we are able to derive them from the dependencies.

For the first cut at this we just work through dependencies. It will be too cumbersome to continue working with the long names. We are getting close enough to the physical design to assign abbreviations.

Here is our list of abbreviations. We've attempted to be fairly logical in developing them but haven't gone overboard in setting up an elaborate structure of abbreviations and rules. We've operated on the premise that we will work with a DBMS which restricts us to 8-character names. This makes it really difficult to do a lot. We've also decided that since we carried the full names up to this point, have some good definitions, and provide a cross reference, these will be adequate.

ALP = Dollar Amount Of Last Purchase

ALY = Dollar Amount Purchased Last Year

ATY = Dollar Amount Purchased This Year

BOOK_AUT = Book Author

BOOK_CPY = Book Copyright Date

BOOK_PUB = Book Publisher

BOOK_SUB = Book Subject

BOOK_TIT = Book Title

CD_ART = Compact Disc Artist

CD_CAT = Compact Disc Category

CD_PNUM = Compact Disc Publisher Catalog Number

CD_TITLE = Compact Disc Title

CD_PUB = Compact Disc Publisher

CONF_NUM = Confirmation Number

CRED_EXP = Customer Credit Card Expiration Date

CRED_NUM = Customer Credit Card Number

CRED_TYP = Customer Credit Card Type

CUST_ADD = Customer Street Address

CUST_BAL = Customer Current Balance

CUST_NO = Customer Priority Number

CUST_CTY = Customer City

CUST_FRS = Customer First and Middle Name

CUST_LST = Customer Last Name

CUST_PH = Customer Phone

CUST_ST = Customer State

CUST_TYP = Customer Type

DLP = Date of Last Purchase

ISBN = ISBN Number

ITEM_VAL = Order Item Value

LIST = Manufacturer's List Price

LOC = Line Of Credit

M_CAT = Montoni Catalog Number

NLY = Number Of Purchases Last Year

NTY = Number Of Purchases This Year

PRICE = Montoni's Bargain Price

ORD_NUM = Order Number
ORD_DATE = Date Of Order
ORD_QTY = Quantity Ordered
P_MFR = Piano Manufacturer
P_MOD = Piano Model Number
P_STAT = Status Of Piano
P_TYPE = Product Type
PO = Purchase Order Number
QTY_AVAL = Quantity Available
QTY_OH = Quantity On Hand
SERIAL = Piano Serial Number
SHP_DATE = Date Of Shipment
TOT_AMT = Order Total Amount
UNIT_AVL = Unit Availability
WHSE_LOC = Warehouse Location
ZIP = Zip Code

Here is the *first cut* at a set of *relations*. It is illustrated by Figure 10.5. You should be able to see that we have derived these directly from the dependencies.

> BOOK(BOOK_AUT, BOOK_CPY, BOOK_PUB, BOOK_SUB, BOOK_TIT, ISBN, LIST, <u>M_CAT</u>, PRICE, QTY_AVAL, QTY_OH, WHSE_LOC)

This is derived from the entity BOOK.

> CD(CD_ART, CD_CAT, CD_PNUM, CD-PUB, CD_TITLE, LIST, <u>M_CAT</u>, PRICE, QTY_AVAL, QTY_OH, WHSE_LOC)

This is derived from the entity DISC.

> CUST(ALP, ALY, ATY, CRED_EXP, CRED_NUM, CRED_TYP, CUST_ADD, CUST_BAL, CUST_CTY, CUST_FRS, CUST_LST, <u>CUST_NO</u>, CUST_PH, CUST_ST, CUST_TYP, DLP, LOC, ZIP)

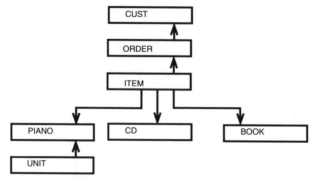

Figure 10.5 Normalization from FDs

This is derived from the entity CUST.

ITEM(ITEM_VAL, <u>M_CAT</u>, <u>ORD_NUM</u>, ORD_QTY, PRICE)

This is derived from the entity ITEM.

ORDER(CONF_NUM, CRED_EXP, CRD_NUM, CRED_TYP, <u>CUST_NO</u>,
ORD_DATE, <u>ORD_NUM</u>, PO, TOT_AMT

This is derived from the entity ORDER.

PIANO(LIST, <u>M_CAT</u>, P_MFR, P_MOD, PRICE, QTY_AVAL, QTY_OH)

This is derived from the entity PIANO.

UNIT(<u>M_CAT</u>, P_MOD, P_STAT, <u>SERIAL</u>, UNIT_AVL, WHSE_LOC)

This is derived from the entity UNIT.

Now, let's review in light of the other information we have.

So far we have a separate relation for each subtype of product, but no relation for the supertype. We really have several choices to evaluate on this.

We can stay with our first arrangement. We'd favor this if the subtypes had no attributes in common.

We can combine all three into one relation as shown by Figure 10.6. We'd favor this if all the attributes were common to all.

PRODUCT(BOOK_AUT, BOOK_CPY, BOOK_PUB, BOOK_SUB,
BOOK_TIT, ISBN, LIST, <u>M_CAT</u>, PRICE, QTY_AVAL, QTY_OH,
WHSE_LOC, CD_ART, CD_CAT, CD_PNUM, CD-PUB, CD_TITLE,
P_MFR, P_MOD)

The only *candidate key* we can seriously consider would be M_CAT because ISBN, CD_PNUM + CD_PUB, and P_MFR + P_MOD will be NULL in many rows.

We still need a separate relation for unit, since WHSE_LOC for a PIANO is determined by SERIAL.

We can adopt a mixed approach, providing one relation for the attributes the three types have in common plus one for each subtype as shown by Figure 10.7. We favor this

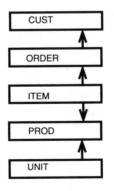

Figure 10.6   Supertype only

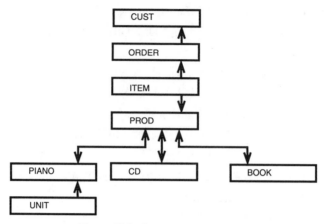

Figure 10.7 Supertype and subtypes

because neither of the above seems appropriate. We will add an attribute for product type, called P_TYPE. This is not strictly needed but it will be a convenience.

> BOOK(<u>M_CAT</u>, BOOK_AUT, BOOK_CPY, BOOK_PUB, BOOK_SUB, BOOK_TIT, ISBN)
>
> CD(<u>M_CAT</u>, CD_ART, CD_CAT, CD_PNUM, CD-PUB, CD_TITLE)
>
> PIANO(<u>M_CAT</u>, P_MFR, P_MOD)
>
> PRODUCT(<u>M_CAT</u>, LIST, PRICE, P_TYPE, QTY_AVAL, QTY_OH, WHSE_LOC)

M_CAT will be the *key* for each of these. ISBN, CD_PNUM + CD_PUB, and P_MFR + P_MOD are also *candidate keys*.

As in the above, we also need a separate relation for UNIT.

> UNIT(<u>M_CAT</u>, P_MOD, P_STAT, <u>SERIAL</u>, UNIT_AVL, WHSE_LOC)

It is very tempting to start looking at physical design issues and make the final decision now. Let's wait a little longer.

We have one relation for Customer.

> CUST(ALP, ALY, ATY, CRED_EXP, CRED_NUM, CRED_TYP, CUST_ADD, CUST_BAL, CUST_CTY, CUST_FRS, CUST_LST, <u>CUST_NO</u>, CUST_PH, CUST_ST, CUST_TYP, DLP, LOC, ZIP)

We can observe that this is normalized with CUST_NO as *key*.

We might perform extensive analysis to determine if there should be separate relations for the subtypes CORP and IND. We can note that INDividual CUSTomers do not have CUST_BAL or LOC while CORPorate CUSTomers do not have CRED_EXP, CRED_NUM, or CRED_TYP.

The alternative looks like this.

> CUST(<u>CUST_NO</u>, ALP, ALY, ATY, CUST_ADD, CUST_CTY, CUST_FRS, CUST_LST, CUST_PH, CUST_ST, CUST_TYP, DLP, ZIP)

IND_CUST(<u>CUST_NO</u>, CRED_EXP, CRED_NUM, CRED_TYP)

CORP_CST(<u>CUST_NO</u>, CUST_BAL, LOC)

We have one relation each for ORDERs and ITEMs.

ORDER(CONF_NUM, CRED_EXP, CRD_NUM, CRED_TYP, CUST_NO, ORD_DATE, <u>ORD_NUM</u>, PO, TOT_AMT

ITEM(ITEM_VAL, <u>M_CAT, ORD_NUM</u>, ORD_QTY, PRICE)

These appear to be normalized with ORD_NUM and M_CAT + ORD_NUM as the respective *keys*.

We might consider introducing a new attribute to identify ITEM within order. Use of M_CAT as a component of the *key* would not be appropriate if there could ever be two ITEMs consisting of the same PRODUCT on one ORDER. If this could be the case, our dependencies are incorrect, and ITEM is not normalized. We have never explicitly stated this. It requires investigation. In addition, our users may be uncomfortable without some sort of item numbers. They could be a convenience in performing maintenance on the order data. At this point we'll note the point but leave things as they are.

We might analyze the possibility of different relations for different order types. Orders from INDividual CUSTomers have no PO, those for CORPorate CUSTomers have no Credit Card Data. It doesn't appear to be worth it.

We seem to have lost CARDCO, CREDCARD, PO, and SHIP.

We might include a relation for CARDCO. The attributes would be things like Credit Card Company Telephone Number. We haven't dealt with this much and we choose to omit it for now.

We really have no information to store about CREDCARD or PO. We'd have relations with no attributes save the *keys*. Everything seems to hang together the way it is. We omit these.

SHIP has a ONE to ONE relationship with ORDER. The only difference in attributes involves SHP_DATE. We don't retain this information in the database after the ORDER is shipped. We can safely omit this.

By the way, how do we determine that these relations are really normalized?

There are no *repeating groups*. First Normal Form is satisfied.

There are *no partial key dependencies*. Second Normal Form is satisfied.

There are *no nonkey or transitive dependencies*. Third Normal Form is satisfied.

There are *no multi-valued dependencies*. Fourth Normal Form is satisfied.

Each relation represents one or more of the specific facts we want to store. We can not detect any possibility of a lossy join. We have done our best to satisfy Fifth Normal Form.

We can also look at referential integrity constraints here.

- An ORDER can not exist without a corresponding CUST. We'd want a delete option of restrict to prevent deletion of an active customer.

- An ORDER with no ITEMs wouldn't make much sense either. We can't specify this one as an SQL constraint. We'll have to program it ourselves.

- An ITEM can't exist without a corresponding ORDER and a corresponding PRODUCT. Restrict appears to be the right delete option for PRODUCT. Cascade could be appropriate for ORDER. This requires some discussion with the users.
- A PRODUCT should have a corresponding BOOK, CD, or PIANO and the converse is also true. We'll have to program this ourselves too.
- A UNIT must have a corresponding PIANO. A delete option of restrict seems right here.

Many people call what we have now a *logical design*. This means we have a sound understanding of the data. We've arranged it in a way that makes sense based on the data alone. *We have not yet committed to a physical arrangement.* If there were no physical issues, we would go with what we have.

10.9 DETERMINE VOLUMES, ACCESS PATTERNS

Now we start looking at some physical design issues. Figure 10.8 is an access map comparable to Figure 7.13. The volumes are shown for each entity. The numbers of entities participating in each relationship are also shown. We've made some assumptions in doing this. We show one to four open orders for a single product and one to two open orders for a single customer. Remember, we get rid of orders once they are shipped. If we retained them, these numbers would be very different. Because this is a simple database, the diagram is simple. It is still worth having.

Figure 10.9 is indicative of the processing involved in producing a packing list. It shows that in order to produce the packing list we access the order by order number, access customer by customer number, access each item by order number, and access the product for each item.

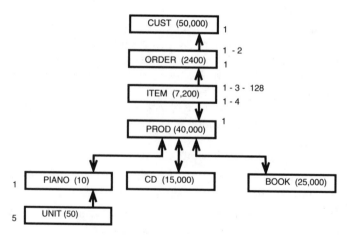

Figure 10.8 Access map one

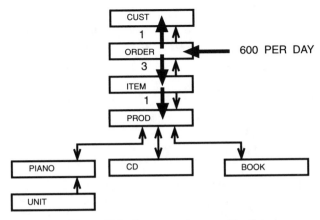

Figure 10.9 Access map two—packing list

We might prepare a diagram like this for every process and add the numbers to determine the total traffic on each path and record.

We might elect to work out the details of some processes by prototyping. If we do this, we won't have all the numbers until the prototyping activity is complete. But we'll have to define and populate a test database in order to create the prototype. If we subsequently come up with numbers which indicate the physical database should be different from the logical, we'll have to change the database. This may force us to redefine and regenerate our transaction and screen definitions. There is no easy way to determine what the impact of this will be. It's going to depend on the exact nature of the changes and the exact nature of the tools we use to generate the system. But don't let anyone tell you that relational systems are so flexible there will be no impact!

In lieu of working out all the transactions and all the numbers, let's take a look at another approach. The matrix shown in Figure 10.10 indicates which product-related data elements are used in which transactions.

This shows that some attributes are used by all transactions, some are used only for order entry, and some are used only for shipping. We can use this to reevaluate the decision we made about the subtypes and supertype.

If we follow Figure 10.5, there will be occasions when we want to determine if a given M_CAT exists in our database or if there is a nonzero QTY_AVAL. Given the three separate relations we must either know the product type, query all three, or form a *union*. It will also be difficult to detect duplicate M_CAT values when adding new products.

If we follow Figure 10.7, we will waste a lot of storage space. We also note that we have a requirement to search by ISBN, CD_PUB + CD_PNUM, and P_MFR + P_MOD. We'll most likely want to provide indexes on these items, and indexes on columns with many NULL values are not efficient. We may also search on other attributes unique to one of the three types, and this will be more efficient given separate relations for each.

		Sell Book	Sell CD	Sell Piano	Ship Book	Ship CD	Ship Piano
All Shipments	WHSE_LOC				X	X	X
	QTY_OH				X	X	X
All	M_CAT	X	X	X	X	X	X
Sales Only	QTY_AVAL	X	X	X			
	PRICE	X	X	X			
	LIST	X	X	X			
Book Sales Only	BOOK_TIT	X					
	BOOK_PUB	X					
	BOOK_AUT	X					
	ISBN	X					
	BOOK_CPY	X					
	BOOK_SUB	X					
CD Sales Only	CD_ART		X				
	CD_TITLE		X				
	CD_PUB		X				
	CD_PNUM		X				
	CD_CAT		X				
Piano Sales Only	P_MFR			X			
	P_MOD			X			

Figure 10.10   Matrix of data used by transaction

We can conclude that we'd do best to follow Figure 10.6. But even here we can benefit from rearranging the assignment of attributes to relations.

Let's assume that we've done a similar analysis for customer data and order data and concluded that an approach similar to Figure 10.7 is appropriate for these. We'll end up with these relations:

BOOK(M_CAT, BOOK_AUT, BOOK_CPY, BOOK_PUB, BOOK_SUB, BOOK_TIT, ISBN, LIST, PRICE, QTY_AVAL).

CD(M_CAT, CD_ART, CD_CAT, CD_PNUM, CD_PUB, CD_TITLE, LIST, PRICE, QTY_AVAL)

PIANO(M_CAT, LIST, PRICE, QTY_AVAL, P_MFR, P_MOD)

PRODUCT(M_CAT, P_TYPE, QTY_OH, WHSE_LOC)

UNIT(<u>M_CAT</u>, P_MOD, P_STAT, <u>SERIAL</u>, UNIT_AVL, WHSE_LOC)

CUST(ALP, ALY, ATY, CRED_EXP, CRED_NUM, CRED_TYP, CUST_ADD, CUST_BAL, CUST_CTY, CUST_FRS, CUST_LST, <u>CUST_NO</u>, CUST_PH, CUST_ST, CUST_TYP, DLP, LOC, ZIP)

ORDER(CONF_NUM, CRED_EXP, CRD_NUM, CRED_TYP, <u>CUST_NO</u>, ORD_DATE, <u>ORD_NUM</u>, PO, TOT_AMT

ITEM(ITEM_VAL, <u>M_CAT</u>, <u>ORD_NUM</u>, ORD_QTY, PRICE)

It's time for some more observations.

The ideal thing to do is work out all the details, compile all the numbers, and perform elaborate optimization calculations for everything. We'd really like to do this. But designing a methodology like this is a little like implementing a perfectly normalized database—it may not always be practical.

The solution is to exercise informed and reasonable judgment based on the costs and risks of the situation. (There are people who will interpret this as encouragement for a haphazard approach. That is *not* what is intended!)

- The costs associated with collecting every minute detail are the time and energy which must be expended. Sometimes it is really impossible to get some information in advance. Sometimes too much time spent *without producing anything* will alienate users or management.

- The costs associated with failure to perform adequate analysis range from the hidden cost of running an inefficient system to the cost of expensive rework. And, this may cost much more than the original analysis would have! There is also a risk that the system will never work.

We recommend that you always look at at least as much as we have here. And, if you must err, err on the side of too much analysis. In this particular case, we'd like to do at least as much work on customer and order as we have on product.

Since our real purpose has been to point the way, and not to design a complete system, we'll stop here. Note that our design is still normalized. We see no reason to introduce any redundancies.

There is one more thing we need to consider—calculated data items. TOT_AMT and ITEM_VAL could be eliminated. They could be calculated when required. In the case of TOT_AMT it would be necessary to add all ITEM_VALs for the order. If there were no physical considerations we could omit both of these. Because there are physical issues, we must make a decision. For the purpose of this example we'll say we decide to retain TOT_AMT but not ITEM_VAL.

10.10 FINAL DATABASE DESIGN

The final steps will involve allocating disc space, selecting indexes, and coding CREATE TABLE and CREATE INDEX statements.

We refer you to preceding chapters for two out of three. But we will discuss indexes. You might review Section 7.4 before you proceed.

Our extensive analysis of the data, the processing, and the volumes, coupled with our *feel* for the situation and our understanding of our particular hardware and software, lead us to initially establish indexes as follows.

BOOK(M_CAT, BOOK_AUT, BOOK_CPY, BOOK_PUB, BOOK_SUB, BOOK_TIT, ISBN, LIST, PRICE, QTY_AVAL)

Index the *primary key*, M_CAT and also on ISBN.

The title and author searches are going to involve substrings and the use of LIKE. Indexes won't help here. Also, indexes on long strings and variable length strings can be very inefficient. If this is an important enough problem, we'll need a really elaborate key word indexing scheme.

CD(M_CAT, CD_ART, CD_CAT, CD_PNUM, CD-PUB, CD_TITLE, LIST, PRICE, QTY_AVAL)

Index the *primary key*, M_CAT and also on CD_PUB plus CD_PNUM. The considerations discussed for book also apply here.

PIANO(M_CAT, LIST, PRICE, QTY_AVAL, P_MFR, P_MOD)

There is so little data that we really don't need to do anything here. If there were more data we'd index the *primary key*, M_CAT and also P_MFR plus P_MOD. We'd need to consider abbreviating P_MFR to a more reasonable length. It won't cost much either way.

PRODUCT(M_CAT, P_TYPE, QTY_OH, WHSE_LOC)

Index the *primary key*, M_CAT.

UNIT(M_CAT, P_MOD, P_STAT, SERIAL, UNIT_AVL, WHSE_LOC)

Once again, there is so little data we might well do nothing. If there were more data we might index M_CAT (as long as there won't be more than a few of each model) and also M_CAT plus SERIAL.

CUST(ALP, ALY, ATY, CRED_EXP, CRED_NUM, CRED_TYP, CUST_ADD, CUST_BAL, CUST_CTY, CUST_FRS, CUST_LST, CUST_NO, CUST_PH, CUST_ST, CUST_TYP, DLP, LOC, ZIP)

Index the *primary key*, CUST_NO. We'd consider another index for CUST_LST plus ZIP. There'd be a cost in indexing on the full 20-character name. We might introduce a separate attribute consisting of the first 6 or 8 characters. We'd also look at how often this form of query must be used.

ORDER(CONF_NUM, CRED_EXP, CRD_NUM, CRED_TYP, CUST_NO, ORD_DATE, ORD_NUM, PO, TOT_AMT)

Index the *primary key*, ORD_NUM. Also index the foreign key, CUST_NO.

ITEM(M_CAT, ORD_NUM, ORD_QTY, PRICE)

Index the *primary key*, M_CAT plus ORD_NUM. Provide separate indexes for both M_CAT and ORD_NUM.

10.11 PARTING THOUGHTS

As we've already noted, it is a little startling that we've kept this example unrealistically simple and omitted many details and it is still quite extensive. There really is no information we've included that would not be necessary to the construction of an effective and efficient system!

We've tried to use this example to flesh out the principles presented throughout the book. We've intentionally avoided the temptation to say, "Here, this is exactly the way you must do this." Instead, we've used this as an opportunity to illustrate the reasoning behind the techniques that have been presented and make it possible for you to make them a part of your methodology.

It's been as hard to decide how much detail to include and where to include it as it is when conducting an analysis and design project. We hope we've struck the proper balance for you.

Endnotes

1. This unlikely combination is chosen to introduce a particular data modeling issue.

2. This is a very unrealistic simplifying assumption.

3. Most books are assigned unique International Standard Book Numbers.

4. We have enough customers that a search by name only could retrieve many duplicates in the case of a common last name. Use of zip code as an adjunct will normally restrict the result to a reasonable number. If there are still duplicates, the customer service representative should be able to determine which is the correct customer record.

5. This is another simplification. The activity must take place somehow.

6. We relegate anything else we haven't discussed to this same category.

7. The actual goods shipped are not shown because a data flow diagram, as a representation of the information system, only shows the movement of information. This often causes some consternation for those who are not well versed in structured analysis. It is true that the information system is a subset of what might be called the complete system and that details of the complete system may be very important. However, they are not part of the information system and do not appear on data flow diagrams.

8. In a real case we must identify that there are several credit card companies and that the exact format and means of communication for each may be different from all others. We won't get into that too deeply, especially right now. At the time this is written, the normal processing of a credit card transaction involves two steps. Prior to or as a part of the sale, a merchant contacts the credit card company or its representative and requests an approval. At this time, the credit card company validates that the card number is correct, that the customer has adequate credit, and that the card has not been reported stolen or subjected to some other restraint. Subsequent to the sale, the merchant submits a separate record of the sale and is reimbursed. At one time this was accomplished via telephone calls and paper sales tickets. As time has passed the process has become more and more automated and has incorporated more

and more electronic data transfer. This information is drawn from the author's personal experience. It should be taken as generally correct but subject to verification at a particular time and place.

9. Throughout this example we arbitrarily establish reasonable sounding lengths for character items. In practice we'd carefully review the existing catalog or some similar source to establish these. It would really be important to do this. If Montoni's line is extensive and our DBMS does not provide for variable length character strings, we'll waste a lot of storage.

10. We'll save a little space by omitting the list. We do this for several more lists which follow. Later on, we'd seriously consider making these lists part of the database and using them for data validation. It's much better to make things like this data than can be altered by authorized users than to make it part of a computer program.

11. This is an outright lie! But we must say something.

12. Does Montoni's have any customers outside the United States? We ignore this possibility. We also ignore the possibility of different shipping and billing addresses.

13. It is possible to derive city and state from Zip Code. Many merchandising companies do so. This really is a normalization based on the determination that City (and State) are functionally dependent on Zip Code. A primary motive for this approach is elimination of key strokes and elimination of error.

14. It is possible to identify some credit card companies by careful examination of the form of the customer credit card number. We ignore this here.

15. This information is used to determine which credit card company receives authorization requests and charges. The exact format for submitting the information and manner of submission varies from company to company and from time to time. This is a topic that could require quite a bit of attention. We beg this question as we have several others.

16. We've noted that we prefer to store lists in the database and not in programs. We could consider an exception here because the list of state abbreviations rarely changes. On the other hand, there is less possibility for error if we have but one copy of this.

17. Extension used to be important. It is not a feature of most modern telephone systems.

18. Most relational systems provide a standard date data type which we can use for this and most other dates.

19. This is another "detail" we omit from the process specification.

20. We won't use NULL because we'd like to be able to add to this. However, the use of zero may cause some averages to be slightly misleading because the zero entries will be counted while NULL values would not be.

21. We have not researched the precise nature of the check digit. If we were really building this system, we'd look into it.

22. We observe once again that most methodologies and CASE tools provide very specific formats for recording this information. Within a given organization or project team, standardization is good as long as the form does not become more important than the content. We resist the temptation to dictate an exact format here.

23. It takes a lot of effort even when you are making it up as you go. Obtaining accurate information and making sure it is accurate is even harder.

24. We'd go over this with anyone we could find. Users are frequently very reluctant to go over this much detail. But it can be invaluable to validate all this now— before we get really detailed.

25. We could get into hard cover and paper cover. We ignore this issue.

26. In New York State (in 1992) sales tax is charged on books but not on periodicals. It might be necessary to check the phrasing of the tax law on this. If Montoni's has branches in several different taxing jurisdictions, it will be necessary to check all of them. You guessed it. We ignore this.

27. We doubt we'll store these as separate entities, but we are being very complete. And, this makes the diagram more logical.

28. We show a single attribute here. Probably we'd also have a telephone number, an address, and so on.

29. This is not a great definition. But it doesn't seem necessary to go any further with this one.

30. Sooner or later a decision must be made about this. We can use the product identifier as an item number or we can create an artificial attribute named line number. We don't really have to decide yet. We put this off a while.

31. We could break this down further, but we already have done so elsewhere.

32. These are broken down elsewhere.

33. This also is not a great definition. But it doesn't seem necessary to go any further with this one.

34. Here is a case of an entity which has only an identifier. It is very likely we will not include it in the database as a separate table. We include it here to be complete.

Bibliography

AGELOFF88 *A Primer on SQL*, Roy Ageloff. Times Mirror/Mosby College Publishing, St. Louis, MO, 1988.

AHO79 "The Theory of Joins in Relational Databases," A. V. Aho, C. Beeri, and J. D. Ullman. *ACM Transactions on Database Systems*, Vol. 4, No. 3, 1979.

ANSI86 *American National Standard for Information Systems—Database Language—SQL*, ANSI X3.135-1986. American National Standards Institute, New York, 1986.

ANSI89 *American National Standard for Information Systems—Database Language—SQL*, ANSI X3.135.1-1989. American National Standards Institute, New York, 1989.

ARANOW89 "Developing Good Data Definitions," Eric B. Aranow. *Database Programming & Design*, August 1989.

ATRE88 *Database: Structured Techniques for Design, Performance, and Management*, Shaku Atre. John Wiley & Sons, New York, 1988.

BACHMAN69 "Data Structure Diagrams," C. W. Bachman. *Data Base* (Journal of the ACM SIGMOD), Vol. 1, No. 2, 1969.

BOAR84 *Application Prototyping: A Requirements Definition Strategy for the 80s*, Bernard H. Boar. John Wiley & Sons, New York, 1984.

BOEHM88 "A Spiral Model of Software Development and Enhancement," Barry W. Boehm. *Computer*, May 1988.

BORSOOK88 "New Pains, New Gains: Distributed Database Solutions Are On Their Way," Paulina Borsook. *Data Communications*, March 1988.

BROOKS75 *The Mythical Man-Month*, Frederick P. Brooks, Jr. Addison-Wesley, Reading, MA, 1975.

BROWN88 "Referential Integrity Checking and SQL," Robert G. Brown. *Database Programming & Design*, March 1988.

BUZZARD91 *Database Server Evaluation Guide*, James Buzzard, Hammerhead Systems. Prepared for Oracle Corporation, 5th Edition, Part No. 51211-0491. San Francisco, CA, 1991.

CELKO89 "DBA Shoptalk: Make or Break Your System," Joe Celko. *Database Programming & Design*, March 1989.

CERI84   *Distributed Databases: Principles & Systems*, Stefano Ceri & Giuseppe Pelagatti. McGraw-Hill, New York, 1984.

CHEN77   "The Entity-Relationship Approach to Logical Data Base Design," Peter Chen. *Q.E.D. Information Sciences*, Wellesley, MA, 1977.

CHOUINARD89   "First Normal Form: Don't Overdo It," Paul Chouinard. *Database Programming & Design*, February 1989.

CODD70   "A Relational Model of Data for Large Shared Data Banks," E. F. Codd. *Communications of the ACM*, Vol. 13, No. 6, 1970.

CODD85   "Is Your DBMS Really Relational?," E. F. Codd. This appeared in two parts in *Computerworld* for October 14 and October 21, 1985.

CODD88   "Fatal Flaws in SQL," E. F. Codd. This appeared in two parts in *Datamation* for August 15 and September 1, 1988.

CODD90   *The Relational Model for Database Management, Version 2*, E. F. Codd. Addison-Wesley, Reading, MA, 1990.

COPI61   *Introduction to Logic*, Irving M. Copi. Macmillan, New York, 1961.

DATE86-1   *An Introduction to Database Systems, Volume 1, Fourth Edition*, C. J. Date. Addison-Wesley, Reading, MA, 1986. Note: The fifth edition of Date's Introduction was published while this book was being written. The result is that some references are to the fourth edition and some are to the fifth edition.

DATE86-2   "A Practical Approach to Database Design," C. J. Date. Chapter 19 of *Relational Database: Selected Writings*, C. J. Date. Addison-Wesley, Reading, MA, 1986.

DATE86-3   "An Informal Definition of the Relational Model," C. J. Date. Chapter 2 of *Relational Database: Selected Writings*, C. J. Date. Addison-Wesley, Reading, MA, 1986.

DATE87   *A Guide to the SQL Standard*, C. J. Date. Addison-Wesley, Reading, MA, 1987.

DATE90   *An Introduction to Database Systems, Volume I, Fifth Edition*, C. J. Date. Addison-Wesley, Reading, MA, 1990. Note: The fifth edition of Date's Introduction was published while this book was being written. The result is that some references are to the fourth edition and some are to the fifth edition.

DAVIS82   "Strategies for Information Requirements Determination," G. B. Davis. *IBM Systems Journal*, Vol. 21, No. 1, 1982.

DEMARCO79   *Structured Analysis and System Specification*, Tom DeMarco. Prentice-Hall, Englewood Cliffs, NJ, 1979.

FAGIN77   "Multivalued Dependencies and a New Normal Form for Relational Databases," Ronald Fagin. *ACM Transactions on Database Systems*, Vol. 2, No. 3, 1977.

FERG88   "The Parts Explosion Problem," Stephen Ferg. *Database Programming & Design*, March 1988.

FINKELSTEIN89   *Information Engineering*, Clive Finkelstein. Addison-Wesley, Sydney, Australia, 1989.

FITZGERALD87   *Fundamentals of Systems Analysis*, Jerry Fitzgerald and Ardra Fitzgerald. John Wiley & Sons, New York, 1987.

FRANK88   *Database Theory and Practice*, Lars Frank. Addison-Wesley, Wokingham, England, 1988.

FROST86   *Introduction to Knowledge Base Systems*, Richard Frost. Macmillan, New York, 1986.

GANE79   *Structured Systems Analysis: Tools and Techniques*, Chris Gane and Trish Sarson. Prentice-Hall, Englewood Cliffs, NJ, 1979.

GANE88   *Computer-Aided Software Engineering: the Methodologies, the Products, the Future*, Chris Gane. Rapid System Development, Inc., New York, 1988.

GELLERT75   *The VNR Concise Encyclopedia of Mathematics*, Gellert, Kustner, Helwich, and Kastner, Van Nostrand Reinhold, Leipzeig, 1975.

GILLENSON84   *Strategic Planning, Systems Analysis, and Database Design: The Continuous Flow Approach*, M. Gillenson and R. Goldberg. John Wiley & Sons, New York, 1984.

GOLD90   "Does Client-Server Equal Distributed Database?," Beth Gold-Bernstein. *Database Programming & Design*, September 1990.

GOLDFINE82   *Database Directions: Information Resource Management Strategies and Tools*, Alan H. Goldfine, Ed. U.S. Government Printing Office, Washington, D.C., 1982.

GUIDE81   *IMS DB/DC in a Distributed Environment*, GPP-58. Guide International Corp., Chicago, IL, 1981.

HAYAKAWA78   *Language in Thought and Action, Fourth Edition*, S. I. Hayakawa. Harcourt Brace Jovanovich, New York, 1978.

HAWRYSZKIEWICZ84   *Database Analysis and Design*, I. T. Hawryszkiewic. Science Research Associates, Inc., Chicago, IL, 1984.

HOWE83   *Data Analysis for Data Base Design*, D. R. Howe. Edward Arnold, London, 1983.

IBM86   *IBM DATABASE2 General Information*, GC26-4073. IBM Corporation, San Jose, CA, 1986.

IBM88-1   *IBM DATABASE2 Version 2 SQL Reference Release 1*, SC26 - 4380. IBM Corporation, San Jose, CA, 1988.

IBM88-2   *IBM DATABASE2 Referential Integrity Usage Guide*, GG24 - 3312. IBM Corporation, Santa Teresa, CA, 1988.

IBM88-3   *Using The IBM 3380 Direct Access Storage in an MVS Environment*, GC26-4492-1. IBM Corporation, San Jose, CA, 1988.

IBM88-4   *Distributed Data Library: Concepts of Distributed Data*, SC26-4417. IBM Corporation, San Jose, CA, 1988.

IBM88-5   *IBM DATABASE2 Version 2: General Information*, GC26-4373. IBM Corporation, San Jose, CA, 1988.

IBM88-6   *Introduction to Distributed Relational Data*, GG24-3200. IBM Corporation, San Jose, CA, 1988.

IBM90-1   *Repository Manager/MVS Repository Modeling Guide*, SC26-4619. IBM Corporation, San Jose, CA, 1990.

IBM90-2   *CICS General Information*, GC33-0155. IBM Corporation, Mechanicsburg, PA, 1990.

IBM91-1   *IBM Systems and Products Guide*, G320-6300-17. IBM Corporation, White Plains, NY, 1991.

IBM91-2 *AD/Cycle Information Model Overview,* GC26-4843-01. IBM Corporation, Cary, NC, 1991.

INGRESXX *INGRES Intelligence: Understanding Optimizers*, MBW-129U-001, undated.

INMON87 *Optimizing Performance with Denormalization*, William H. Inmon. Database Programming and Design, 1987.

INMON89 *DB2: Maximizing Performance of On-line Production Systems*, William H. Inmon. QED Information Sciences, Wellesley, MA, 1989.

ISO89 *Information Processing Systems—Database Language SQL with Integrity Enhancement*, ISO Standard 9075. International Standards Organization, Switzerland, 1989.

KENT78 *Data and Reality*, William Kent. North-Holland Publishing, Amsterdam, 1978.

KENT83 "A Simple Guide to Five Normal Forms in Relational Database Theory," William Kent, *Communications of the ACM*, Vol. 26, No. 2, 1983.

KING83 "Centralized versus Decentralized Computing: Organizational Considerations and Management Options," John Leslie King. *ACM Computing Surveys*, Vol. 15, No. 4, December 1983.

KHOSHAFIAN92 *A Guide to Developing Client/Server SQL Applications*, Khoshafian, Chan, Wong, and Wong. Morgan Kaufmann Publishers, San Mateo, CA, 1992.

KRONENBERG87 "The VAXcluster Concept: An Overview of a Distributed System," Kronenberg, et al. *Digital Technical Journal*, Number 5, September 1987.

LARY89 "The Hierarchical Storage Controller, a Tightly Coupled Multiprocessor as Storage Server," Richard F. Lary and Robert G. Bean. *Digital Technical Journal*, Number 8, February 1989.

LIEBOWITZ85 *Multiple Processor Systems For Real-Time Applications*, Burt H. Liebowitz and John H. Carson. Prentice-Hall, Englewood Cliffs, NJ, 1985.

MARTIN82 *Strategic Data Planning Methodologies*, James Martin. Prentice-Hall, Englewood Cliffs, NJ, 1982.

MARTIN83 *Managing the Data-Base Environment*, James Martin. Prentice-Hall, Englewood Cliffs, NJ, 1983.

MARTIN89 "Development of the VAX Distributed Name Service," Sally J. Martin, Janet M. McCann, and David R. Oran. *Digital Technical Journal*, Number 9, June 1989.

MCFADDEN85 *Data Base Management*, Fred R. McFadden and Jeffrey A. Hoffer. Benjamin/Cummings Publishing, Menlo Park, CA, 1985.

MCFADDEN88 *Data Base Management, Second Edition*, Fred R. McFadden and Jeffrey A. Hoffer. Benjamin/Cummings Publishing, Menlo Park, CA, 1988.

MILLS86 *Principles of Information Systems Analysis and Design*, H. Mills, R. Linger, and A. Hevner. Academic Press, Orlando, FL, 1986.

ORACLE86 *ORACLE Database Administrator's Guide, Version 5.1*, Oracle Corporation, Belmont, CA, 1986.

ORACLE87 *SQL*PLUS Reference Guide, Version 2.0*, Oracle Corporation, Belmont, CA, 1987.

ORACLE88 *ORACLE RDBMS Database Administrator's Guide, Version 6.0*, Oracle Corporation, Belmont, CA, 1988.

ORACLE89 *CASE * Method: Tasks and Deliverables*, Barker, et al. ORACLE Corporation, Belmont, CA, 1989.

OZSU91 *Principles of Distributed Database Systems*, M. Tamer Ozsu and Patrick Valdurie. Prentice-Hall, Englewood Cliffs, NJ, 1991.

PAGEJONES88 *The Practical Guide to Structured Systems Design, Second Edition*, Meilor Page-Jones. Yourdon Press, Englewood Cliffs, NJ, 1988.

PARNES81 *The Magic of Your Mind*, Sidney J. Parnes. Creative Education Foundation, Buffalo, NY, 1981.

PECKHAM88 "Semantic Data Models," Joan Peckham and Fred Maryanski. *ACM Computing Reviews*, Vol. 20, No. 3, September 1988.

PRATT91 *Database Systems: Management & Design*, Phillip J. Pratt and Joseph J. Adamski. Boyd & Fraser, Boston, 1991.

PRESSMAN87 *Software Engineering: A Practitioner's Approach, Second Edition*, Roger Pressman. McGraw-Hill, New York, 1987.

ROSS87 *Entity Modeling: Techniques and Application*, Ronald G. Ross. Database Research Group, Inc., Boston, 1987.

SENN89 *Analysis and Design of Information Systems*, James A. Senn. McGraw-Hill, New York, 1989.

SHLAER88 *Object-Oriented Systems Analysis: Modeling the World in Data*, Sally Shlaer and Stephen J. Mellor. Yourdon Press, Englewood Cliffs, NJ, 1988.

SIMORA91 *The Bowker Annual Library and Book Trade Almanac, 35th Edition*, Filomena Simora, Ed. R. R. Bowker, New York, 1991.

SHETH90 "Federated Database Systems for Managing Distributed Heterogeneous, and Autonomous Databases," Amit P. Sheth and James A. Larsen. *ACM Computing Surveys*, Vol. 22, No. 3, September 1990.

SWEET85 "Keyfield Design," Frank Sweet. *Datamation*, October 1, 1985.

TEOREY86 "A Logical Design Methodology for Relational Databases Using the Extended Entity-Relationship Model," Toby J. Teorey, Dongoing Yang, and James P. Fry. *ACM Computing Surveys*, Vol. 18, No. 21986.

TEOREY90 *Database Modeling and Design: The Entity-Relationship Approach*, Toby J. Teorey. Morgan Kaufman, San Mateo, CA, 1990.

WERTZ89 *The Data Dictionary: Concepts and Uses, Second Edition*, Charles J. Wertz. QED Information Sciences, Wellesley, MA, 1989.

WIORKOWSKI88 *DB2 Design and Development Guide*, Gabrielle Wiorkowski and David Kull. Addison-Wesley, Reading, MA, 1988.

WHITENER89 "Primary Identifiers: The Basics of Database Stability," Theresa A. Whitener. *Database Programming & Design*, January 1989.

ZACHMAN87 "A Framework For Information Systems Architecture," John A. Zachman. *IBM Systems Journal*, Vol. 26, No. 3, 1987.

Index